Uganda
a country study

Federal Research Division
Library of Congress
Edited by
Rita M. Byrnes
Research Completed
December 1990

On the cover: A crested crane, the national symbol

Second Edition, First Printing, 1992.

Library of Congress Cataloging-in-Publication Data

Uganda : a country study / Federal Research Division, Library of
Congress ; edited by Rita M. Byrnes.—2nd ed.
    p.   cm. — (Area handbook series, ISSN 1057-5294) (DA
pam ; 550-74)
    "Supersedes the 1969 edition of Area handbook for Uganda
coauthored by Allison Butler Herrick, et al."—T.p. verso.
    "Research completed December 1990."
    Includes bibliographical references (pp. 245-270) and index.
    ISBN 0-8444-0749-6
    1. Uganda. I. Byrnes, Rita M., 1943- . II. Library of
Congress. Federal Research Division. III. Area handbook for
Uganda. IV. Series. V. Series: DA pam ; 550-74.
DT433.222.U35   1992   92-513
967.61—dc20   CIP

Headquarters, Department of the Army
DA Pam 550-74

For sale by the Superintendent of Documents, U.S. Government Printing Office
Washington, D.C. 20402

Foreword

This volume is one in a continuing series of books prepared by the Federal Research Division of the Library of Congress under the Country Studies/Area Handbook Program sponsored by the Department of the Army. The last page of this book lists the other published studies.

Most books in the series deal with a particular foreign country, describing and analyzing its political, economic, social, and national security systems and institutions, and examining the interrelationships of those systems and the ways they are shaped by cultural factors. Each study is written by a multidisciplinary team of social scientists. The authors seek to provide a basic understanding of the observed society, striving for a dynamic rather than a static portrayal. Particular attention is devoted to the people who make up the society, their origins, dominant beliefs and values, their common interests and the issues on which they are divided, the nature and extent of their involvement with national institutions, and their attitudes toward each other and toward their social system and political order.

The books represent the analysis of the authors and should not be construed as an expression of an official United States government position, policy, or decision. The authors have sought to adhere to accepted standards of scholarly objectivity. Corrections, additions, and suggestions for changes from readers will be welcomed for use in future editions.

Louis R. Mortimer
Chief
Federal Research Division
Library of Congress
Washington, D.C. 20540

Acknowledgments

The authors would like to acknowledge the contributions of Allison Butler Herrick, Saone Baron Crocker, Sidney A. Harrison, Howard J. John, Susan R. MacKnight, and Richard F. Nyrop, who wrote the 1969 first edition of *Uganda: A Country Study*. The present volume incorporates portions of their work.

The authors are grateful to numerous individuals in various government agencies and private institutions who generously shared their time, expertise, and knowledge about Uganda. These people include Ralph K. Benesch, who oversees the Country Studies/Area Handbook Program for the Department of the Army. None of these individuals is in any way responsible for the work of the authors, however.

The authors also wish to thank those who contributed directly to the preparation of the manuscript. These include Sandra W. Meditz, who reviewed all textual and graphic materials and served as liaison with the sponsoring agency; Richard F. Nyrop, who reviewed several of the chapters; Marilyn Majeska, who managed editing and production; Reed Isbel, who edited the chapters; Laverle Berry, who updated chapters and helped prepare the manuscript for prepublication review; Tim Merrill, who helped select illustrations and draft maps; and Barbara Edgerton, Janie L. Gilchrist, and Izella Watson, who did the word processing. Beverly Wolpert performed the final prepublication editorial review, and Joan C. Cook compiled the index. Linda Peterson and Malinda B. Neale of the Library of Congress Printing and Processing Section performed phototypesetting, under the supervision of Peggy Pixley.

David P. Cabitto provided invaluable graphics support. Harriett R. Blood prepared the topography map, and Greenhorne and O'Mara prepared the other maps, all of which were reviewed by David P. Cabitto. The charts were prepared by David P. Cabitto, who also deserves special thanks for designing the illustrations for the book's cover and chapter title pages.

Finally, the authors acknowledge the generosity of the individuals and public and private agencies who allowed their photographs to be used in this study. They are indebted especially to those who contributed work not previously published. John A. Rowe also is due special thanks for providing several historical photographs.

Contents

List of Figures

Preface

Like its predecessor, this study is an attempt to treat in a concise and objective manner the dominant social, political, economic, and military aspects of contemporary Uganda. Sources of information included scholarly books, journals, and monographs; official reports of governments and international organizations; foreign and domestic newspapers; and numerous periodicals. Chapter bibliographies appear at the end of the book; brief comments on some of the more valuable sources suggested as possible further reading appear at the end of each chapter. Place-names follow the system adopted by the United States Board on Geographic Names. Measurements are given in the metric system; a conversion table is provided to assist those readers who are unfamiliar with metric measurements (see table 1, Appendix). A glossary is also included.

The body of the text reflects information available as of December 1990. Certain other portions of the text, however, have been updated: the Introduction discusses significant events that have occurred since the information cutoff date; the Country Profile includes updated information as available; and the Bibliography lists recently published sources thought to be particularly helpful to the reader.

Country Profile

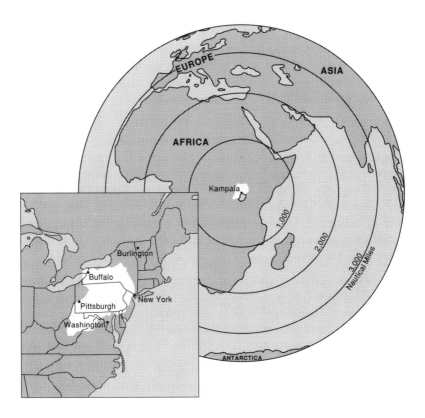

Country

Formal Name: Republic of Uganda.

Short Form: Uganda.

Term for Citizens: Ugandan(s).

Capital: Kampala.

Date of Independence: October 9, 1962, from Britain.

Geography

Size: 241,139 square kilometers, including 44,000 square kilometers of open water or swampland.

Topography: Mostly plateau that slopes gently toward north, with central downwarp occupied by Lake Kyoga. Mountains on east and west. Highest peak of Mount Stanley is Margherita (5,113 meters). Approximately one-half of Lake Victoria (10,200 square kilometers) lies within Uganda and is source of Nile River.

Climate: Equatorial climate, moderated by altitude. Annual rainfall varies from more than 2,100 millimeters around Lake Victoria to about 500 millimeters in northeast. Vegetation heaviest in south; thins to savanna and dry plains in northeast.

Society

Population: In 1990, 16.9 million (government estimate); annual growth rate more than 3.2 percent, increasingly tempered by impact of acquired immune deficiency syndrome (AIDS). Nearly one-half population under age fifteen. Nearly 10 percent urban, almost half in Kampala. Density varies from more than 120 inhabitants per square kilometer in far southeast and southwest to fewer than 30 inhabitants per square kilometer in north-central region.

Languages: Three major language families found in Uganda— Bantu, Central Sudanic, and Nilotic. Lake Kyoga rough boundary between Bantu-speakers in south and Nilotic- and Central Sudanic-speakers of north. Official language: English. Swahili and Arabic also widely spoken.

Religion: 66 percent Christian, equally divided between Roman Catholics and Protestants; largest Christian denomination Anglican (Episcopal). About 15 percent Muslim. Remainder traditional or no religion.

Education: Education not compulsory but highly regarded. Four levels: primary of seven years; lower secondary of three or four years; upper secondary of two years; and postsecondary consisting of university, teachers' colleges, or commercial training. Pupils share expenses with central government on primary and lower secondary levels; thereafter, education free. 1989 primary enrollment more than 2.5 million; secondary, 265,000. Adult literacy rate 50 percent or more.

Health: Large number of infectious diseases, including measles, pertussis, respiratory tract infections, anemia, tetanus, malaria, and tuberculosis. Incidence of AIDS quite high, reaching epidemic proportions in southern areas. Uganda had 20,000 hospital beds, more than 600 health centers, and about 700 doctors in late 1980s. Low expenditures on health care and facilities. Life expectancy in 1989 about fifty-three years.

Economy

Gross Domestic Product (GDP): USh995.6 billion, or about US$4.9 billion in FY 1989; per capita income USh60,7112, or about US$304. About 44 percent of GDP originates outside monetary economy.

Currency: Uganda shilling (USh). USh510 = US$1, official exchange rate, late 1990; parallel market rate USh700 = US$1.

Government Budget: USh169.26 billion in FY 1990, including deficit of USh57.91 billion.

Fiscal Year (FY): July 1 to June 30.

Agriculture: Agricultural activity in monetary sector constituted about 26 percent of GDP and 95 percent of export revenues; in addition, agriculture accounted for over 90 percent of nonmonetary economic activity. Cash crops: coffee, cotton, tea, tobacco. Food crops: plantains, cassava, sweet potatoes, millet, sorghum, corn, beans, peanuts. Fishing important for domestic consumption. Forest areas cover 7.5 million hectares; being rapidly depleted despite attempts at regulation.

Energy: Electric generating plants at Owen Falls and Murchison (Kabalega) Falls; some oil in western Uganda.

Industry: Mostly processing of agricultural produce and production of textiles, wood and paper products, cement, chemicals. Small part of GDP in late 1980s, with much unused capacity.

Mining: Formerly 9 percent of exports; output nil in late 1980s, except for construction materials such as sand and gravel.

Tourism: Third largest source of foreign exchange until destroyed by civil war and unrest during 1970s; slowly reviving in late 1980s.

Exports: Coffee, cotton, tea, tobacco. Coffee chief export crop and foreign exchange earner.

Imports: Machinery, military equipment and supplies, construction materials, oil, vehicles, medical supplies.

Major Trading Partners: Exports to United States and Western Europe; imports from Kenya, Britain, Germany, Italy.

Transport and Telecommunications

Roads: Total of 27,000 kilometers, 6,000 all-weather, 1,800 paved. All areas of country accessible by road; condition of roads poor. Road repair government priority.

Railroads: Total of 1,240 kilometers, in state of severe disrepair. Chief transport link with Indian Ocean ports. Rehabilitation underway in late 1980s.

Civil Aviation: Five airports with paved runways, major one at Entebbe. Little domestic or international service by Uganda Airlines in late 1980s. Complete reorganization and rebuilding in process.

Ports: Two inland ports, Jinja and Port Bell, both on Lake Victoria.

Telecommunications: 61,600 telephones, 9 television stations, 10 AM radio stations; radio-relay systems for long-distance surface communications; international service via Atlantic Ocean and Indian Ocean International Telecommunications Satellite Corporation (Intelsat) links.

Government and Politics

Government: Legal basis of government 1967 constitution modified by decrees of the National Resistance Movement (NRM) after 1986. The National Resistance Council (NRC) wields supreme authority and power as interim government expected to last until January 1995. Resistance councils (RCs) exist on district, county, subcounty, parish, and village levels, each elected by council members of next lower level and by universal suffrage at village level.

Administrative Divisions: Uganda divided into 34 districts, 150 counties, and 129 municipal governing units.

Courts: Legal and court systems heavily influenced by British common law and practice, supplemented by Islamic law and customary institutions and laws. Supreme Court of Uganda highest court, below which are series of appeals courts; civil disputes in hands of local resistance committees.

Politics: Two main parties, Uganda People's Congress (UPC) and Democratic Party (DP). Organized political activity suspended in 1986. In February 1989, elections held for all resistance councils, including some seats on NRC.

Foreign Relations: Nonaligned foreign policy; enthusiastic supporter of African and regional economic and political cooperation. President Yoweri Kaguta Museveni elected chair of Organization of African Unity (OAU) in July 1990.

National Security

Armed Forces: No official figures available, but strength of National Resistance Army (NRA) estimated at 70,000. Recruitment voluntary; no fixed term of service, both men and women serve.

Defense Spending: About USh6.9 billion, or US$40.68 million, in FY 1989. Consumes 35 percent or more of national budget.

Military Organization: Information on organization and composition not officially available. Combat units: six brigades, several battalions, and Police Air Wing.

Major Military Suppliers: Britain (training), Tanzania (training), Libya (training and equipment), Soviet Union (equipment), Democratic People's Republic of Korea (North Korea) (training and equipment), United States (training).

Security Forces: In 1986 NRA assumed responsibility for internal security. Police force reorganized and together with other internal security organs began to enforce law and order in all districts except those experiencing rebel activity in late 1989. Controlled by Ministry of Internal Affairs. In late 1980s, receiving training from Britain, France, and North Korea. Numbered 20,000 by early 1991.

Introduction

IN MID-1992 UGANDA WAS still trying to recover from two decades of instability and civil war. For the majority of the population born after Idi Amin Dada seized power in 1971, a peaceful and prosperous Uganda was difficult to imagine. But many Ugandans saw promising signs of economic and political reform in the nation's fledgling grass-roots democracy, new economic development projects and export initiatives, and the renewed commitment to education and social services. Serious problems remained unresolved, however, and it was clear that efforts to rehabilitate Uganda's devastated economy and return the country to civilian rule would take most of the decade.

Uganda in earlier times had known periods of relative peace, but not quiet isolation. Its early history, told through the archaeological record and accounts of travelers, included centuries of political change, population migration, and the development of cultural diversity. The earliest occupants of the low-lying plateau that stretches north from the shores of Lake Victoria had been joined by new migrants from the north and west by about the fourth century A.D. These new arrivals, ancestors of today's Bantu-speaking societies, came under pressure from the expansion of non-Bantu-speaking warriors and herders from the northeast by about the tenth century A.D. The gradual population movement to the southwest was slowed by the formation of new societies comprising farmers and herders. Several of them competed for regional control, assimilating and dominating their neighbors to varying degrees, and several evolved into complex centralized societies marked by economic and social stratification. During the nineteenth century, the strongest among them, Bunyoro, began to lose power to its breakaway neighbor, Buganda. By the end of the nineteenth century, Buganda dominated the region, but the rivalry between Buganda and Bunyoro remained strong enough to be exploited by colonial agents who established the Uganda Protectorate in 1894.

Representatives of Islam and Christianity, who had also competed for social, spiritual, and economic advantage over one another, also left a lasting imprint on Ugandan society. Political developments throughout the twentieth century have reflected the divisions between Uganda's centralized and noncentralized societies, and among the diverse ethnic groups in each of these categories, their different responses to the colonial experience, and the impact of world religions.

Uganda had been brought into the world economic system gradually over the centuries, first through trade in ivory, and later through trade in slaves and agricultural products. In the early twentieth century, colonial officials, with the help of Baganda (people of Buganda; sing., Muganda) agents, established cash crops, especially cotton, and later coffee, to help finance economic development according to world market demands. Buganda prospered and drew farm workers from other areas of the protectorate. Buganda's schools also developed ahead of those in other regions, helping fuel existing rivalries between the Baganda and their neighbors.

Agricultural production increased dramatically during World War I, and during the 1920s and 1930s, farmers were able to weather the fluctuations in world market prices by cutting cash-crop production and reverting to subsistence agriculture. Protectorate laws carefully regulated the use of land and other resources, often allocating economic rights according to racial categories. Protests against such restrictions increased after World War II, but, unlike much of Africa, Uganda was preparing peacefully for independence well before it arrived.

At independence in October 1962, ethnic and regional rivalries were crystallized in several newly formed political parties and in the federal system that gave substantial autonomy to the four large kingdoms in the south, plus the highly centralized society of Busoga. The central government maintained control over the northern region. The army flourished under the first independent government led by Milton Obote and pressed its demands for higher pay and improved conditions of service. A military coup in 1971, however, plunged Uganda into eight years of terror and disintegration under the government of Idi Amin. Uganda's once-developing economy disintegrated, and its once-thriving education system suffered lasting damage. Government-sanctioned brutality became commonplace. Many of Uganda's intellectuals and entrepreneurs were forced to flee. A brief but tumultuous political transition followed the nightmare of the Amin years, and the early 1980s became a time of revenge-seeking and despair under the second government led by Milton Obote. Growing rebellions finally forced Obote from office in 1985, but Ugandans had little cause for confidence in their political future.

The government led by Yoweri Kaguta Museveni that seized power in January 1986 had not inspired overwhelming public confidence in its ability to rule. Museveni's National Resistance Army (NRA), however, had shown greater military discipline than other armed forces in recent years, and Museveni declared that

establishing a peaceful and secure environment was his highest priority as president. For this goal, Museveni had strong popular backing.

The NRA's hastily formed political arm, the National Resistance Movement (NRM), set out its political program in the Ten-Point Program, which advocated a broad-based democracy and a hierarchy of popular assemblies, or resistance councils (RCs), from the village through district levels to mediate between the national government and the village. After initial doubts about embracing Western economic reforms, the NRM also embarked on ambitious structural adjustment and export diversification programs. Museveni took seriously the notion of accountability in government service and set about improving standards of behavior among public-sector employees.

But the NRM had few politically educated people in its ranks, and Museveni's policy of appointing members of previous governments to high office cost him political support. In addition, the NRM's political ideas were new and lacked support in the northern and eastern regions, where popular insurgencies continued to plague his rule even after six years in power. And the army, with its intense recruitment drives and policy of incorporating former rebel opponents into its ranks, was unable to eliminate the human rights abuses for which it had become infamous. Campaigns to pacify and stabilize rebel-occupied areas turned into army assaults on peaceful residents of the north and east, and the judicial system was slow to deal with those accused of serious atrocities. At the same time, the cost of maintaining the military escalated rapidly, and pressures to reduce the size of the army posed the dilemma of escalating unemployment among former members of the military.

Since research on this volume was completed in 1990, the government has continued its program of political reform in an effort to meet its own deadline for returning to civilian rule by 1995. Progress, however, has been slow. The central institutions of grassroots democracy, the RCs, improved their ability to function as part of the government, but in some areas the RCs' exact responsibilities were not well understood. In a few cases, their efforts to maintain order degenerated into vigilantism.

A twenty-one-member constitutional commission appointed in 1988 completed its nationwide consultations in late 1991, but it postponed submitting a draft constitution to the government until November 1992. The government also planned a nationwide referendum on the draft constitution in mid-1993.

Nationwide RC elections, held from February 29 to March 9, 1992, were generally considered a success. Voters in more than

30,000 villages elected RCs for their villages, and indirect elections were held for RC members at the parish, subcounty, county, and district levels. Partisan campaigning and explicitly soliciting votes were legally prohibited; candidates who violated this prohibition were disqualified, although candidates were able to use other avenues to make their views known. In several areas, staunch critics of the government were elected to the RCs, confirming the widespread belief that the elections were generally free and fair. About half of the incumbent RC members were removed from office, and several members of the national legislature lost in elections for village RCs.

In a few areas, such as Bushenyi, elections were delayed because of conditions caused by religious feuding, political violence, or the spreading drought. In a few localities, election irregularities led to the annulment and rescheduling of the balloting. But when the votes were counted, more than 400,000 Ugandans had been elected to various levels of political office, and the new office-holders represented nearly every ethnic, religious, and political identity in the country. The next elections were planned for late 1994, when the government pledged it would provide secret ballots and the direct election of legislators at all levels.

Despite well-publicized human rights abuses by the military that continued through early 1991, President Museveni's New Year's message for 1992 emphasized his commitment to improving this record. By mid-1992, the courts had begun to hear the cases of eighteen prominent northern politicians who had been accused of treason in April 1991, and charges against several of the accused had been dropped. The government had disciplined soldiers for human rights abuses in unsettled areas of the north and east, and the army response to the unrest was more restrained in 1992. An inspector general of government (IGG) was appointed to serve as a "watchdog" on government, but the incumbent's effectiveness was undermined by the IGG's large caseload and the fact that the inspector general served at the president's pleasure.

The government declared northern Uganda "pacified" in late 1991, following a three-month-long army sweep that included house-to-house searches in Gulu, Lira, Kitgum, and Apac districts. Residents were asked to produce poll tax receipts and other documents to prove their identity. In some cases, civilians were assaulted, and a few were executed for failing to comply.

Museveni also attempted to bring order to Uganda's foreign relations. He met in Nairobi with Kenyan president Daniel T. arap Moi and Tanzanian president Ali Hassan Mwinyi in late 1991, and they agreed to develop closer ties among the three countries.

Relations with Kenya had been strained, primarily because of continuing clashes along their common border. Most of the attacks were provoked by banditry and cross-border skirmishes among isolated groups of soldiers or herders, but the two leaders harbored mutual suspicions of one another. Moi feared Museveni's close ties with Libyan leader Muammar Qadhafi could contribute to destabilization in Kenya, where ethnic and political tensions were already high. (This fear probably diminished, however, following Libya's reported June 1992 termination of its military relationship with Uganda.) The three leaders agreed to coordinate policies in security, trade, transportation, agriculture, and industry, and to pursue other avenues for regional cooperation.

Relations with Rwanda remained strained as of mid-1992. Fighting continued along the Uganda-Rwanda border following the October 1990 invasion of Rwanda by Rwandan exiles in Uganda. Many members of the invading rebel army, the Rwandan Patriotic Front (RPF), had been members of the Ugandan army. Rwandan president Juvénal Habyarimana continued to accuse Museveni of allowing, and even supporting, RPF operations from Ugandan territory, and Rwandan forces struck back across the border several times in 1991 and early 1992. Ugandan officials estimated that several thousand Ugandans had been killed, and more than 30,000 displaced, by the conflict. Representatives of the Organization of African Unity (OAU), along with officials from Rwanda, Burundi, Tanzania, and Zaire, met several times in 1991 and 1992 and urged the warring parties to observe the ceasefire agreed to in March 1991, but fighting continued as of mid-1992.

Unrest in Zaire arising out of economic deterioration and a stalemate over political reform also contributed to the security crisis in southwestern Uganda in 1992. Ugandan officials claimed more than 20,000 Zairian refugees had entered Uganda, seeking refuge from marauding Zairian troops and antigovernment rebel banditry.

In northern Uganda, similar problems arose out of civil war and drought conditions in Sudan. In 1991 and 1992, Sudanese army assaults on antigovernment rebel units near the Ugandan border were forcing southern Sudanese to seek refuge in the increasingly drought-stricken area of northern Uganda, and in a few cases Sudanese attacks extended into Ugandan territory.

The influx of refugees strained an already struggling Ugandan economy. Uganda's overall economic growth continued in 1992, but fell from the impressive rate of nearly 6 percent in 1990 and almost 5 percent in 1991 to a projected 4.5 percent in 1992. The government attributed the positive performance to the nation's returning political stability and an increasingly favorable investment environment. Foreign assistance also continued to play a significant role in economic growth. Inflation fell from triple-digit levels to about 25 percent in 1990 but rose to 38 percent in 1991. Targeted inflation for 1992 was 15 percent.

The fiscal year (FY—see Glossary) 1992 budget included total government spending of 674.35 billion Uganda shillings (USh; for value of the Uganda shilling—see Glossary), or about US$911.3 million, of which the government claimed defense spending would constitute about 20 percent. Educational expenditures would constitute 12 percent; health care, 6.5 percent; 3 percent was earmarked for providing safe drinking water. Roughly one-third of expenditures were to be financed by government revenues; one-third by foreign grants; and one-third by borrowing, debt rescheduling, and the sale of treasury bills.

Agricultural growth reached 2.8 percent in 1991 and was expected to exceed that in 1992. Cotton production doubled in 1991 over 1990 levels; production of tea and tobacco also increased. Coffee earnings fell to about US$140 million in 1991—largely the result of the collapse of the International Coffee Agreement, which had regulated world market prices—but coffee still accounted for about 70 percent of merchandise export earnings. Nontraditional export earnings, although small in comparison with traditional exports, doubled between 1990 and 1992 to more than US$50 million, largely because of government support programs that included low-interest loans and expanded credit opportunities to encourage the production of a wider variety of agricultural products.

Nevertheless, Uganda's trade deficit remained high in 1991, with imports roughly three times the value of exports. Combined with high interest payments, the unfavorable trade deficit produced a current account deficit of almost US$500 million. Debt service requirements reached roughly 75 percent of export earnings, with arrears mounting steadily. Most of Uganda's external debt was owed to multilateral creditors and therefore could not be rescheduled.

The government continued to implement features of the 1987–91 economic rehabilitation program, such as liberalizing the marketing of agricultural produce. In 1992 a few coffee producers' groups were handling coffee marketing, although the government's Coffee Marketing Board remained active. In early 1992, the government introduced an auction system for allocating foreign exchange on the basis of market dictates rather than government selection among importers. To help improve Uganda's investment climate, the government also began restoring to its original owners the property that had been expropriated during the 1970s, and negotiating compensation in a few other cases.

The government announced that it would privatize, at least in part, 100 of the country's 116 public enterprises and eliminate 16 parastatals. It would retain majority shares in commercial banking; copper mining; housing; airlines; breweries; grain milling; pharmaceutical distribution; steel and cement production; textile and sugar manufacturing; and the marketing of coffee, cotton, and most agricultural produce. Private investors, including foreigners, would be able to purchase shares in companies in which the government was a major shareholder. The government planned to retain full ownership of electric utilities, railroads, air cargo services, development finance banking, posts and telecommunications, insurance agencies, tourist agencies, and newspaper publishing. To improve accountability among these enterprises, it intended to reduce the number of political appointments and increase its oversight of recordkeeping practices.

Civil service reform was also an important goal for the early 1990s. With the elimination of "ghost" employees from government rolls in mid-1991, the number of public employees outside the education sector was reduced from 90,000 to roughly 64,000, and teachers' rolls were reduced to roughly 80,000. The salaries of remaining government employees were increased, some by as much as 40 percent, after these payroll cuts were announced.

Uganda continued to experience a devastating epidemic of infection with the human immunodeficiency virus (HIV) and acquired immune deficiency syndrome (AIDS), despite government and private-sector initiatives to reduce the rate of transmission and the impact of the disease. In 1991 the internationally funded AIDS Information Center (AIC) in Kampala began the first free, anonymous HIV testing and counseling program in sub-Saharan Africa. The AIC planned to test 280,000 Ugandans by mid-1993. After it had conducted 30,000 tests, the center recorded seropositive rates of approximately 26 percent, but the total number of AIDS cases nationwide could not be estimated with certainty. The government established the AIDS Commission Secretariat to coordinate AIDS prevention strategies nationwide. Government officials and medical and social workers met in Kampala in mid-1992 to address the needs of the several hundred thousand children who had been orphaned by the AIDS epidemic.

Despite significant progress and ambitious planning, Uganda faced serious economic and political problems in 1992. Lingering insurgency campaigns in the north and east, increased defense spending, and serious military abuses reinforced one another to erode public confidence. The government's commitment to economic development provided hope of improved living standards, but the combined economic and security problems, along with the effects of two decades of neglect of education and social services, led many people to question whether Museveni could deliver on his pledge to restore broad-based democracy to Uganda.

June 15, 1992   Rita M. Byrnes

Chapter 1. Historical Setting

The baobab tree, ancient symbol of the African plains

UGANDA WAS ONE of the lesser-known African countries until the 1970s when Idi Amin Dada rose to the presidency. His bizarre public pronouncements—ranging from gratuitous advice for Richard Nixon to his proclaimed intent to raise a monument to Adolf Hitler—fascinated the popular news media. Beneath the facade of buffoonery, however, the darker reality of massacres and disappearances was considered equally newsworthy. Uganda became known as an African horror story, fully identified with its field marshal president. Even a decade after Amin's flight from Uganda in 1979, popular imagination still insisted on linking the country and its exiled former ruler.

But Amin's well-publicized excesses at the expense of Uganda and its citizens were not unique, nor were they the earliest assaults on the rule of law. They were foreshadowed by Amin's predecessor, Milton Obote, who suspended the 1962 constitution and ruled part of Uganda by martial law for five years before a military coup in 1971 brought Amin into power. Amin's bloody regime was followed by an even bloodier one—Obote's second term as president during the civil war from 1981 to 1985, when government troops carried out genocidal sweeps of the rural populace in a region that became known as the Luwero Triangle. The dramatic collapse of coherent government under Amin and his plunder of his nation's economy, followed by the even greater failure of the second Obote government in the 1980s, raised the essential question—"what went wrong?"

At Uganda's independence in October 1962 there was little indication that the country was headed for disaster. On the contrary, it appeared a model of stability and potential progress. Unlike neighboring Kenya, Uganda had no European settler class attempting to monopolize the rewards of the cash-crop economy. Nor was there any recent legacy of bitter and violent conflict in Uganda to compare with the 1950s Mau Mau rebellion in Kenya. In Uganda it was African producers who grew the cotton and coffee that brought a higher standard of living, financed the education of their children, and led to increased expectations for the future.

Unlike neighboring Tanzania, Uganda enjoyed rich natural resources, a flourishing economy, and an impressive number of educated and prosperous middle-class African professionals, including business people, doctors, lawyers, and scientists. And unlike neighboring Zaire (the former Belgian Congo), which descended into chaos and misrule immediately after independence, Uganda's first few years of self-rule saw a series of successful development projects. The new government built many new schools, modernized the transportation network, and increased manufacturing output as well as national income. With its prestigious national Makerere University, its gleaming new teaching hospital at Mulago, its Owen Falls hydroelectric project at Jinja—all gifts of the departing British—Uganda at independence looked optimistically to the future.

Independence came without a struggle and was caused by British actions as much as it was a response to an indigenous independence movement. The British determined a timetable for withdrawal before local groups had organized an effective nationalist movement. Uganda's political parties emerged in response to impending independence rather than as a means of winning it.

In part the result of its fairly smooth transition to independence, the near absence of nationalism among Uganda's diverse ethnic groups led to a series of political compromises. The first was a government made up of coalitions of local and regional interest groups loosely organized into political parties. The national government was presided over by a prime minister whose principal role appeared to be that of a broker, trading patronage and development projects—such as roads, schools, and dispensaries—to local or regional interest groups in return for political support. It was not the strong, directive, ideologically clothed central government desired by most African political leaders, but it worked. And it might reasonably have been expected to continue to work, because there were exchanges and payoffs at all levels and to all regions.

Historical Legacies and Social Divisions

As Uganda's first prime minister, Obote displayed a talent for acting as a broker for groups divided from each other by distance, language, cultural tradition, historical enmities, and rivalries in the form of competing religions—Islam, Roman Catholicism, and Protestantism.

Observers with a powerfully developed sense of hindsight could point to a series of divisions within Ugandan society that contributed to its eventual national disintegration. First, the language gulf between the Nilotic-speaking people of the north and the Bantu-speaking peoples of the south was as wide as that between speakers of Slavic and of Romance languages in Europe. Second, there was an economic divide between the pastoralists, who occupied the drier rangelands of the west and north, and the agriculturalists, who cultivated the better-watered highland or lakeside regions. Third, there was a long-standing division between the centralized and sometimes despotic rule of the ancient African kingdoms and the kinship-based politics of recent times, which were characterized by a greater sense of equality and participation. Furthermore, there was a historical political division among the kingdoms themselves. They were often at odds—as in the case of Buganda and Bunyoro and other precolonial polities that disputed among themselves over control of particular lands. There also were the historical complaints of particular religious groups that had lost ground to rivals in the past; for example, the eclipse of the Muslims at the end of the nineteenth century by Christians allied to British colonialism created an enduring grievance. In addition, Bunyoro's nineteenth-century losses of territory to an expanding Buganda kingdom, allied to British imperialism, gave rise to a problem that would emerge after independence as the "lost counties" issue. Another divisive factor was the uneven development in the colonial period, whereby the south secured railroad transport, cash crops, mission education, and the seat of government, seemingly at the expense of other regions, which were still trying to catch up after independence. Conflicting local nationalism (often misleadingly termed "tribalism") also contributed to social divisions. The most conspicuous example was Buganda, whose population of over one million, extensive territory in the favored south of Uganda, and self-proclaimed superiority created a serious backlash among other peoples. The presence of Nubians, an alien community of professional military people clustered around military encampments, added to the disharmony. Nubians had been brought in from Sudan to serve as a colonial coercive force to suppress local tax revolts. This community shared little sense of identification with Uganda. Another alien community that dominated commercial life in the cities and towns was composed of Asians, who had arrived with British colonial rule. Finally, the closely related peoples of nearby Belgian Congo and Sudan soon became embroiled in their own civil wars during the colonial period, drawing in ethnically related Ugandans.

This formidable list of obstacles to national integration, coupled with the absence of nationalist sentiment, left the newly independent Uganda vulnerable to political instability in the 1960s. It was by no means inevitable that the government by consensus and compromise that characterized the early 1960s would devolve into the military near-anarchy of the 1970s. The conditions contributing to such a debacle, however, were already present at independence.

Uganda Before 1900

Uganda's strategic position along the Great Rift Valley, its favorable climate at an altitude of 1,200 meters and above, and the reliable rainfall in the Lake Victoria Basin made it attractive to African cultivators and herders as early as the fourth century B.C. Core samples from the bottom of Lake Victoria have revealed that dense rainforest once covered the land around the lake. Centuries of cultivation removed almost all the original tree cover.

The cultivators who gradually cleared the forest were probably Bantu-speaking people, who, with their slow but inexorable expansion, gradually populated most of Africa south of the Sahara Desert. Their knowledge of agriculture and use of iron technology permitted them to clear the land and feed ever larger numbers of settlers. They displaced small bands of indigenous hunter-gatherers, who relocated to the less accessible mountains. Meanwhile, by the fourth century B.C., the Bantu-speaking metallurgists were perfecting iron smelting to produce medium-grade carbon steel in preheated forced draft furnaces. Although most of these developments were taking place southwest of modern Ugandan boundaries, iron was mined and smelted in many parts of the country not long afterward.

Early Political Systems

As the Bantu-speaking agriculturalists multiplied over the centuries, they evolved a form of government by clan (see Glossary) chiefs. This kinship-organized system was useful for coordinating work projects, settling internal disputes, and carrying out religious observances to clan deities, but it could effectively govern only a limited number of people. Larger polities began to form states by the end of the first millennium A.D., some of which would ultimately govern over a million subjects each.

The stimulus to the formation of states may have been the meeting of people of differing cultures. The lake shores became densely settled by Bantu-speakers, particularly after the introduction of the banana, or plantain, as a basic food crop around A.D. 1000; farther north in the short grass uplands, where rainfall was intermittent, pastoralists were moving south from the area of the Nile River in search of better pastures. Indeed, a short grass "corridor" existed north and west of Lake Victoria through which successive waves of herders may have passed on the way to central and southern Africa. The meeting of these peoples resulted in trade across various ecological zones and evolved into more permanent relationships.

Nilotic-speaking pastoralists were mobile and ready to resort to arms in defense of their own cattle or raids to appropriate the cattle of others. But their political organization was minimal, based on kinship and decision making by kin-group elders. In the meeting of cultures, they may have acquired the ideas and symbols of political chiefship from the Bantu-speakers, to whom they could offer military protection. A system of patron-client relationships developed, whereby a pastoral elite emerged, entrusting the care of cattle to subjects who used the manure to improve the fertility of their increasingly overworked gardens and fields. The earliest of these states may have been established in the fifteenth century by a group of pastoral rulers called the Chwezi. Although legends depicted the Chwezi as supernatural beings, their material remains at the archaeological sites of Bigo and Mubende have shown that they were human and the probable ancestors of the modern Hima or Tutsi (Watutsi) pastoralists of Rwanda and Burundi. During the fifteenth century, the Chwezi were displaced by a new Nilotic-speaking pastoral group called the Bito. The Chwezi appear to have moved south of present-day Uganda to establish kingdoms in northwest Tanzania, Rwanda, and Burundi.

From this process of cultural contact and state formation, three different types of states emerged. The Hima type was later to be seen in Rwanda and Burundi. It preserved a caste system whereby the rulers and their pastoral relatives attempted to maintain strict separation from the agricultural subjects, called Hutu. The Hima rulers lost their Nilotic language and became Bantu-speakers, but they preserved an ideology of superiority in political and social life and attempted to monopolize high status and wealth. In the twentieth century, the Hutu revolt after independence led to the expulsion from Rwanda of the Hima elite, who became refugees in Uganda. A counterrevolution in Burundi secured power for the Hima through periodic massacres of the Hutu majority.

The Bito type of state, in contrast with that of the Hima, was established in Bunyoro, which for several centuries was the dominant political power in the region. Bito immigrants displaced the influential Hima and secured power for themselves as a royal clan, ruling over Hima pastoralists and Hutu agriculturalists alike. No rigid caste lines divided Bito society. The weakness of the Bito ideology was that, in theory, it granted every Bito clan member royal status and with it the eligibility to rule. Although some of these ambitions might be fulfilled by the Bunyoro king's (*omukama*) granting his kin offices as governors of districts, there was always the danger of a coup d'état or secession by overambitious relatives. Thus, in Bunyoro periods of political stability and expansion were interrupted by civil wars and secessions.

The third type of state to emerge in Uganda was that of Buganda, on the northern shores of Lake Victoria. This area of swamp and hillside was not attractive to the rulers of pastoral states farther north and west. It became a refuge area, however, for those who wished to escape rule by Bunyoro or for factions within Bunyoro who were defeated in contests for power. One such group from Bunyoro, headed by Prince Kimera, arrived in Buganda early in the fifteenth century. Assimilation of refugee elements had already strained the ruling abilities of Buganda's various clan chiefs, and a supraclan political organization was already emerging. Kimera seized the initiative in this trend and became the first effective king (*kabaka*) of the fledgling state. Ganda (root word and adjective for Buganda) oral traditions later sought to disguise this intrusion from Bunyoro by claiming earlier, shadowy, quasi-supernatural *kabakas*.

Unlike the Hima caste system or the Bunyoro royal clan political monopoly, Buganda's kingship was made a kind of state lottery in which all clans could participate. Each new king was identified with the clan of his mother, rather than that of his father. All clans readily provided wives to the ruling *kabaka*, who had eligible sons by most of them. When the ruler died, his successor was chosen by clan elders from among the eligible princes, each of whom belonged to the clan of his mother. In this way, the throne was never the property of a single clan for more than one reign.

Consolidating their efforts behind a centralized kingship, the Baganda (people of Buganda; sing., Muganda) shifted away from defensive strategies and toward expansion. By the mid-nineteenth century, Buganda had doubled and redoubled its territory. Newly conquered lands were placed under chiefs nominated by the king. Buganda's armies and the royal tax collectors traveled swiftly to all parts of the kingdom along specially constructed roads which crossed streams and swamps by bridges and viaducts. On Lake Victoria (which the Baganda called Nnalubale), a royal navy of outrigger canoes, commanded by an admiral who was chief of the Lungfish clan, could transport Baganda commandos to raid any shore of the lake. The journalist Henry M. Stanley visited Buganda in 1875 and provided an estimate of Buganda's troop strength. Stanley counted 125,000 troops marching off on a single campaign to the east, where a fleet of 230 war canoes waited to act as auxiliary naval support.

At Buganda's capital, Stanley found a well-ordered town of about 40,000 surrounding the king's palace, which was situated atop a commanding hill. A wall more than four kilometers in circumference surrounded the palace compound, which was filled with grass-roofed houses, meeting halls, and storage buildings. At the entrance to the court burned the royal fire (*gombolola*), which would be extinguished only when the *kabaka* died. Thronging the grounds were foreign ambassadors seeking audiences, chiefs going to the royal

*Drawing of the royal capital of Buganda
at the time of journalist Henry M.
Stanley's visit in 1875*

advisory council, messengers running errands, and a corps of young
pages, who served the *kabaka* while training to become future chiefs.
For communication across the kingdom, the messengers were supplemented by drum signals.

Most communities in Uganda, however, were not organized on
such a vast political scale. To the north, the Nilotic-speaking Acholi
people adopted some of the ideas and regalia of kingship from
Bunyoro in the eighteenth century. Chiefs (*rwots*) acquired royal
drums, collected tribute from followers, and redistributed it to those
who were most loyal. The mobilization of larger numbers of subjects permitted successful hunts for meat. Extensive areas of bush-
land were surrounded by beaters, who forced the game to a central
killing point in a hunting technique that was still practiced in areas
of central Africa in 1990. But these Acholi chieftaincies remained
relatively small in size, and within them the power of the clans remained strong enough to challenge that of the *rwot*.

Long-Distance Trade and Foreign Contact

Until the middle of the nineteenth century, Uganda remained
relatively isolated from the outside world. The central African lake
region was, after all, a world in miniature, with an internal trade

system, a great power rivalry between Buganda and Bunyoro, and its own inland seas. When intrusion from the outside world finally came, it was in the form of long-distance trade for ivory.

Ivory had been a staple trade item from the East Africa coast since before the Christian era. But growing world demand in the nineteenth century, together with the provision of increasingly efficient firearms to hunters, created a moving "ivory frontier" as elephant herds near the coast were nearly exterminated. Leading large caravans financed by Indian moneylenders, coastal Arab traders based on Zanzibar (united with Tanganyika in 1964 to form Tanzania) had reached Lake Victoria by 1844. One trader, Ahmad bin Ibrahim, introduced Buganda's *kabaka* to the advantages of foreign trade: the acquisition of imported cloth and, more important, guns and gunpowder. Ibrahim also introduced the religion of Islam, but the *kabaka* was more interested in guns. By the 1860s, Buganda was the destination of ever more caravans, and the *kabaka* and his chiefs began to dress in cloth called *mericani*, which was woven in Massachusetts and carried to Zanzibar by American traders. It was judged finer in quality than European or Indian cloth, and increasing numbers of ivory tusks were collected to pay for it. Bunyoro sought to attract foreign trade as well, in an effort to keep up with Buganda in the burgeoning arms race.

Bunyoro also found itself threatened from the north by Egyptian-sponsored agents who sought ivory and slaves but who, unlike the Arab traders from Zanzibar, were also promoting foreign conquest. Khedive Ismail of Egypt aspired to build an empire on the Upper Nile; by the 1870s, his motley band of ivory traders and slave raiders had reached the frontiers of Bunyoro. The khedive sent a British explorer, Samuel Baker, to raise the Egyptian flag over Bunyoro. The Banyoro (people of Bunyoro) resisted this attempt, and Baker had to fight a desperate battle to secure his retreat. Baker regarded the resistance as an act of treachery, and he denounced the Banyoro in a book that was widely read in Britain. Later British empire builders arrived in Uganda with a predisposition against Bunyoro, which eventually would cost the kingdom half its territory until the "lost counties" were restored to Bunyoro after independence.

Farther north the Acholi responded more favorably to the Egyptian demand for ivory. They were already famous hunters and quickly acquired guns in return for tusks. The guns permitted the Acholi to retain their independence but altered the balance of power within Acholi territory, which for the first time experienced unequal distribution of wealth based on control of firearms.

Meanwhile, Buganda was receiving not only trade goods and guns, but also a stream of foreign visitors. The explorer J.H. Speke

*Kabaka Mutesa I,
who reigned from 1856 to 1884*

passed through Buganda in 1862 and claimed he had discovered the source of the Nile. Both Speke and Stanley (based on his 1875 stay in Uganda) wrote books that praised the Baganda for their organizational skills and willingness to modernize. Stanley went further and attempted to convert the king to Christianity. Finding Kabaka Mutesa I apparently receptive, Stanley wrote to the Church Missionary Society (CMS) in London and persuaded it to send missionaries to Buganda in 1877. Two years after the CMS established a mission, French Catholic White Fathers also arrived at the king's court, and the stage was set for a fierce religious and nationalist rivalry in which Zanzibar-based Muslim traders also participated. By the mid-1880s, all three parties had been successful in converting substantial numbers of Baganda, some of whom attained important positions at court. When a new young *kabaka,* Mwanga, attempted to halt the dangerous foreign ideologies that he saw threatening the state, he was deposed by the armed converts in 1888. A four-year civil war ensued in which the Muslims were initially successful and proclaimed an Islamic state. They were soon defeated, however, and were not able to renew their effort.

The victorious Protestant and Roman Catholic converts then divided the Buganda kingdom, which they ruled through a figurehead *kabaka* dependent on their guns and goodwill. Thus, outside religion had disrupted and transformed the traditional state. Soon afterwards, the arrival of competing European imperialists—the

11

German Doctor Karl Peters (an erstwhile philosophy professor) and the British Captain Frederick Lugard—broke the Christian alliance; the British Protestant missionaries urged acceptance of the British flag, while the French Catholic mission either supported the Germans (in the absence of French imperialists) or called for Buganda to retain its independence. In January 1892, fighting broke out between the Protestant and Catholic Baganda converts. The Catholics quickly gained the upper hand, until Lugard intervened with a prototype machine gun, the Maxim (named after its American inventor, Hiram Maxim). The Maxim decided the issue in favor of the pro-British Protestants; the French Catholic mission was burned to the ground, and the French bishop fled. The resultant scandal was settled in Europe when the British government paid compensation to the French mission and persuaded the Germans to relinquish their claim to Uganda.

With Buganda secured by Lugard and the Germans no longer contending for control, the British began to enlarge their claim to the "headwaters of the Nile," as they called the land north of Lake Victoria. Allying with the Protestant Baganda chiefs, the British set about conquering the rest of the country, aided by Nubian mercenary troops who had formerly served the khedive of Egypt. Bunyoro had been spared the religious civil wars of Buganda and was firmly united by its king, Kabarega, who had several regiments of troops armed with guns. After five years of bloody conflict, the British occupied Bunyoro and conquered Acholi and the northern region, and the rough outlines of the Uganda Protectorate came into being. Other African polities, such as the Ankole kingdom to the southwest, signed treaties with the British, as did the chiefdoms of Busoga, but the kinship-based peoples of eastern and northeastern Uganda had to be overcome by military force.

A mutiny by Nubian mercenary troops in 1897 was only barely suppressed after two years of fighting, during which Baganda Christian allies of the British once again demonstrated their support for the colonial power. As a reward for this support, and in recognition of Buganda's formidable military presence, the British negotiated a separate treaty with Buganda, granting it a large measure of autonomy and self-government within the larger protectorate. One-half of Bunyoro's conquered territory was awarded to Buganda as well, including the historical heartland of the kingdom containing several Nyoro (root word and adjective for Bunyoro) royal tombs. Buganda doubled in size from ten to twenty counties (*sazas*), but the "lost counties" of Bunyoro remained a continuing grievance that would return to haunt Buganda in the 1960s.

The Colonial Era

Although momentous change occurred during the colonial era in Uganda, some characteristics of late-nineteenth century African society survived to reemerge at the time of independence. Colonial rule affected local economic systems dramatically, in part because the first concern of the British was financial. Quelling the 1897 mutiny had been costly—units of the Indian army had been transported to Uganda at considerable expense. The new commissioner of Uganda in 1900, Sir Harry H. Johnston, had orders to establish an efficient administration and to levy taxes as quickly as possible. Johnston approached the chiefs in Buganda with offers of jobs in the colonial administration in return for their collaboration. The chiefs, whom Johnston characterized in demeaning terms, were more interested in preserving Buganda as a self-governing entity, continuing the royal line of *kabakas,* and securing private land tenure for themselves and their supporters. Hard bargaining ensued, but the chiefs ended up with everything they wanted, including one-half of all the land in Buganda. The half left to the British as "Crown Land" was later found to be largely swamp and scrub.

Johnston's Buganda Agreement of 1900 imposed a tax on huts and guns, designated the chiefs as tax collectors, and testified to the continued alliance of British and Baganda interests. The British signed much less generous treaties with the other kingdoms (Toro in 1900, Ankole in 1901, and Bunyoro in 1933) without the provision of large-scale private land tenure. The smaller chiefdoms of Busoga were ignored.

The Baganda immediately offered their services to the British as administrators over their recently conquered neighbors, an offer that was attractive to the economy-minded colonial administration. Baganda agents fanned out as local tax collectors and labor organizers in areas such as Kigezi, Mbale, and, significantly, Bunyoro. This subimperialism and Ganda cultural chauvinism were resented by the people being administered. Wherever they went, Baganda insisted on the exclusive use of their language, Luganda, and they planted bananas as the only proper food worth eating. They regarded their traditional dress—long cotton gowns called *kanzus*—as civilized; all else was barbarian. They also encouraged and engaged in mission work, attempting to convert locals to their form of Christianity or Islam. In some areas, the resulting backlash aided the efforts of religious rivals—for example, Catholics won converts in areas where oppressive rule was identified with a Protestant Muganda chief.

The people of Bunyoro were particularly aggrieved, having fought the Baganda and the British; having a substantial section of their heartland annexed to Buganda as the ''lost counties''; and finally having ''arrogant'' Baganda administrators issuing orders, collecting taxes, and forcing unpaid labor. In 1907 the Banyoro rose in a rebellion called *nyangire,* or ''refusing,'' and succeeded in having the Baganda subimperial agents withdrawn.

Meanwhile, in 1901 the completion of the Uganda railroad from the coast at Mombasa to the Lake Victoria port of Kisumu moved colonial authorities to encourage the growth of cash crops to help pay the railroad's operating costs. Another result of the railroad construction was the 1902 decision to transfer the eastern section of the Uganda Protectorate to the Kenya Colony, then called the East Africa Protectorate, to keep the entire railroad line under one local colonial administration. Because the railroad experienced cost overruns in Kenya, the British decided to justify its exceptional expense and pay its operating costs by introducing large-scale European settlement in a vast tract of land that became a center of cash-crop agriculture known as the ''white highlands.''

In many areas of Uganda, by contrast, agricultural production was placed in the hands of Africans, if they responded to the opportunity. Cotton was the crop of choice, largely because of pressure by the British Cotton Growing Association, textile manufacturers who urged the colonies to provide raw materials for British mills. Even the CMS joined the effort by launching the Uganda Company (managed by a former missionary) to promote cotton planting and to buy and transport the produce.

Buganda, with its strategic location on the lakeside, reaped the benefits of cotton growing. The advantages of this crop were quickly recognized by the Baganda chiefs who had newly acquired freehold estates, which came to be known as *mailo* land because they were measured in square miles. In 1905 the initial baled cotton export was valued at £2,200; in 1906, £21,000; in 1907; £211,000; and in 1908, £252,000. By 1915 the value of cotton exports had climbed to £2,369,000, and Britain was able to end its subsidy of colonial administration in Uganda. In Kenya, by contrast, the white settlers required continuing subsidies by the home government.

The income generated by cotton sales made Buganda relatively prosperous, compared with the rest of colonial Uganda, although before World War I cotton was also being grown in the eastern regions of Busoga, Lango, and Teso. Many Baganda spent their new earnings on imported clothing, bicycles, metal roofing, and even automobiles. They also invested in their children's educations. The Christian missions emphasized literacy skills, and

African converts quickly learned to read and write. By 1911 two popular journals, *Ebifa* (News) and *Munno* (Your Friend), were published monthly in Luganda. Heavily supported by African funds, new schools were soon turning out graduating classes at Mengo High School, St. Mary's Kisubi, Namilyango, Gayaza, and King's College Budo—all in Buganda. The chief minister of the kingdom, Sir Apolo Kagwa, personally awarded a bicycle to the top graduate at King's College Budo, together with the promise of a government job. The schools, in fact, had inherited the educational function formerly performed in the *kabaka*'s palace, where generations of young pages had been trained to become chiefs. Now the qualifications sought were literacy and skills, including typing and English translation.

Two important principles of precolonial political life carried over into the colonial era: clientage, whereby ambitious younger officeholders attached themselves to older high-ranking chiefs, and generational conflict, which resulted when the younger generation sought to expel their elders from office in order to replace them. After World War I, the younger aspirants to high office in Buganda became impatient with the seemingly perpetual tenure of Sir Apolo and his contemporaries, who lacked many of the skills that members of the younger generation had acquired through schooling. Calling themselves the Young Baganda Association, members of the new generation attached themselves to the young *kabaka,* Daudi Chwa, who was the figurehead ruler of Buganda under indirect rule. But Kabaka Daudi never gained real political power, and after a short and frustrating reign, he died at the relatively young age of forty-three.

Far more promising as a source of political support were the British colonial officers, who welcomed the typing and translation skills of school graduates and advanced the careers of their favorites. The contest was decided after World War I, when an influx of British ex-military officers, now serving as district commissioners, began to feel that self-government was an obstacle to good government. Specifically, they accused Sir Apolo and his generation of inefficiency, abuse of power, and failure to keep adequate financial accounts—charges that were not hard to document. Sir Apolo resigned in 1926, at about the same time that a host of elderly Baganda chiefs were replaced by a new generation of officeholders. The Buganda treasury was also audited that year for the first time. Although it was not a nationalist organization, the Young Baganda Association claimed to represent popular African dissatisfaction with the old order. As soon as the younger Baganda had replaced the older generation in office, however, their objections to privilege accompanying power ceased. The pattern persisted in Ugandan politics up to and after independence.

The commoners, who had been laboring on the cotton estates of the chiefs before World War I, did not remain servile. As time passed, they bought small parcels of land from their erstwhile land-lords. This land fragmentation was aided by the British, who in 1927 forced the chiefs to limit severely the rents and obligatory labor they could demand from their tenants. Thus the oligarchy of landed chiefs who had emerged with the Buganda Agreement of 1900 declined in importance, and agricultural production shifted to in-dependent smallholders, who grew cotton, and later coffee, for the export market.

Unlike Tanganyika, which was devastated during the prolonged fighting between Britain and Germany in the East African cam-paign of World War I, Uganda prospered from wartime agricul-tural production. After the population losses during the era of conquest and the losses to disease at the turn of the century (par-ticularly the devastating sleeping sickness epidemic of 1900–06), Uganda's population was growing again. Even the 1930s depres-sion seemed to affect smallholder cash farmers in Uganda less se-verely than it did the white settler producers in Kenya. Ugandans simply grew their own food until rising prices made export crops attractive again.

Two issues continued to create grievances through the 1930s and 1940s. The colonial government strictly regulated the buying and processing of cash crops, setting prices and reserving the role of intermediary for Asians, who were thought to be more efficient. The British and Asians firmly repelled African attempts to break into cotton ginning. In addition, on the Asian-owned sugar plan-tations established in the 1920s, labor for sugarcane and other cash crops was increasingly provided by migrants from peripheral areas of Uganda and even from outside Uganda.

The Issue of Independence

In 1949 discontented Baganda rioted and burned down the houses of progovernment chiefs. The rioters had three demands: the right to bypass government price controls on the export sales of cotton, the removal of the Asian monopoly over cotton ginning, and the right to have their own representatives in local government replace chiefs appointed by the British. They were critical as well of the young *kabaka*, Frederick Walugembe Mutesa II (also known as Kabaka Freddie), for his inattention to the needs of his people. The British governor, Sir John Hall, regarded the riots as the work of communist-inspired agitators and rejected the suggested reforms.

Kabaka Daudi Chwa, with regents (left) and British administrators (right)

Far from leading the people into confrontation, Uganda's would-be agitators were slow to respond to popular discontent. Nevertheless, the Uganda African Farmers Union, founded by I.K. Musazi in 1947, was blamed for the riots and was banned by the British. Musazi's Uganda National Congress replaced the farmers union in 1952, but because the congress remained a casual discussion group more than an organized political party, it stagnated and came to an end just two years after its inception.

Meanwhile, the British began to move ahead of the Ugandans in preparing for independence. The effects of Britain's postwar withdrawal from India, the march of nationalism in West Africa, and a more liberal philosophy in the Colonial Office geared toward future self-rule all began to be felt in Uganda. The embodiment of these issues arrived in 1952 in the person of a new and energetic reformist governor, Sir Andrew Cohen (formerly undersecretary for African affairs in the Colonial Office). Cohen set about preparing Uganda for independence. On the economic side, he removed obstacles to African cotton ginning, rescinded price discrimination against African-grown coffee, encouraged cooperatives, and established the Uganda Development Corporation to promote and finance new projects. On the political side, he reorganized the Legislative Council, which had consisted of an unrepresentative selection of interest groups heavily favoring the European community, to include African representatives elected from districts throughout Uganda. This system became a prototype for the future parliament.

Power Politics in Buganda

The prospect of elections caused a sudden proliferation of new political parties. This development alarmed the old-guard leaders within the Uganda kingdoms because they realized that the center of power would be at the national level. The spark that ignited wider opposition to Governor Cohen's reforms was a 1953 speech in London in which the secretary of state for colonies referred to the possibility of a federation of the three East African territories (Kenya, Uganda, and Tanganyika), similar to that established in central Africa. Many Ugandans were aware of the Federation of Rhodesia and Nyasaland (later Zimbabwe, Zambia, and Malawi) and its domination by white settler interests. Ugandans deeply feared the prospect of an East African federation dominated by the racist settlers of Kenya, which was then in the midst of the bitter Mau Mau uprising. They had vigorously resisted a similar suggestion by the 1930 Hilton Young Commission. Confidence in Cohen vanished just as the governor was preparing to urge Buganda to recognize that its special status would have to be sacrificed in the interests of a new and larger nation-state.

Kabaka Freddie, who had been regarded by his subjects as uninterested in their welfare, now refused to cooperate with Cohen's plan for an integrated Buganda. Instead, he demanded that Buganda be separated from the rest of the protectorate and transferred to Foreign Office jurisdiction. Cohen's response to this crisis was to deport the *kabaka* to a comfortable exile in London. His forced departure made the *kabaka* an instant martyr in the eyes of the Baganda, whose latent separatism and anticolonial sentiments set off a storm of protest. Cohen's action had backfired, and he could find no one among the Baganda prepared or able to mobilize support for his schemes. After two frustrating years of unrelenting Ganda hostility and obstruction, Cohen was forced to reinstate Kabaka Freddie.

The negotiations leading to the *kabaka*'s return had an outcome similar to the negotiations of Commissioner Johnston in 1900; although appearing to satisfy the British, they were a resounding victory for the Baganda. Cohen secured the *kabaka*'s agreement not to oppose independence within the larger Uganda framework. Not only was the *kabaka* reinstated in return, but for the first time since 1889, the monarch was also given the power to appoint and dismiss his chiefs (Buganda government officials) instead of acting

18

as a mere figurehead while they conducted the affairs of government. The *kabaka*'s new power was cloaked in the misleading claim that he would be only a "constitutional monarch," while in fact he was a leading player in deciding how Uganda would be governed. A new grouping of Baganda calling themselves the "King's Friends" rallied to the *kabaka*'s defense. They were conservative, fiercely loyal to Buganda as a kingdom, and willing to entertain the prospect of participation in an independent Uganda only if it were headed by the *kabaka*. Baganda politicians who did not share this vision or who were opposed to the "King's Friends" found themselves branded as the "King's Enemies," which meant political and social ostracism.

The major exception to this rule were the Roman Catholic Baganda who had formed their own party, the Democratic Party (DP), led by Benedicto Kiwanuka. Many Catholics had felt excluded from the Protestant-dominated establishment in Buganda ever since Lugard's Maxim had turned the tide in 1892. The *kabaka* had to be Protestant, and he was invested in a coronation ceremony modeled on that of British monarchs (who are invested by the Church of England's Archbishop of Canterbury) that took place at the main Protestant church. Religion and politics were equally inseparable in the other kingdoms throughout Uganda. The DP had Catholic as well as other adherents and was probably the best organized of all the parties preparing for elections. It had printing presses and the backing of the popular newspaper *Munno,* which was published at the St. Mary's Kisubi mission.

Elsewhere in Uganda, the emergence of the *kabaka* as a political force provoked immediate hostility. Political parties and local interest groups were riddled with divisions and rivalries, but they shared one concern: they were determined not to be dominated by Buganda. In 1960 a political organizer from Lango, Milton Obote, seized the initiative and formed a new party, the Uganda People's Congress (UPC), as a coalition of all those outside the Roman Catholic-dominated DP who opposed Buganda hegemony.

The steps Cohen had initiated to bring about the independence of a unified Uganda state had led to a polarization between factions from Buganda and those opposed to its domination. Buganda's population in 1959 was 2 million, out of Uganda's total of 6 million. Even discounting the many non-Baganda resident in Buganda, there were at least 1 million people who owed allegiance to the *kabaka*—too many to be overlooked or shunted aside, but too few to dominate the country as a whole. It was obvious that autonomy for Buganda and a strong unitary government were incompatible, but no compromise emerged, and the decision on the form of government was postponed. The British announced that elections would be held in March 1961 for "responsible government," the next-to-last stage of preparation before the formal granting of independence. It was assumed that those winning the election would gain valuable experience in office, preparing them for the probable responsibility of governing after independence.

In Buganda the "King's Friends" urged a total boycott of the election because their attempts to secure promises of future autonomy had been rebuffed. Consequently, when the voters went to the polls throughout Uganda to elect eighty-two National Assembly members, in Buganda only the Roman Catholic supporters of the DP braved severe public pressure and voted, capturing twenty of Buganda's twenty-one allotted seats. This artificial situation gave the DP a majority of seats, although it had a minority of 416,000 votes nationwide versus 495,000 for the UPC. Benedicto Kiwanuka became the new chief minister of Uganda.

Shocked by the results, the Baganda separatists, who formed a political party called Kabaka Yekka (KY), had second thoughts about the wisdom of their election boycott. They quickly welcomed the recommendations of a British commission that proposed a future federal form of government. According to these recommendations, Buganda would enjoy a measure of internal autonomy if it participated fully in the national government. For its part, the UPC was equally anxious to eject its DP rivals from government before they became entrenched. Obote reached an understanding with Kabaka Freddie and the KY, accepting Buganda's special federal relationship and even a provision by which the *kabaka* could appoint Buganda's representatives to the National Assembly, in return for a strategic alliance to defeat the DP. The *kabaka* was also promised the largely ceremonial position of head of state of Uganda, which was of great symbolic importance to the Baganda.

This marriage of convenience between the UPC and the KY made inevitable the defeat of the DP interim administration. In the aftermath of the April 1962 final election leading up to independence, Uganda's national parliament consisted of forty-three UPC delegates, twenty-four KY delegates, and twenty-four DP delegates. The new UPC–KY coalition led Uganda into independence in October 1962, with Obote as prime minister and the *kabaka* as head of state.

Independence: The Early Years

Uganda's approach to independence was unlike that of most other colonial territories where political parties had been organized to force self-rule or independence from a reluctant colonial regime. Whereas these conditions would have required local and regional differences to be subordinated to the greater goal of winning independence, in Uganda parties were forced to cooperate with one another, with the prospect of independence already assured. One of the major parties, KY, was even opposed to independence unless its particular separatist desires were met. The UPC–KY partnership represented a fragile alliance of two fragile parties.

In the UPC, leadership was factionalized. Each party functionary represented a local constituency, and most of the constituencies were ethnically distinct. For example, Obote's strength lay among his Langi kin in eastern Uganda; George Magezi represented the local interests of his Banyoro compatriots; Grace S.K. Ibingira's strength was in the Ankole kingdom; and Felix Onama was the northern leader of the largely neglected West Nile District in the northwest corner of Uganda. Each of these regional political bosses and those from the other Uganda regions expected to receive a ministerial post in the new Uganda government, to exercise patronage, and to bring the material fruits of independence to local supporters. Failing these objectives, each was likely either to withdraw from the UPC coalition or realign within it.

Moreover, the UPC had had no effective urban organization before independence, although it was able to mobilize the trade unions, most of which were led by non-Ugandan immigrant workers from Kenya (a situation that contributed to the independent Uganda government's almost immediate hostility toward the trade unions). No common ideology united the UPC, the composition of which ranged from the near reactionary Onama to the radical John Kakonge, leader of the UPC Youth League. As prime minister, Obote was responsible for keeping this loose coalition of divergent interest groups intact.

Obote also faced the task of maintaining the UPC's external alliances, primarily the coalition between the UPC and the *kabaka*, who led Buganda's KY. Obote proved adept at meeting the diverse demands of his many partners in government. He even temporarily acceded to some demands that he found repugnant, such as Buganda's claim for special treatment. This accession led to demands by other kingdoms for similar recognition. The Busoga chiefdoms banded together to claim that they, too, deserved recognition under the rule of their newly defined monarch, the *kyabasinga*. Not to be outdone, the Iteso people, who had never recognized a precolonial king, claimed the title *kingoo* for Teso District's political boss, Cuthbert Obwangor. Despite these separatist pressures,

Obote's long-term goal was to build a strong central government at the expense of entrenched local interests, especially those of Buganda.

The first major challenge to the Obote government came not from the kingdoms, nor the regional interests, but from the military. In January 1964, units of the Ugandan army mutinied, demanding higher pay and more rapid promotions (see The First Obote Regime: The Growth of the Military, ch. 5). Minister of Defense Onama, who courageously went to speak to the mutineers, was seized and held hostage. Obote was forced to call in British troops to restore order, a humiliating blow to the new regime. In the aftermath, Obote's government acceded to all the mutineers' demands, unlike the governments of Kenya and Tanganyika, which responded to similar demands with increased discipline and tighter control over their small military forces.

The military then began to assume a more prominent role in Ugandan life. Obote selected a popular junior officer with minimal education, Idi Amin Dada, and promoted him rapidly through the ranks as a personal protégé. As the army expanded, it became a source of political patronage and of potential political power.

Later in 1964, Obote felt strong enough to address the critical issue of the "lost counties," which the British had conveniently postponed until after independence. The combination of patronage offers and the promise of future rewards within the ruling coalition gradually thinned opposition party ranks, as members of parliament "crossed the floor" to join the government benches. After two years of independence, Obote finally acquired enough votes to give the UPC a majority and free himself of the KY coalition. The turning point came when several DP members of parliament (MPs) from Bunyoro agreed to join the government side if Obote would undertake a popular referendum to restore the "lost counties" to Bunyoro. The *kabaka,* naturally, opposed the plebiscite. Unable to prevent it, he sent 300 armed Baganda veterans to the area to intimidate Banyoro voters. In turn, 2,000 veterans from Bunyoro massed on the frontier. Civil war was averted, and the referendum was held. The vote demonstrated an overwhelming desire by residents in the counties annexed to Buganda in 1900 to be restored to their historical Bunyoro allegiance, which was duly enacted by the new UPC majority despite KY opposition.

This triumph for Obote and the UPC strengthened the central government and threw Buganda into disarray. KY unity was weakened by internal recriminations, after which some KY stalwarts, too, began to "cross the floor" to join Obote's victorious government. By early 1966, the result was a parliament composed of seventy-four UPC, nine DP, eight KY, and one independent MP. Obote's efforts to produce a one-party state with a powerful executive prime minister appeared to be on the verge of success.

Paradoxically, however, as the perceived threat from Buganda diminished, many non-Baganda alliances weakened. And as the possibility of an opposition DP victory faded, the UPC coalition itself began to come apart. The one-party state did not signal the end of political conflict, however; it merely relocated and intensified that conflict within the party. The issue that brought the UPC disharmony to a crisis involved Obote's military protégé, Idi Amin.

In 1966 Amin caused a commotion when he walked into a Kampala bank with a gold bar (bearing the stamp of the government of the Belgian Congo) and asked the bank manager to exchange it for cash. Amin's account was ultimately credited with a deposit of £217,000. Obote rivals questioned the incident, and it emerged that the prime minister and a handful of close associates had used Colonel Amin and units of the Ugandan army to intervene in the neighboring Congo crisis. Former supporters of Congolese leader Patrice Lumumba, led by a "General Olenga," opposed the American-backed government and were attempting to lead the eastern region into secession. These troops were reported to be trading looted ivory and gold for arms supplies secretly smuggled to them by Amin. The arrangement became public when Olenga later claimed that he had failed to receive the promised munitions. This claim appeared to be supported by the fact that in mid-1965, a seventy-five-ton shipment of Chinese weapons was intercepted by the Kenyan government as it was being moved from Tanzania to Uganda.

Obote's rivals for leadership within the UPC, supported by some Baganda politicians and others who were hostile to Obote, used the evidence revealed by Amin's casual bank deposit to claim that the prime minister and his closest associates were corrupt and had conducted secret foreign policy for personal gain, in the amount of £225,000 each. Obote denied the charge and said the money had been spent to buy the munitions for Olenga's Congolese troops. On February 4, 1966, while Obote was away on a trip to the north of the country, an effective "no confidence" vote against Obote was passed by the UPC MPs. This attempt to remove Obote appeared to be organized by UPC Secretary General Grace S.K. Ibingira, closely supported by the UPC leader from Bunyoro, George Magezi, and a number of other southern UPC notables. Only the radical UPC member, John Kakonge, voted against the motion.

Because he was faced with a nearly unanimous disavowal by his governing party and national parliament, many people expected Obote to resign. Instead, Obote turned to Idi Amin and the army, and, in effect, carried out a coup d'état against his own government in order to stay in power. Obote suspended the constitution, arrested the offending UPC ministers, and assumed control of the state. He forced a new constitution through parliament without a reading and without the necessary quorum. That constitution abolished the federal powers of the kingdoms, most notably the internal autonomy enjoyed by Buganda, and concentrated presidential powers in the prime minister's office. The *kabaka* objected, and Buganda prepared to wage a legal battle. Baganda leaders rhetorically demanded that Obote's "illegal" government remove itself from Buganda soil.

Buganda, however, once again miscalculated, for Obote was not interested in negotiating. Instead, he sent Idi Amin and loyal troops to attack the *kabaka*'s palace on nearby Mengo Hill. The palace was defended by a small group of bodyguards armed with rifles and shotguns. Amin's troops had heavy weapons but were reluctant to press the attack until Obote became impatient and demanded results. By the time the palace was overrun, the *kabaka* had taken advantage of a cloudburst to exit over the rear wall. He hailed a passing taxi and was driven off to exile. After the assault, Obote was reasonably secure from open opposition. The new republican 1967 constitution abolished the kingdoms altogether. Buganda was divided into four districts and ruled through martial law, a forerunner of the military domination over the civilian population that all of Uganda would experience after 1971.

Obote's success in the face of adversity reclaimed for him the support of most members of the UPC, which then became the only legal political party. The original independence election of 1962, therefore, was the last one held in Uganda until December 1980. On the homefront, Obote issued the "Common Man's Charter," echoed the call for African Socialism by Tanzanian president Julius Nyerere, and proclaimed a "move to the left" to signal new efforts to consolidate power. His critics noted, however, that he placed most control over economic nationalization in the hands of an Asian millionaire who was also a financial backer of the UPC. Obote created a system of secret police, the General Service Unit (GSU). Headed by a relative, Akena Adoko, the GSU reported on suspected subversives (see Internal Security Services, ch. 5). The Special Force Units of paramilitary police, heavily recruited from Obote's own region and ethnic group, supplemented the security forces within the army and police.

Although Buganda had been defeated and occupied by the military, Obote was still concerned about security there. His concerns were well founded; in December 1969, he was wounded in an assassination attempt and narrowly escaped more serious injury when a grenade thrown near him failed to explode. He had retained power by relying on Idi Amin and the army, but it was not clear that he could continue to count on their loyalty.

Obote appeared particularly uncertain of the army after Amin's sole rival among senior army officers, Brigadier Acap Okoya, was murdered early in 1970. (Amin later promoted the man rumored to have recruited Okoya's killers.) A second attempt was made on Obote's life when his motorcade was ambushed later that year, but the vice president's car was mistakenly riddled with bullets. Obote began to recruit more Acholi and Langi troops, and he accelerated their promotions to counter the large numbers of soldiers from Amin's home, which was then known as West Nile District. Obote also enlarged the paramilitary Special Force Units as a counterweight to the army.

Amin, who at times inspected his troops wearing an outsized sport shirt with Obote's face across the front and back, protested his loyalty. But in October 1970, Amin was placed under temporary house arrest while investigators looked into his army expenditures, reportedly several million dollars over budget. Another charge against Amin was that he had continued to aid southern Sudan's Anya Nya rebels in opposing the regime of Jafaar Numayri even after Obote had shifted his support away from the Anya Nya to Numayri. This foreign policy shift provoked an outcry from Israel, which had been supplying the Anya Nya rebels. Amin was close friends with several Israeli military advisers who were in Uganda to help train the army, and their eventual role in Amin's efforts to oust Obote remained the subject of continuing controversy.

Military Rule under Amin

By January 1971, Obote was prepared to rid himself of the potential threat posed by Amin. Departing for the Commonwealth Conference of Heads of Government at Singapore, he relayed orders to loyal Langi officers that Amin and his supporters in the army were to be arrested. Various versions emerged of the way this news was leaked to Amin; in any case, Amin decided to strike first. In the early morning hours of January 25, 1971, mechanized units loyal to him attacked strategic targets in Kampala and the airport at Entebbe, where the first shell fired by a pro-Amin tank commander killed two Roman Catholic priests in the airport waiting room. Amin's troops easily overcame the disorganized opposition to the coup, and Amin almost immediately initiated mass executions of Acholi and Langi troops, whom he believed to be pro-Obote.

The Amin coup was warmly welcomed by most of the people of the Buganda kingdom, which Obote had attempted to dismantle. They seemed willing to forget that their new president, Idi Amin, had been the tool of that military suppression. Amin made the usual statements about his government's intent to play a mere "caretaker role" until the country could recover sufficiently for civilian rule. Amin repudiated Obote's nonaligned foreign policy, and his government was quickly recognized by Israel, Britain, and the United States. By contrast, presidents Julius Nyerere of Tanzania, Kenneth Kaunda of Zambia, Jomo Kenyatta of Kenya, and the Organization of African Unity (OAU) initially refused to accept the legitimacy of the new military government. Nyerere, in particular, opposed Amin's regime, and he offered hospitality to the exiled Obote, facilitating his attempts to raise a force and return to power.

Amin's military experience, which was virtually his only experience, determined the character of his rule. He renamed Government House "the Command Post," instituted an advisory defense council composed of military commanders, placed military tribunals above the system of civil law, appointed soldiers to top government posts and parastatal agencies, and even informed the newly inducted civilian cabinet ministers that they would be subject to military discipline. Uganda was, in effect, governed from a collection of military barracks scattered across the country, where battalion commanders, acting like local warlords, represented the coercive arm of the government. The GSU was disbanded and replaced by the State Research Bureau (SRB; see Idi Amin and Military Rule, ch. 5). SRB headquarters at Nakasero became the scene of torture and grisly executions over the next several years.

Despite its outward display of a military chain of command, Amin's government was arguably more riddled with rivalries, regional divisions, and ethnic politics than the UPC coalition that it had replaced. The army itself was an arena of lethal competition, in which losers were usually eliminated. Within the officer corps, those trained in Britain opposed those trained in Israel, and both stood against the untrained, who soon eliminated many of the army's most experienced officers. In 1966, well before the Amin era, northerners in the army had assaulted and harassed soldiers from the south. In 1971 and 1972, the Lugbara and Kakwa (Amin's ethnic group) from the West Nile District were slaughtering northern Acholi and Langi, who were identified with Obote. Then the

*Idi Amin addresses the United Nations General Assembly
in New York, October 1975.
Courtesy United Nations (T. Chen)*

Kakwa fought the Lugbara. Amin came to rely on Nubians and on former Anya Nya rebels from southern Sudan.

The army, which had been progressively expanded under Obote, was further doubled and redoubled under Amin. Recruitment was largely, but not entirely, in the north. There were periodic purges, when various battalion commanders were viewed as potential problems or became real threats. Each purge provided new opportunities for promotions from the ranks. The commander of the air force, Smuts Guweddeko, had previously worked as a telephone operator; the unofficial executioner for the regime, Major Malyamungu, had formerly been a nightwatch officer. By the mid-1970s, only the most trustworthy military units were allowed ammunition, although this prohibition did not prevent a series of mutinies and murders. An attempt by an American journalist, Nicholas Stroh, and his colleague, Robert Siedle, to investigate one of these barracks outbreaks in 1972 at the Simba Battalion in Mbarara led to their disappearances and later deaths.

Amin never forgot the source of his power. He spent much of his time rewarding, promoting, and manipulating the army. Financing his ever-increasing military expenditures was a continuing concern. Early in 1972, he reversed foreign policy—never a

27

major issue for Amin—to secure financial and military aid from Muammar Qadhafi of Libya. Amin expelled the remaining Israeli advisers, to whom he was much indebted, and became vociferously anti-Israel. To induce foreign aid from Saudi Arabia, he rediscovered his previously neglected Islamic heritage. He also commissioned the construction of a great mosque on Kampala Hill in the capital city, but it was never completed because much of the money intended for it was embezzled.

In September 1972, Amin expelled almost all of Uganda's 50,000 Asians and seized their property. Although Amin proclaimed that the "common man" was the beneficiary of this drastic act—which proved immensely popular—it was actually the army that emerged with the houses, cars, and businesses of the departing Asian minority. This expropriation of property proved disastrous for the already declining economy. Businesses were run into the ground, cement factories at Tororo and Fort Portal collapsed from lack of maintenance, and sugar production literally ground to a halt, as unmaintained machinery jammed permanently. Uganda's export crops were sold by government parastatals, but most of the foreign currency they earned went for purchasing imports for the army. The most famous example was the so-called "whiskey run" to Stansted Airport in Britain, where planeloads of Scotch whiskey, transistor radios, and luxury items were purchased for Amin to distribute among his officers and troops. An African proverb, it was said, summed up Amin's treatment of his army: "A dog with a bone in its mouth can't bite."

The rural African producers, particularly of coffee, turned to smuggling, especially to Kenya. The smuggling problem became an obsession with Amin; toward the end of his rule, he appointed his mercenary adviser, the former British citizen Bob Astles, to take all necessary steps to eliminate the problem. These steps included orders to shoot smugglers on sight.

Another near-obsession for Amin was the threat of a counterattack by former president Obote. Shortly after the expulsion of Asians in 1972, Obote did launch such an attempt across the Tanzanian border into southwestern Uganda. His small army contingent in twenty-seven trucks set out to capture the southern Ugandan military post at Masaka but instead settled down to await a general uprising against Amin, which did not occur. A planned seizure of the airport at Entebbe by soldiers in an allegedly hijacked East African Airways passenger aircraft was aborted when Obote's pilot blew out the aircraft's tires and it remained in Tanzania. Amin was able to mobilize his more reliable Malire Mechanical Regiment and expel the invaders.

Although jubilant at his success, Amin realized that Obote, with Nyerere's aid, might try again. He had the SRB and the newly formed Public Safety Unit (PSU) redouble their efforts to uncover subversives and other imagined enemies of the state. General fear and insecurity became a way of life for the populace, as thousands of people disappeared. In an ominous twist, people sometimes learned by listening to the radio that they were ''about to disappear.'' State terrorism was evidenced in a series of spectacular incidents; for example, High Court Judge Benedicto Kiwanuka, former head of government and leader of the banned DP, was seized directly from his courtroom. Like many other victims, he was forced to remove his shoes and then bundled into the trunk of a car, never to be seen alive again. Whether calculated or not, the symbolism of a pair of shoes by the roadside to mark the passing of a human life was a bizarre yet piercing form of state terrorism.

Amin did attempt to establish ties with an international terrorist group in July 1976, when he offered the Palestinian hijackers of an Air France flight from Tel Aviv a protected base at the old airport at Entebbe, from which to press their demands in exchange for the release of Israeli hostages. The dramatic rescue of the hostages by Israeli commandos was a severe blow to Amin, unassuaged by his murder of a hospitalized hostage, Dora Block, and his mass execution of Entebbe airport personnel.

Amin's government, conducted by often erratic personal proclamation, continued on. Because he was illiterate—a disability shared with most of his higher ranking officers—Amin relayed orders and policy decisions orally by telephone, over the radio, and in long rambling speeches to which civil servants learned to pay close attention. The bureaucracy became paralyzed as government administrators feared to make what might prove to be a wrong decision. The minister of defense demanded and was given the Ministry of Education office building, but then the decision was reversed. Important education files were lost during their transfer back and forth by wheelbarrow. In many respects, Amin's government in the 1970s resembled the governments of nineteenth-century African monarchs, with the same problems of enforcing orders at a distance, controlling rival factions at court, and rewarding loyal followers with plunder. However, Amin's regime was possibly less efficient than those of the precolonial monarchs.

Religious conflict was another characteristic of the Amin regime that had its origins in the nineteenth century. After rediscovering his Islamic allegiance in the effort to gain foreign aid from Libya and Saudi Arabia, Amin began to pay more attention to the formerly deprived Muslims in Uganda, a move that turned out to be a mixed blessing for them. Muslims began to do well in what economic opportunities yet remained, the more so if they had relatives in the army. Construction work began on Kibule Hill, the site of Kampala's most prominent mosque. Many Ugandan Muslims with a sense of history believed that the Muslim defeat by Christians in 1889 was finally being redressed. Christians, in turn, perceived that they were under siege as a religious group; it was clear that Amin viewed the churches as potential centers of opposition. A number of priests and ministers disappeared in the course of the 1970s, but the matter reached a climax with the formal protest against army terrorism in 1977 by Church of Uganda ministers, led by Archbishop Janan Luwum. Although Luwum's body was subsequently recovered from a clumsily contrived "auto accident," subsequent investigations revealed that Luwum had been shot to death by Amin himself. This latest in a long line of atrocities was greeted with international condemnation, but apart from the continued trade boycott initiated by the United States in July 1978, verbal condemnation was not accompanied by action.

By 1978 Amin's circle of close associates had shrunk significantly—the result of defections and executions. It was increasingly risky to be too close to Amin, as his vice president and formerly trusted associate, General Mustafa Adrisi, discovered. When Adrisi was injured in a suspicious auto accident, troops loyal to him became restive. The once reliable Malire Mechanized Regiment mutinied, as did other units. In October 1978, Amin sent troops still loyal to him against the mutineers, some of whom fled across the Tanzanian border. Amin then claimed that Tanzanian president Nyerere, his perennial enemy, had been at the root of his troubles. Amin accused Nyerere of waging war against Uganda, and, hoping to divert attention from his internal troubles and rally Uganda against the foreign adversary, Amin invaded Tanzanian territory and formally annexed a section across the Kagera River boundary on November 1, 1978 (see Idi Amin and Military Rule, ch. 5).

Nyerere mobilized his citizen army reserves and counterattacked, joined by Ugandan exiles united as the Uganda National Liberation Army (UNLA). The Ugandan army retreated steadily, expending much of its energy by looting along the way. Libya's Qadhafi sent 3,000 troops to aid fellow Muslim Amin, but the Libyans soon found themselves on the front line, while behind them Ugandan army units were using supply trucks to carry their newly plundered wealth in the opposite direction. Tanzania and the UNLA took Kampala in April 1979, and Amin fled by air, first to Libya and later to a seemingly permanent exile at Jiddah, Saudi

Arabia. The war that had cost Tanzania an estimated US$1 million per day was over. What kind of government would attempt the monumental task of rebuilding the economically and psychologically devastated country, which had lost an estimated 300,000 victims to Amin's murderous eight-year regime?

Uganda after Amin

The Interim Period, 1979–80

A month before the liberation of Kampala, representatives of twenty-two Ugandan civilian and military groups were hastily called together at Moshi, Tanzania, to try to agree on an interim civilian government once Amin was removed. Called the Unity Conference in the hope that unity might prevail, it managed to establish the Uganda National Liberation Front (UNLF) as the political representative of the UNLA. Dr. Yusuf Lule, former principal of Makerere University, became head of the UNLF executive committee. As an academic rather than a politician, Lule was not regarded as a threat to any of the contending factions. Shortly after Amin's departure, Lule and the UNLF moved to Kampala, where they established an interim government. Lule became president, advised by a temporary parliament, the National Consultative Council (NCC). The NCC, in turn, was composed of representatives from the Unity Conference.

Conflict surfaced immediately between Lule and some of the more radical of the council members who saw him as too conservative, too autocratic, and too willing as a Muganda to listen to advice from other Baganda. After only three months, with the apparent approval of Nyerere, whose troops still controlled Kampala, Lule was forcibly removed from office and exiled. He was replaced by Godfrey Binaisa, a Muganda like Lule, but one who had previously served as a high-ranking member of Obote's UPC. It was not an auspicious start to the rebuilding of a new Uganda, which required political and economic stability. Indeed, the quarrels within the NCC, which Binaisa enlarged to 127 members, revealed that many rival and would-be politicians who had returned from exile were resuming their self-interested operating styles. Ugandans who endured the deprivations of the Amin era became even more disillusioned with their leaders. Binaisa managed to stay in office longer than Lule, but his inability to gain control over a burgeoning new military presence proved to be his downfall.

At the beginning of the interim government, the military numbered fewer than 1,000 troops who had fought alongside the Tanzanian People's Defence Force (TPDF) to expel Amin. The army

31

was back to the size of the original King's African Rifles (KAR) at independence in 1962. But in 1979, in an attempt to consolidate support for the future, such leaders as Yoweri Kaguta Museveni and Major General (later Chief of Staff) David Oyite Ojok began to enroll thousands of recruits into what were rapidly becoming their private armies. Museveni's 80 original soldiers grew to 8,000; Ojok's original 600 became 24,000. When Binaisa sought to curb the use of these militias, which were harassing and detaining political opponents, he was overthrown in a military coup on May 10, 1980. The coup was engineered by Ojok, Museveni, and others acting under the general direction of Paulo Muwanga, Obote's right-hand man and chair of the Military Commission (see The Second Obote Regime: Repression Continues, ch. 5). The TPDF was still providing necessary security while Uganda's police force—which had been decimated by Amin—was rebuilt, but Nyerere refused to help Binaisa retain power. Many Ugandans claimed that although Nyerere did not impose his own choice on Uganda, he indirectly facilitated the return to power of his old friend and ally, Milton Obote. In any case, the Military Commission headed by Muwanga effectively governed Uganda during the six months leading up to the national elections of December 1980.

Further evidence of the militarization of Ugandan politics was provided by the proposed expenditures of the newly empowered Military Commission. Security and defense were to be allotted more than 30 percent of the national revenues. For a country desperately seeking funds for economic recovery from the excesses of the previous military regime, this allocation seemed unreasonable to civilian leaders.

Shortly after Muwanga's 1980 coup, Obote made a triumphant return from Tanzania. In the months before the December elections, he began to rally his former UPC supporters. Ominously, in view of recent Ugandan history, he often appeared on the platform with General Ojok, a fellow Langi. Obote also began to speak of the need to return to a UPC one-party state.

The national election on December 10, 1980, was a crucial turning point for Uganda. It was, after all, the first election in eighteen years. Several parties contested, the most important of which were Obote's UPC and the DP led by Paul Kawanga Ssemogerere. Most of Uganda's Roman Catholics were DP members, along with many others whose main concern was to prevent the return of another Obote regime. Because the Military Commission, as the acting government, was dominated by Obote supporters (notably chairman Paulo Muwanga), the DP and other contenders faced formidable obstacles. By election day, the UPC had achieved some exceptional advantages, summarized by Minority Rights Group Report Number 66 as follows. Seventeen UPC candidates were declared "unopposed" by the simple procedure of not allowing DP or other candidates to run against them. Fourteen district commissioners, who were expected to supervise local polling, were replaced with UPC nominees. The chief justice of Uganda, to whom complaints of election irregularities would have to be made, was replaced with a UPC member. In a number of districts, non-UPC candidates were arrested, and one was murdered. Even before the election, the government press and Radio Uganda appeared to treat the UPC as the victor. Muwanga insisted that each party have a separate ballot box on election day, thus negating the right of secret ballot. There were a number of other moves to aid the UPC, including Muwanga's statement that the future parliament would also contain an unspecified number of unelected representatives of the army and other interest groups.

Polling appeared to be heavy on election day, and by the end of the voting, the DP, on the basis of its own estimates, declared victory in 81 of 126 constituencies. The British Broadcasting Corporation and Voice of America broadcast the news of the DP triumph, and Kampala's streets were filled with DP celebrants. At this point, Muwanga seized control of the Electoral Commission, along with the power to count the ballots, and declared that anyone disputing his count would be subject to a heavy fine and five years in jail. Eighteen hours later, Muwanga announced a UPC victory, with seventy-two seats. Some DP candidates claimed the ballot boxes were simply switched to give their own vote tally to the UPC runner-up. Nevertheless, a small contingent of neutral election watchers, the Commonwealth Observer Group, declared itself satisfied with the validity of the election. Some Ugandans criticized the Commonwealth Observer Group, suggesting that members of the group measured African elections by different standards than those used elsewhere or that they feared civil war if the results were questioned. Indeed, popular perception of a stolen election actually helped bring about the civil war the Commonwealth Observer Group may have feared.

The Second Obote Regime, 1981–85

In February 1981, shortly after the new Obote government took office, with Paulo Muwanga as vice president and minister of defense, a former Military Commission member, Yoweri Museveni, and his armed supporters declared themselves the National Resistance Army (NRA). Museveni vowed to overthrow Obote by means of a popular rebellion, and what became known as "the war in the bush'' began. Several other underground groups also emerged to attempt to sabotage the new regime, but they were eventually crushed. Museveni, who had guerrilla war experience with the Front for the Liberation of Mozambique (Frente de Libertação de Moçambique—Frelimo), campaigned in rural areas hostile to Obote's government, especially central and western Buganda and the western regions of Ankole and Bunyoro.

The Obote government's four-year military effort to destroy its challengers resulted in vast areas of devastation and greater loss of life than during the eight years of Amin's rule. The UNLA's many Acholi and Langi had been hastily enrolled with minimal training and little sense of discipline. Although they were survivors of Amin's genocidal purges of northeast Uganda, in the 1980s they were armed and in uniform, conducting similar actions against Bantu-speaking Ugandans in the south, with whom they appeared to feel no empathy or even pity. In early 1983, to eliminate rural support for Museveni's guerrillas, the area of Luwero District, north of Kampala, was targeted for a massive population removal affecting almost 750,000 people. These artificially created refugees were packed into several internment camps subject to military control, which in reality meant military abuse. Civilians outside the camps, in what came to be known as the "Luwero Triangle," were presumed to be guerrillas or guerrilla sympathizers and were treated accordingly. The farms of this highly productive agricultural area were looted—roofs, doors, and even door frames were stolen by UNLA troops. Civilian loss of life was extensive, as evidenced some years later by piles of human skulls in bush clearings and alongside rural roads.

The army also concentrated on the northwestern corner of Uganda, in what was then West Nile District. Bordering Sudan, West Nile had provided the ethnic base for much of Idi Amin's earlier support and had enjoyed relative prosperity under his rule. Having borne the brunt of Amin's anti-Acholi massacres in previous years, Acholi soldiers avenged themselves on inhabitants of Amin's home region, whom they blamed for their losses. In one famous incident in June 1981, Ugandan army soldiers attacked a Catholic mission where local refugees had sought sanctuary. When the International Committee of the Red Cross (ICRC) reported a subsequent massacre, the government expelled it from Uganda.

Despite these activities, Obote's government, unlike Amin's regime, was sensitive to its international image and realized the importance of securing foreign aid for the nation's economic recovery. Obote had sought and followed the advice of the International Monetary Fund (IMF—see Glossary), even though the austerity measures ran counter to his own ideology. He severely devalued the Uganda shilling, attempted to facilitate the export of cash crops, and postponed any plans he may once have entertained for reestablishing one-party rule. The continued sufferance of the DP, although much harried and abused by UPC stalwarts, became an important symbol to international donors. The government's inability to eliminate Museveni and win the civil war, however, sapped its economic strength, and the occupation of a large part of the country by an army hostile to the Ugandans living there furthered discontent with the regime. Abductions by the police, as well as the detentions and disappearances so characteristic of the Amin period, recurred. In place of torture at the infamous State Research Bureau at Nakasero, victims met the same fate at so-called "Nile Mansions." Amnesty International, a human rights organization, issued a chilling report of routine torture of civilian detainees at military barracks scattered across southern Uganda. The overall death toll from 1981 to 1985 was estimated as high as 500,000. Obote, once seen by the donor community as the one man with the experience and will to restore Uganda's fortunes, now appeared to be a liability to recovery.

In this deteriorating military and economic situation, Obote subordinated other matters to a military victory over Museveni. North Korean military advisers were invited to take part against the NRA rebels in what was to be a final campaign that won neither British nor United States approval. But the army was war-weary, and after the death of the highly capable General Ojok in a helicopter accident at the end of 1983, it began to split along ethnic lines. Acholi soldiers complained that they were given too much frontline action and too few rewards for their services. Obote delayed appointing a successor to Ojok for as long as possible. In the end, he appointed a Langi to the post and attempted to counter the objection of Acholi officers by spying on them, reviving his old paramilitary counterweight, the mostly Langi Special Force Units, and thus repeating some of the actions that led to his overthrow by Amin. As if determined to replay the January 1971 events, Obote once again left the capital after giving orders for the arrest of a leading Acholi commander, Brigadier (later Lieutenant General) Basilio Olara Okello, who mobilized troops and entered Kampala on July 27, 1985. Obote, together with a large entourage, fled the country for Zambia. This time, unlike the last, Obote allegedly took much of the national treasury with him.

The Return of Military Rule, 1985

The military government of General Tito Lutwa Okello ruled from July 1985 to January 1986 with no explicit policy except the natural goal of self-preservation—the motive for their defensive coup. To stiffen the flagging efforts of his army against the NRA, Okello invited former soldiers of Amin's army to reenter Uganda from the Sudanese refugee camps and participate in the civil war on the government side. As mercenaries fresh to the scene, these units fought well, but they were equally interested in looting and did not discriminate between supporters and enemies of the government. The reintroduction of Amin's infamous cohorts was poor international public relations for the Okello government and helped create a new tolerance of Museveni.

In 1986 a cease-fire initiative from Kenya was welcomed by Okello, who could hardly expect to govern the entire country with only war-weary and disillusioned Acholi troops to back him. Negotiations dragged on, but with Okello and the remnants of the UNLA army thoroughly discouraged, Museveni had only to wait for the regime to disintegrate. In January 1986, welcomed enthusiastically by the local civilian population, Museveni moved against Kampala. Okello and his soldiers fled northward to their ethnic base in Acholi. Yoweri Museveni formally claimed the presidency on January 29, 1986. Immense problems of reconstruction awaited the new regime.

*　*　*

The best general introductions to Uganda in the precolonial and colonial periods are S. Karugire's *A Political History of Uganda* and J. Jørgensen's *Uganda: A Modern History.* For the place of Uganda in the larger context of East African and African history, see B. Davidson's *A History of East and Central Africa to the Late 19th Century; Zamani: A Survey of East African History,* edited by B. Ogot and J. Kieran; and the relevant chapters in *History of East Africa,* published by Oxford University, and *The Cambridge History of Africa.*

More specialized treatment of Ugandan issues can be found in T. Sathyamurthy's *The Political Development of Uganda, 1900–1986;* D. Rothchild and M. Rogin's "Uganda" in G. Carter's *National Unity and Regionalism in Eight African States;* D. Apter's *The Political Kingdom in Uganda,* F. Welbourn's *Religion and Politics in Uganda, 1952–1962;* N. Kasfir's *The Shrinking Political Arena;* and C. Gertzel's *Party and Locality in Northern Uganda.*

The destructive period of Amin in the 1970s produced a series of studies, among them D. Martin's *General Amin,* H. Kyemba's *A State of Blood,* A. Mazrui's *Soldiers and Kinsmen in Uganda,* M. Twaddle's *Expulsion of a Minority,* G.I. Smith's *Ghosts of Kampala,* and the International Commission of Jurists' *Uganda and Human Rights.*

Sources for Uganda since the fall of Amin are T. Avirgan and M. Honey's *War in Uganda,* H. Hansen and M. Twaddle's *Uganda Now,* P. Wiebe and C. Dodge's *Beyond Crisis,* K. Rupesinghe's *Conflict Resolution in Uganda,* and the Minority Rights Group's *Uganda and Sudan—North and South.* (For further information and complete citations, see Bibliography.)

Chapter 2. The Society and Its Environment

A fisherman casting his net

UGANDA'S LOCATION between the two arms of the Great Rift Valley provides the country with an alluvial plateau and plentiful lakes and rivers. Mountain peaks mark geological fault lines along its eastern and western boundaries and provide cooler temperatures and ample rainfall. This environment was peopled by successive waves of immigrants, some of whom displaced indigenous hunting societies during the first millennium A.D. Most of the newcomers eventually settled in the region that would become southern Uganda, and their evolving political and cultural diversity contributed to conflicts that flared up over several centuries. These enmities still simmered in the twentieth century, but none of them seriously derailed the modernization process that was occurring in Uganda as it approached independence in 1962.

Some local beliefs reinforced the process of acculturation, emphasizing patronage as a means of advancement and valuing education as a necessary step toward that advancement. British educational systems and world religions were readily accepted in the nineteenth and twentieth centuries. The focus of modernization was clearly in Buganda, however, and during the decades after independence, national progress toward modernization slowed as the nation's non-Baganda (people of Buganda; sing., Muganda) majority attempted to adjust this balance in their favor. Military rule—a precarious alternative to dominance by the Baganda—failed to implant a sense of nationhood because the notion of government as a mechanism for expropriating wealth was merely replaced by that of government as a brutalizing force.

In the late 1980s, Uganda's recovery from the damage of more than two decades of corrupt government and civil war was slowed by the scourge of acquired immune deficiency syndrome (AIDS). This disease shook but did not destroy most people's confidence in human institutions as the major determinants of their future, and it also provided a fertile environment for new religions that might claim to control the disease. Religions provided channels for political organization and protest, especially the Holy Spirit Movement (HSM), which challenged government controls in the northeast.

One of the challenges facing the National Resistance Movement (NRM) government was balancing traditional forces against pressures for modernization brought to bear by Uganda's growing educated elite. Women, too, have often been a force for modernization, as they demanded educational and economic opportunities denied under traditional and colonial rulers. The focus of these pressures in the 1980s was Uganda's still strong educational system. Through education, people struggled to bolster the institutions that underlay civil society in an environment that bore scars from government neglect and abuse.

Physical Setting

Location and Size

Uganda is a landlocked country astride the equator, about 800 kilometers inland from the Indian Ocean (see fig. 1). It lies on the northwestern shores of Lake Victoria, extending from 1° south to 4° north latitude and 30° to 35° east longitude.

Uganda is bordered by Tanzania and Rwanda to the south, Zaire to the west, Sudan to the north, and Kenya to the east. With a land surface of 241,139 square kilometers (roughly twice the size of the state of Pennsylvania), Uganda occupies most of the Lake Victoria Basin, which was formed by the geological shifts that created the Great Rift Valley during the Pleistocene era. The Sese Islands and other small islands in Lake Victoria also lie within Uganda's borders.

Land Use

In the southern half of the country, rich soil and rainfall permit extensive agriculture, and in the drier and less fertile northern areas, pastoral economies are common. Approximately 21 percent of the land is cultivated and 45 percent is woodland and grassland, some of which has been cleared for roads, settlements, and farmland in the south. Approximately 13 percent of the land is set aside as national parks, forests, and game reserves. Swampland surrounding lakes in the southern and central regions supports abundant papyrus growth. The central region's woodlands and savanna give way to acacia and cactus growth in the north. Valuable seams of copper, cobalt, and other minerals have been revealed along geological fault lines in the southeast and southwest (see Mining, ch. 3). Volcanic foothills in the east contain phosphates and limestone.

Mountains

Most of south-central Uganda lies at an altitude of about 1,100 meters above sea level (see fig. 3). The plateau that stretches northward from Lake Victoria declines to an altitude of approximately 900 meters on the Sudan border. The gradually sloping terrain is

interrupted by a shallow basin dipping toward the center of the country and hilly areas toward the west and southwest.

Both eastern and western borders are marked by mountains. The Ruwenzori Mountains (often called the Mountains of the Moon) form about eighty kilometers of the border between Uganda and Zaire. The highest peaks of Mount Stanley in the Ruwenzoris are snow-capped. Foremost among these are Margherita (5,113 meters) and Alexandra (5,094 meters). Farther south the northernmost of the Virunga Mountains reach 4,132 meters on Mount Muhavura; 3,648 meters on Mount Mgahinga; and 3,477 meters on Mount Sabinio, which marks the border with Rwanda and Zaire.

In eastern Uganda, the border with Kenya is also marked by volcanic hills. Dominating these, roughly 120 kilometers north of the equator, is Mount Elgon, which rises from the 1,200-meter plains to reach a height of 4,324 meters. Mount Elgon is the cone of an extinct volcano, with ridges radiating thirty kilometers from its crater. Rich soil from its slopes is eroded into the plains below. North of Mount Elgon are Kadam (also known as Debasien or Tabasiat) Peak, which reaches a height of 3,054 meters, and Mount Moroto, at 3,085 meters. In the far northeast, Mount Zulia, Mount Morungole, and the Labwor and Dodoth Hills reach heights in excess of 2,000 meters. The lower Imatong Mountains and Mount Langia, at 3,029 meters, mark the border with Sudan.

Lakes and Rivers

Uganda is a well-watered country. Nearly one-fifth of the total area, or 44,000 square kilometers, is open water or swampland. Four of East Africa's Great Lakes—Lake Victoria, Lake Kyoga, Lake Albert, and Lake Edward—lie within Uganda or on its borders. Lake Victoria dominates the southeastern corner of the nation, with almost one-half of its 10,200-square-kilometer area lying inside Ugandan territory. It is the second largest freshwater lake in area in the world (after Lake Superior), and it feeds the upper waters of the Nile River, which is referred to in this region as the Victoria Nile.

Lake Kyoga and the surrounding basin dominate central Uganda. Extensions of Lake Kyoga include Lake Kwania, Lake Bugondo, and Lake Opeta. These "finger lakes" are surrounded by swampland during rainy seasons. All lakes in the Lake Kyoga Basin are shallow, usually reaching a depth of only eight or nine meters, and Lake Opeta forms a separate lake during dry seasons. Along the border with Zaire, Lake Albert and Lake Edward occupy troughs in the western Great Rift Valley.

Leaving Lake Victoria at Owen Falls, the Victoria Nile descends as it travels toward the northwest. Widening to form Lake Kyoga, the Nile receives the Kafu River from the west before flowing north to Lake Albert. From Lake Albert, the Nile is known as the Albert Nile as it travels roughly 200 kilometers to the Sudan border. In southern and western Uganda, geological activity over time has shifted drainage patterns. The land west of Lake Victoria is traversed by valleys that were once rivers carrying the waters of Lake Victoria into the Congo River system. The Katonga River flows westward from Lake Victoria to Lake George. Lake George and Lake Edward are connected by the Kazinga Channel. The Semliki River flows north out of Lake Edward to Lake Albert, draining parts of Zaire and forming a portion of the Uganda-Zaire border.

Spectacular waterfalls occur at Murchison (Kabalega) Falls on the Victoria Nile River just east of Lake Albert. At the narrowest point on the falls, the waters of the Nile pass through an opening barely seven meters wide. One of the tributaries of the Albert Nile, the Zoka River, drains the northwestern corner of Uganda, a region still popularly known as the West Nile although that name was not officially recognized in 1990. Other major rivers include the Achwa River (called the Aswa in Sudan) in the north, the Pager River and the Dopeth-Okok River in the northeast, and the Mpologoma River, which drains into Lake Kyoga from the southeast.

Climate

Uganda's equatorial climate provides plentiful sunshine, moderated by the relatively high altitude of most areas of the country. Mean annual temperatures range from about 16°C in the southwestern highlands to 25°C in the northwest; but in the northeast, temperatures exceed 30°C about 254 days per year. Daytime temperatures average about eight to ten degrees warmer than nighttime temperatures in the Lake Victoria region, and temperatures are generally about fourteen degrees lower in the southwest.

Except in the northeastern corner of the country, rainfall is well distributed. The southern region has two rainy seasons, usually beginning in early April and again in October. Little rain falls in June and December. In the north, occasional rains occur between April and October, while the period from November to March is often very dry. Mean annual rainfall near Lake Victoria often exceeds 2,100 millimeters, and the mountainous regions of the southeast and southwest receive more than 1,500 millimeters of rainfall yearly. The lowest mean annual rainfall in the northeast measures about 500 millimeters.

Population

Size

In 1990 the Ugandan government estimated the nation's population to be 16.9 million people; international estimates ranged as high as 17.5 million (see table 2, Appendix). Most estimates were based on extrapolations from the 1969 census, which enumerated approximately 9.5 million people. The results of the 1980 census, which counted 12.6 million people, were cast in doubt by the loss of census data in subsequent outbreaks of violence.

Life expectancy in 1989 averaged fifty-three years, roughly two years higher for women than men. The population was increasing by over 3.2 percent per year, a substantial increase over the rate of 2.5 percent in the 1960s and significantly more than the 2.8 percent growth rate estimated for most of East Africa. At this rate, Uganda's population was expected to double between 1989 and the year 2012. The crude birth rate, estimated to be 49.9 per 1,000 population, was equivalent to other regional estimates. Fertility ratios, defined as the number of live births per year per 1,000 women between the ages of sixteen and forty-five years, ranged from 115 in the south to more than 200 in the northeast. In general, fertility declined in more developed areas, and birth rates were lower among educated women.

The crude death rate was 18 per 1,000 population, equivalent to the average for East Africa as a whole. Infant mortality in the first year of life averaged 120 per 1,000 population, but some infant deaths were not reported to government officials. Deaths from AIDS were increasing in the late 1980s (see Health and Welfare, this ch.). Death rates were generally lower in high-altitude areas, in part because of the lower incidence of malaria.

Composition and Distribution

Ministry of Planning and Economic Development officials estimated that nearly 50 percent of the population was under the age of 15 and the median age was only 15.7 years in 1989 (see fig. 4). The sex ratio was 101.8 males per 100 females. The dependency ratio—a measure of the number of young and old in relation to 100 people between the ages of fifteen and sixty—was estimated at 104.

Uganda's population density was found to be relatively high in comparison with that of most of Africa, estimated to be fifty-three per square kilometer nationwide. However, this figure masked a range from fewer than 30 per square kilometer in the north-central region to more than 120 in the far southeast and southwest, and

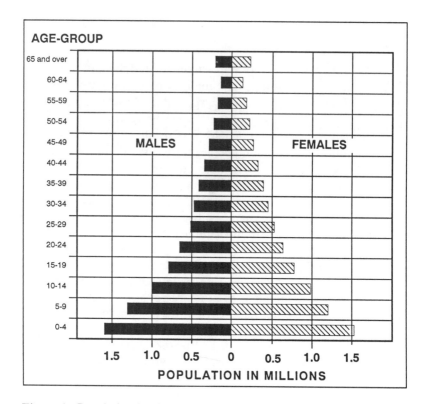

Figure 4. Population by Age and Sex, 1989

even these estimates overlooked some regions that were depopulated by warfare.

In late 1989, nearly 10 percent of the population lived in urban centers of more than 2,000 people. This figure was increasing in the late 1980s but remained relatively low in comparison with the rest of Africa and was only slightly higher than Uganda's 1969 estimate of 7.3 percent. Rural-to-urban migration declined during the 1970s as a result of deteriorating security and economic conditions. Kampala, with about 500,000 people, accounted for almost one-half of the total urban population but recorded a population increase of only 3 percent during the 1980s. Jinja, the main industrial center and second largest city, registered a population of about 55,000—an increase of 10,000 from the 1980 population estimate. Six other cities—Kabale, Kabarole, Entebbe, Masaka, Mbarara, and Mbale—had populations of more than 20,000 in 1989. Urban migration was expected to increase markedly during the 1990s.

Uganda was the focus of migration from surrounding African countries until 1970, with most immigrants coming from Rwanda, Burundi, and Sudan. In the 1970s, immigrants were estimated to make up 11 percent of the population. About 23,000 Ugandans were living in Kenya, and a smaller number had fled to other neighboring countries. Emigration increased dramatically during the 1970s and was believed to slow during the 1980s.

In 1989 Uganda reported 163,000 refugees to the United Nations High Commissioner for Refugees (UNHCR). Most of these were from Rwanda, but several other neighboring countries were also represented. At the same time, Zaire and Sudan registered a total of nearly 250,000 refugees from Uganda.

Ethnic Diversity and Language

All governments after independence declared their opposition to discrimination on the basis of ethnicity. Neither the 1969 nor the 1980 census recorded ethnic identity. However, Ugandans continued to take pride in their family histories, and government officials, like many other people, continued to consider ethnic factors in decision making. Moreover, much of Uganda's internal upheaval traditionally was based in part on historical differences among ethnic groups.

The forty or more distinct societies that constitute the Ugandan nation are usually classified according to linguistic similarities. Most Ugandans speak either Nilo-Saharan or Congo-Kordofanian languages. Nilo-Saharan languages, spoken across the north, are further classified as Eastern Nilotic (formerly Nilo-Hamitic), Western Nilotic, and Central Sudanic. The many Bantu languages in the south are within the much larger Congo-Kordofanian language grouping.

Lake Kyoga in central Uganda serves as a rough boundary between the Bantu-speaking south and the Nilotic and Central Sudanic language speakers in the north. Despite the popular image of north-versus-south in political affairs, however, this boundary runs roughly from northwest to southeast near the course of the Nile River, and many Ugandans live among people who speak other languages. Some sources describe regional variation in terms of physical characteristics, clothing, bodily adornments, and mannerisms, but others also claim that these differences are disappearing.

Bantu-speakers probably entered southern Uganda by the end of the first millennium A.D. and developed centralized kingdoms by the fifteenth or sixteenth century. Following independence,

Figure 5. Major Ethnic Groups

Bantu-language speakers comprised roughly two-thirds of the population. They were classified as Eastern Lacustrine and Western Lacustrine Bantu, referring to the populous region around East Africa's Great Lakes (Victoria, Kyoga, Edward, and Albert in Uganda; Kivu and Tanganyika to the south). Eastern Lacustrine Bantu-speakers included the Baganda (people of Buganda, whose language is Luganda), Basoga, and many smaller societies in Uganda, Tanzania, and Kenya. Western Lacustrine Bantu-speakers included the Banyoro (people of Bunyoro), Batoro, Banyankole, and several smaller populations (see fig 5).

Nilotic-language speakers probably entered the area from the north beginning about A.D. 1000. They were the first cattle-herding people in the area but relied on crop cultivation to supplement livestock herding for subsistence. The largest Nilotic populations in Uganda in the 1980s were the Iteso and Karamojong cluster of ethnic groups, who speak Eastern Nilotic languages, and the Acholi, Langi, and Alur, who speak Western Nilotic languages.

Central Sudanic languages, which also arrived in Uganda from the north over a period of centuries, are spoken by the Lugbara, Madi, and a few small groups in the northwestern corner of the country.

One of the most recent major languages to arrive in Uganda is English. Introduced by the British in the late nineteenth century, it was the language of the colonial administration. After independence English became the official language of Uganda; it is used in government and commerce and is the primary medium of educational instruction. Official publications and most major newspapers appear in English, and English is often employed in radio and television broadcasts. Most Ugandans also speak at least one African language. Swahili and Arabic are also widely spoken.

Eastern Lacustrine Bantu

Baganda

The Baganda (sing., Muganda; often referred to simply by the root word and adjective, Ganda) make up the largest Ugandan ethnic group, although they represent only about 16.7 percent of the population. (The name Uganda, the Swahili term for Buganda, was adopted by British officials in 1894 when they established the Uganda Protectorate, centered in Buganda.) Buganda's boundaries are marked by Lake Victoria on the south, the Victoria Nile River on the east, and Lake Kyoga on the north. This region was never conquered by colonial armies; rather the powerful king (*kabaka*), Mutesa, agreed to protectorate status. At the time, Mutesa claimed territory as far west as Lake Albert, and he considered the agreement with Britain to be an alliance between equals. Baganda armies went on to help establish colonial rule in other areas, and Baganda agents served as tax collectors throughout the protectorate. Trading centers in Buganda became important towns in the protectorate, and the Baganda took advantage of the opportunities provided by European commerce and education. At Uganda's independence in 1962, Buganda had achieved the highest standard of living and the highest literacy rate in the country.

Authoritarian control is an important theme of Ganda culture. In precolonial times, obedience to the king was a matter of life and death. A second important theme of Ganda culture, however, is the emphasis on individual achievement. An individual's future is not entirely determined by status at birth. Instead, individuals carve out their fortunes by hard work as well as by choosing friends, allies, and patrons carefully.

The traditional Ganda economy relied on crop cultivation. In contrast with many other East African economic systems, cattle played only a minor role. Many Baganda hired laborers from the north as herders. Bananas were the most important staple food, providing the economic base for the region's dense population growth. This crop does not require shifting cultivation or bush fallowing to maintain soil fertility, and, as a result, Ganda villages were quite permanent. Women did most of the agricultural work, whereas men often engaged in commerce and politics (and in precolonial times, warfare).

Ganda social organization emphasized descent through males. Four or five generations of descendants of one man, related through male forebears, constituted a patrilineage (see Glossary). A group of related lineages constituted a clan (for lineage and clan—see Glossary). Clan leaders could summon a council of lineage heads, and council decisions affected all lineages within the clan. Many of these decisions regulated marriage, which had always been between two different lineages, forming important social and political alliances for the men of both lineages. Lineage and clan leaders also helped maintain efficient land use practices, and they inspired pride in the group through ceremonies and remembrances of ancestors.

Ganda villages, sometimes as large as forty or fifty homes, were generally located on hillsides, leaving hilltops and swampy lowlands uninhabited, to be used for crops or pastures. Early Ganda villages surrounded the home of a chief or headman, which provided a common meeting ground for members of the village. The chief collected tribute from his subjects, provided tribute to the *kabaka,* distributed resources among his subjects, maintained order, and reinforced social solidarity through his decision-making skills. Late nineteenth-century Ganda villages became more dispersed as the role of the chiefs diminished in response to political turmoil, population migration, and occasional popular revolts.

Most lineages maintained links to a home territory (*butaka*) within a larger clan territory, but lineage members did not necessarily live on *butaka* land. Men from one lineage often formed the core of a village; their wives, children, and in-laws joined the village. People were free to leave if they became disillusioned with the local leader to take up residence with other relatives or in-laws, and they often did so.

The twentieth-century influence of the Baganda in Uganda has reflected the impact of eighteenth- and nineteenth-century developments (see Uganda Before 1900, ch. 1). A series of *kabakas* amassed military and political power by killing rivals to the throne, abolishing hereditary positions of authority, and exacting higher taxes from their subjects. Ganda armies also seized territory held by Bunyoro, the neighboring kingdom to the west. Ganda cultural norms also prevented the establishment of a royal clan by assigning the children of the *kabaka* to the clan of their mother. At the same time, this practice allowed the *kabaka* to marry into any clan in the society.

One of the most powerful appointed advisers of the *kabaka* was the *katikiro,* who was in charge of the kingdom's administrative and judicial systems—effectively serving as both prime minister and chief justice. The *katikiro* and other powerful ministers formed an inner circle of advisers who could summon lower-level chiefs and other appointed advisers to confer on policy matters. By the end of the nineteenth century, the *kabaka* had replaced many clan heads with appointed officials and claimed the title "head of all the clans."

The power of the *kabaka* impressed British officials, but political leaders in neighboring Bunyoro were not receptive to British officials who arrived with Baganda escorts. Buganda became the centerpiece of the new protectorate, and many Baganda were able to take advantage of opportunities provided by schools and businesses in their area. Baganda civil servants also helped administer other ethnic groups, and Uganda's early history was written from the perspective of the Baganda and the colonial officials who became accustomed to dealing with them.

The family in Buganda is often described as a microcosm of the kingdom. The father is revered and obeyed as head of the family. His decisions are generally unquestioned. A man's social status is determined by those with whom he establishes patron-client relationships, and one of the best means of securing this relationship is through one's children. Baganda children, some as young as three years old, are sent to live in the homes of their social superiors, both to cement ties of loyalty among parents and to provide avenues for social mobility for their children. Even in the 1980s, Baganda children were considered psychologically better prepared for adulthood if they had spent several years living away from their parents at a young age.

Baganda recognize at a very young age that their superiors, too, live in a world of rules. Social rules require a man to share his wealth by offering hospitality, and this rule applies more stringently to those of higher status. Superiors are also expected to behave with impassivity, dignity, self-discipline, and self-confidence, and adopting these mannerisms sometimes enhances a man's opportunities for success.

Ganda culture tolerates social diversity more easily than many other African societies. Even before the arrival of Europeans, many Ganda villages included residents from outside Buganda. Some had arrived in the region as slaves, but by the early twentieth century, many non-Baganda migrant workers stayed in Buganda to farm. Marriage with non-Baganda was fairly common, and many Baganda marriages ended in divorce. After independence, Ugandan officials estimated that one-third to one-half of all adults married more than once during their lives.

Basoga

The traditional territory of the Basoga (people of Busoga; sing., Musoga; adj. Soga) is in southeastern Uganda, east of the Victoria Nile River. The Basoga make up about 8 percent of the population. Before the arrival of Europeans, the Basoga were subsistence farmers who also kept cattle, sheep, and goats. Basoga often had gardens for domestic use close to the homestead. There the women of the household cared for the most common staple foods—bananas, millet, cassava, and sweet potatoes. Men generally cared for cash crops—coffee, cotton, peanuts, and corn.

Traditional Soga society consisted of a number of small kingdoms not united under a single paramount leader. Society was organized around a number of principles, the most important of which was descent. Descent was traced through male forebears, leading to the formation of the patrilineage, which included an individual's closest relatives. This group provided guidance and support for each individual and united related homesteads for economic, social, and religious purposes. Lineage membership determined marriage choices, inheritance rights, and obligations to the ancestors. An individual usually attempted to improve on his economic and social position, which was initially based on lineage membership, by skillfully manipulating patron-client ties within the authority structure of the kingdom. A man's patrons, as much as his lineage relatives, influenced his status in society.

Unlike the *kabakas* of Buganda, Basoga kings are members of a royal clan, selected by a combination of descent and approval by royal elders. In northern Busoga, near Bunyoro, the royal clan, the Babito, is believed to be related to the Bito aristocracy in Bunyoro (see Western Lacustrine Bantu, this ch.). Some Basoga in this area maintain that they are descended from people of Bunyoro.

Bagisu

The Bagisu (people of Bugisu; adj., Gisu) constitute roughly 5 percent of the population. They occupy the well-watered western slopes of Mount Elgon, where they grow millet, bananas, and corn for subsistence, and coffee and cotton as cash crops. Bugisu has the highest population density in the nation, rising to 250 per square kilometer. As a result, almost all land in Bugisu is cultivated, and land pressure causes population migration and social conflicts.

A large number of Bagisu were drawn into the cash economy in 1912, with the organization of smallholder production of arabica coffee and the extension of Uganda's administrative network into Bugisu. After that, the Bagisu were able to exploit their fertile environment by producing large amounts of coffee and threatening to withhold their produce from the market when confronted with unreasonable government demands. One of the mechanisms for organizing coffee production was the Bugisu Cooperative Union (BCU), which became one of the most powerful and most active agricultural cooperatives in Uganda. Bugisu's economic strength was based in part on the fact that coffee grown on Mount Elgon was of the highest quality in Uganda, and total output in this small region constituted more than 10 percent of the coffee produced nationwide (see Crops, ch. 3).

Land pressure during the early decades of colonial rule caused the Bagisu to move northward, impinging on the territory of the Sebei people, who have fought against Gisu dominance for over a century. The Bagwere and Bakedi people to the south have also claimed distinct cultural identities and have sought political autonomy.

Western Lacustrine Bantu

The Banyoro, Batoro, and Banyankole people of western Uganda are classified as Western Lacustrine Bantu language speakers. Their complex kingdoms are believed to be the product of acculturation between two different ethnic groups, the Hima (Bahima) and the Iru (Bairu). In each of these three societies, two distinct physical types are identified as Hima and Iru. The Hima are generally tall and are believed to be the descendants of pastoralists who migrated into the region from the northeast. The Iru are believed to be descendants of agricultural populations that preceded the Hima as cultivators in the region.

Banyoro

Bunyoro lies in the plateau of western Uganda. The Banyoro (people of Bunyoro; sing., Munyoro; adj. Nyoro) constitute roughly 3 percent of the population. Their economy is primarily agricultural, with many small farms of two or three hectares. Many people also keep goats, sheep, and chickens. People often say that the Banyoro once possessed large herds of cattle, but their herds were reduced by disease and warfare. Cattle raising is still a prestigious occupation, generally reserved for people of Hima descent. The traditional staple is millet, and sweet potatoes, cassava, and legumes of various kinds are also grown. Bananas are used for making beer and occasionally as a staple food. Cotton and tobacco are important cash crops.

Nyoro homesteads typically consist of one or two mud-and-wattle houses built around a central courtyard, surrounded by banana trees and gardens. Homesteads are not gathered into compact villages; rather, they form clustered settlements separated from each other by uninhabited areas. Each Munyoro belongs to a clan, or large kinship group based on descent through the male line. A woman retains her membership in her clan of birth after marriage, even though she lives in her husband's home. Adult men usually live near, but not in, their father's homestead. Men of the same clan are also dispersed throughout Bunyoro, as a result of generations of population migration based on interpersonal loyalties and the demand for farmland.

The traditional government of Bunyoro consisted of a hereditary ruler, or king (*omukama*), who was advised by his appointed council consisting of a prime minister, chief justice, and treasurer. The *omukama* occupied the apex of a graded hierarchy of territorial chiefs, of whom the most important were four county chiefs. Below them in authority were subcounty chiefs, parish chiefs, and village heads.

The Nyoro *omukama* was believed to be descended from the first ruler, Kintu, whose three sons were tested to determine the relationship that would endure among their descendants. As a result of a series of trials, the oldest son became a servant and cultivator, the second became a herder, and the third son became the ruler over all the people. This tale served to legitimize social distinctions in Nyoro society that viewed pastoral life-styles as more prestigious than peasant agriculture and to emphasize the belief that socioeconomic roles were divinely ordained.

During colonial times, the king was a member of the Bito clan. Bito clan members, especially those closest to the king, were considered members of royalty, based on their putative descent from Kintu's youngest son, who was chosen to rule. The pastoralist Hima were believed to be descended from Kintu's second son, and the Iru, or peasant cultivators, were said to be descended from Kintu's eldest son, the cultivator. Even during the twentieth century, when many Banyoro departed from their traditional occupations, these putative lines of descent served to justify some instances of social behavior.

Among the most important of the *omukama*'s advisers were his "official brother" (*okwiri*) and "official sister" (*kalyota*), who represented

Murchison (Kabalega) Falls on the Victoria Nile River near Lake Albert
Lake Victoria at Entebbe
Courtesy Carl Fleischhauer

his authority within the royal clan, effectively removing the king from the demands of his family. The *kalyota* was forbidden to marry or bear children, protecting the king against challenges from her offspring. The king's mother, too, was a powerful relative, with her own property, court, and advisers. The king had numerous other retainers, including custodians of royal graves, drums, weapons, stools, and other regalia, as well as cooks, musicians, potters, and other attendants. Most of these were his close relatives and were given land as a symbol of their royalty; a few palace advisers were salaried.

Almost all Nyoro political power derived from the king, who appointed territorial chiefs at all levels. High-ranking chiefs were known as the "king's men" and were obligated to live in the royal homestead, or capital. The chief's advisers, messengers, and delegates administered his territory according to his dictates. During colonial times, the three highest ranks of chiefs were assigned county, subcounty, and parish-level responsibilities to conform with the system British officials used in Buganda. Most kings appointed important Hima cattle farmers to be chiefs. People provided the chiefs with tribute—usually grain, beer, and cattle—most of which was supposed to be delivered to the king. Failure to provide generous tribute weakened a man's standing before the throne and jeopardized his family's security.

Batoro

The Toro kingdom evolved out of a breakaway segment of Bunyoro some time before the nineteenth century. The Batoro (people of Toro) and Banyoro speak closely related languages, Lutoro and Lunyoro, and share many other similar cultural traits. The Batoro live on Uganda's western border, south of Lake Albert. They constitute roughly 3.2 percent of the population, but the Toro king (also called *omukama*) also claims to rule over the Bakonjo and Baamba people in the more fertile highlands above the plains of Toro. These highlands support cultivation of coffee as well as cotton, rice, sugarcane, and cocoa. Jurisdictional disputes have erupted into violence many times during colonial and independent rule and led to the formation of the Ruwenzururu political movement that was still disrupting life in Toro in the late 1980s.

Toro is a highly centralized kingdom like Buganda but similar in stratification to Bunyoro. The *omukama* has numerous retainers and royal advisers. Chiefs govern at several levels below the king, and like the *kabaka* of Buganda, the Toro ruler can appoint favored clients to these positions of power. Clientship—often involving cattle exchange—is an important means of social advancement.

Banyankole

Ankole (Nkole) is a large kingdom in southwestern Uganda, where the pastoralist Hima established dominion over the agricultural Iru some time before the nineteenth century. The Hima and Iru established close relations based on trade and symbolic recognition, but they were unequal partners in these relations. The Iru were legally and socially inferior to the Hima, and the symbol of this inequality was cattle, which only the Hima could own. The two groups retained their separate identities through rules prohibiting intermarriage and, when such marriages occurred, making them invalid.

The Hima provided cattle products that otherwise would not have been available to Iru farmers. Because the Hima population was much smaller than the Iru population, gifts and tribute demanded by the Hima could be supplied fairly easily. These factors probably made Hima-Iru relations tolerable, but they were nonetheless reinforced by the superior military organization and training of the Hima.

The kingdom of Ankole expanded by annexing territory to the south and east. In many cases, conquered herders were incorporated into the dominant Hima stratum of society, and agricultural populations were adopted as Iru or slaves and treated as legal inferiors. Neither group could own cattle, and slaves could not herd cattle owned by the Hima.

Ankole society evolved into a system of ranked statuses, where even among the cattle-owning elite, patron-client ties were important in maintaining social order. Men gave cattle to the king (*mugabe*) to demonstrate their loyalty and to mark life-cycle changes or victories in cattle-raiding. This loyalty was often tested by the king's demands for cattle or for military service. In return for homage and military service, a man received protection from the king, both from external enemies and from factional disputes with other cattle owners.

The *mugabe* authorized his most powerful chiefs to recruit and lead armies on his behalf, and these warrior bands were charged with protecting Ankole borders. Only Hima men could serve in the army, however, and the prohibition on Iru military training almost eliminated the threat of Iru rebellion. Iru legal inferiority was also symbolized in the legal prohibition against Iru owning cattle. And, because marriages were legitimized through the exchange of cattle, this prohibition helped reinforce the ban on Hima-Iru intermarriage. The Iru were also denied high-level political appointments, although they were often appointed to assist local administrators in Iru villages.

The Iru had a number of ways to redress grievances against Hima overlords, despite their legal inferiority. Iru men could petition the king to end unfair treatment by a Hima patron. Iru people could not be subjugated to Hima cattle-owners without entering into a patron-client contract.

A number of social pressures worked to destroy Hima domination of Ankole. Miscegenation took place despite prohibitions on intermarriage, and children of these unions (*abambari*) often demanded their rights as cattle owners, leading to feuding and cattle-raiding. From what is present-day Rwanda, groups launched repeated attacks against the Hima during the nineteenth century. To counteract these pressures, several Hima warlords recruited Iru men into their armies to protect the southern borders of Ankole. And, in some outlying areas of Ankole, people abandoned distinctions between Hima and Iru after generations of maintaining legal distinctions that had begun to lose their importance.

Eastern Nilotic Language Groups

Historians believe that Uganda's northeastern districts were inhabited by herders migrating from the east over a period of several centuries. Their twentieth-century descendants live in Kenya, Sudan, and Uganda, where the largest groups are the Karamojong (people of Karamoja) ethnic groups. These include the Karamojong proper, as well as the Jie, Dodoth, and several small related groups, constituting about 12 percent of the population. All Karamojong peoples speak almost the same language (Akaramojong), with different pronunciations. The Iteso (people of Teso) south of Karamoja also speak an Eastern Nilotic language (Ateso) and are historically related to the Karamojong, but the Iteso are sometimes classified separately, based on cultural differences (many of which are recently acquired). The small Teuso (Ik), Tepeth, and Labwor populations in the northeast also speak Eastern Nilotic languages but maintain separate cultural identities. In northwestern Uganda, the Kakwa are also classified as Eastern Nilotic, based on linguistic similarities to the Karamojong, despite the fact that Kakwa society is surrounded by Western Nilotic and Central Sudanic language speakers.

Karamojong Cluster

The relatively sparse rainfall in northeastern Uganda supports a pastoralist economy, and most people also raise crops to supplement their diet, which centers around meat, milk, and blood from cattle. Even after independence in 1962, most Ugandan governments dealt with the Karamojong as rather difficult rural citizens who sometimes impeded administration of the region. Most Karamojong resisted government pressures to abandon their herding life-styles, but officials estimated that as many as 20 percent of the population may have died in the drought and famine that swept through much of the African Sahel in the early 1980s.

Karamojong, Jie, and Dodoth oral historians have recounted their forebears' arrival in the region from the north. According to these accounts, they found an indigenous society, the Oropom, who were forced to move southward, leaving an Oropom clan among the Karamojong as an apparent remnant of this society. The Dodoth people are believed to have separated from the Karamojong proper in the mid-eighteenth century. They migrated northward into more mountainous territory. As a result, their culture resembles that of the Karamojong in many respects. Dodoth homesteads are generally in valleys, with dry-season pastures on nearby hillsides. As a result, the Dodoth do not practice the transhumant migration patterns that required other Karamojong peoples to establish dry-season cattle camps.

Cattle are of great symbolic and economic importance, and people recalled the devastating rinderpest epidemic that swept the area in the late nineteenth century. Using that tragedy to educate the young, they also told of cattle herds that were saved by being moved to highland grazing areas.

British control of the region was fairly ineffective well into the twentieth century, although successful trading centers had been established as early as 1890. Traders brought ivory and, occasionally, cattle to augment local herds, and received grain, spears, and other metal products in return.

Most Karamojong peoples supplement their pastoral economy with crop cultivation, which is almost entirely in the hands of women. Millet is an important staple, but many people also grow corn and peanuts. Tobacco is often grown within the stockade that surrounds most homesteads. The homestead is usually a circular configuration, and within this enclosure, each married woman has a house built of mud and brushwood walls with a thatched roof. The center of this is a cattle kraal, usually with only one opening to the outside.

Wives live in their husband's homestead after marriage. Each wife has a separate, small house that serves as a kitchen, and some women also cultivate plots of ground several hours' walk away from their homes. Men were traditionally scornful of widowers and old men who cared for their own gardens, but after plows were introduced in the 1950s and farming became more financially rewarding, many young men claimed plots of ground for their own use and hired women to work in them.

Dodoth homesteads are larger than those of the Karamojong proper and more isolated from one another. Surrounding the homestead, upright poles are thrust into the earth, intertwined with branches and packed with mud and cow dung, forming a sturdy wall with only one or two small openings to the outside. As many as forty people often live in one homestead. Each wife has her own hut and hearth, and adolescent girls often build huts of their own next to their mothers' huts. Adolescent boys also build a larger "men's house," where they live before marriage. People keep cattle and other animals inside the fortified wall at night. A woman often keeps a small garden near her hut, but fields and pastures are outside the homestead.

Among most Karamojong peoples, men living within a homestead are related by descent through male forebears. This group, the patrilineage, is augmented by wives and children, and occasionally by unmarried brothers of the lineage head. A group of brothers usually shares the ownership of a herd of cattle, although animals are divided among individuals for milking and other domestic purposes. Cattle are usually branded with clan markings, although a man normally knows each animal in his family herd. Only when the last surviving brother dies is the herd divided among the next generation, with each set of full brothers inheriting a small herd.

Grazing areas are common ground outside the stockade, although milk cows sometimes stay near the homestead. During the driest months, usually February and March, cattle are moved to seasonal camps some distance from the homestead. In these camps, men live almost entirely on milk and blood drawn from live cattle, and, occasionally, meat. In the homestead, women, children, and old people forage for food, including flying ants, if stores of grain are depleted. In very lean times, milk is reserved for children and calves before adults.

Most societies of northeastern Uganda are organized into kinship groups larger than the lineage. Among the Jie, patrilineages maintaining the belief that they are distantly related often keep homesteads near one another, but this practice is less common among other Karamojong. The clan comprises related lineages, often numbering over 100 people. Jie clans are exogamous, meaning that two people of the same clan cannot marry one another. In addition, men generally avoid marriage with a woman of their mother's clan or that of her close relatives. Jie clan members share some symbolic recognition of their common identity, such as jewelry,

Residents relax in the evening at a park in downtown Kampala.
Conducting business in a fabric shop in Kampala
Courtesy Carl Fleischhauer

63

but they do not observe the ritual taboos of animals or foods that are characteristic of many other African clan groupings.

Two important sources of social solidarity link members of unrelated lineages to one another. Intermarriage forms bonds based on brideprice cattle, which are given by a man's family to that of his bride, and children, who are important to their own lineage and to that of their mother. Age-sets (see Glossary) form bonds among groups of men close in age. (Clan leaders establish a new age-set about every twenty-five years.) Members of an age-set are generally obligated to maintain ties of friendship and assist each other when in need.

Cattle are so vital in Karamoja that it is often difficult for Westerners to understand the attitudes surrounding them. Owning cattle is a mark of adulthood for men. Being without cattle is almost as onerous as being seriously ill; it threatens life. Moreover, a man can lose his entire herd of cattle in a brief raid. A mistake in judgment, such as a poor choice of pastures or travel routes, can cost a life's work. At the same time, outsiders are sometimes surprised to realize that these herders perceive themselves as poverty-ridden or uncivilized. In fact, the value of their cattle is often much greater than the value of the salaries received by government civil servants who come from the south to administer the region of the Karamojong.

Living among the Karamojong peoples in the far northeast are several small ethnic groups who rely on hunting and cattle-raiding for much of their subsistence, but some have also gained a reputation as spies and informers in the local system of raiding and warfare. One such group, the Teuso, were moved from their homeland in the 1960s to clear land for Kidepo National Park. Most of their Karamojong neighbors despised the Teuso, so much so that people were willing to see them starve rather than allow them to join nearby villages. Some Teuso died, and others left the area to become low-wage earners in nearby towns. The social system that developed in response to depopulation and deprivation emphasized individual survival at the expense of other people. The Uganda government reacted strongly against the unfavorable publicity generated by one anthropological account of this society in the early 1970s, and security problems limited travel in the area. As a result, by the late 1980s, information about their society was scarce.

The Tepeth also lived among the Karamojong, although they were usually classified as a separate Eastern Nilotic-speaking group. Oral histories relate that they were forced by government edict to vacate their homes in caves high in the mountains in northeastern

Uganda. The move increased their vulnerability to attack by people and disease, and an influx of refugees from Sudan further disrupted life. Warfare and conflict increased, and the Tepeth developed a variety of religious cults and rituals to maintain their cultural integrity in the face of Karamojong and Sudanese influence. In the late 1980s, little was known of the life-style of the remaining Tepeth people.

The Labwor people, who live on the border between Acholi and Karamoja, are historically and linguistically related to the Karamojong but have adopted much of the life-style of the Acholi. The Labwor region is also a center of trade between cultivators to the west and pastoralists to the east. The local economy centers around crops—chiefly sorghum, eleusine (finger millet, a cereal), corn, gourds, sweet potatoes, beans, and peanuts—but people also raise cattle and goats. A small number of men from Labwor have achieved substantial wealth as itinerant traders in northeastern Uganda. Labwor society is organized into homesteads centered around the core of patrilineally related men and their wives and children. In addition, age-sets are important stabilizing factors, forming cross-cutting ties among lineages.

Iteso

The Iteso (people of Teso) are an acculturated branch of the Eastern Nilotic language speakers. With roughly 8.1 percent of the population of Uganda, they are believed to be the nation's second largest ethnic group. Teso territory stretches south from Karamoja into the well-watered region of Lake Kyoga. The traditional economy emphasizes crop growing. Many Iteso joined Uganda's cash economy when coffee and cotton were introduced in 1912, and the region has thrived through agriculture and commerce.

Traditional Teso settlements consist of scattered homesteads, each organized around a stockade and several granaries. Groups of homesteads are united around a hearth, where men who form the core of the settlement gather for ritual and social purposes. These groups usually consist of patrilineally related males, whose wives, children, and other relatives form the remainder of the settlement. Several groups of lineages form a clan. Clans are only loosely organized, but clan elders maintain ritual observances in honor of their ancestors. Men of the clan consult the elders about social customs, especially marriage. Much of the agricultural work is performed by women. Women may also own land and granaries, but after the introduction of cash-crop agriculture, most land was claimed by men and passed on to their sons.

All Iteso men within a settlement, both related and unrelated, are organized according to age. Each age-set spans fifteen to twenty years, providing a generational framework for sharing the work of the settlement. Age-sets exercise social control by recognizing status distinctions based on seniority, both between and within age-groups. They also share responsibility for resolving disputes within the settlement or among neighboring settlements.

The small population of Kumam people living on the western border of Teso are historically related to the Iteso, but the Kumam have adopted many cultural features of their neighbors to the west, the Langi. The Kumam economy is based on mixed farming and cotton, but little other information was available regarding their culture in the 1980s.

Kakwa

Although Kakwa people speak an Eastern Nilotic language, they are geographically separated from other Eastern Nilotic speakers. Kakwa society occupies the region of extreme northwestern Uganda that borders southern Sudan and northeastern Zaire. Those living in Uganda constitute less than 1 percent of the population, but Kakwa society has achieved widespread notoriety because the father of Idi Amin Dada, president of Uganda from 1971 to 1979, was Kakwa. (Amin's mother was from a neighboring society, the Lugbara.) The Kakwa are believed to have migrated to the region from the northeast. Their indigenous political system features small villages centered around a group of men who are related by descent. A council of male elders wields political and judicial authority. Most land is devoted to cultivating corn, millet, potatoes, and cassava. Cattle are part of the economy but not central to it. After Amin was deposed in 1979, many Kakwa people fled. Government and rebel troops inflicted a wave of revenge on the area, even though Amin had lived in Buganda as a child and had spent little time among Kakwa villagers.

Western Nilotic Language Groups

Western Nilotic language groups in Uganda include the Acholi, Langi, Alur, and several smaller ethnic groups. Together they comprise roughly 15 percent of the population. Most Western Nilotic languages in Uganda are classified as Lwo, closely related to the language of the Luo society in Kenya. The two largest ethnic groups, the Acholi and Langi, speak almost identical languages, which vary slightly in pronunciation, suggesting that the two groups divided as recently as the early or mid-nineteenth century. The Alur, who live west of the Acholi and Langi, are culturally similar to neighboring societies of the West Nile region, where most people speak Central Sudanic languages.

Langi and Acholi

The Langi and Acholi occupy north-central Uganda. The Langi represent roughly 6 percent of the population. Despite their linguistic affiliation with other Lwo speakers, the Langi reject the "Lwo" label. The Acholi represent 4 percent of the population but suffered severe depopulation and dislocation in the violence of the 1970s and 1980s.

By about the thirteenth century A.D., Lwo-speaking peoples migrated from territory now in Sudan into Uganda and Kenya. They were probably pastoralists, organized in segmentary patrilineages rather than highly centralized societies, but with some positions of ritual or political authority. They encountered horticultural Bantu-speakers, organized under the authority of territorial chiefs. The newcomers probably claimed to be able to control rain, fertility, and supernatural forces through ritual and sacrifice, and they may have established positions of privilege for themselves based on their spiritual expertise. Some historians believe the Langi represent the descendants of fifteenth-century dissenters from Karamojong society to the east.

Both societies are organized into localized patrilineages and further grouped into clans, which are dispersed throughout the territory. Clan members claim descent from a common ancestor, but they are seldom able to recount the nature of their relationship to the clan founder. Acholi lineages are ranked according to their proximity to a royal lineage, and the head of this lineage is recognized as a king, although his power is substantially less than that of monarchs in the south.

Acholi and Langi societies rely on millet cultivation and animal husbandry for subsistence. In some areas, people also cultivate corn, eleusine, peanuts, sesame seed, sweet potatoes, and cassava. Both Langi and Acholi generally assign agricultural tasks either to men or women; in many cases men are responsible for cattle while women work in the fields. (In some villages, only adult men may milk cows.) An Acholi or Langi man may marry more than one wife, but he may not marry within his lineage or that of his mother. A woman normally leaves her own family to live in her husband's homestead, which may include his brothers and their families. Each wife has a separate house and hearth for cooking.

Alur

The Alur political system is a series of overlapping, interlocking chiefdoms, which were never unified in a single polity during precolonial times. Related lineages from different chiefdoms performed some religious ceremonies together, and intermarriage among chiefdoms was also fairly common. People also recognized other Alur speakers as neighbors. The Acholi claimed land east of Alur territory, and the Alur lost land in 1952, with the creation of Murchison (Kabalega) National Game Park. The Alur subsequently incorporated some Sudanic-speaking groups into their society as they expanded to the west.

Alur territory was remote from British commerce during colonial times, but once colonial boundaries were set, people found ways to profit from cross-border smuggling. Only a few churches, schools, and medical dispensaries were established, and many Alur became migrant laborers in Buganda to earn money to pay their taxes. Despite its geographical isolation, Alur territory in the 1980s showed signs of substantial but uneven acculturation, influenced by Sudanese, Zairian, and other Ugandan cultures. Alur society also became the object of some of the anti-Amin revenge that swept through the region in the 1980s.

Central Sudanic Language Groups

Central Sudanic languages are spoken by about 6 percent of Ugandans, most of whom live in the northwest. The Lugbara (roughly 3.8 percent of the total) and the Madi (roughly 1.2 percent) are the largest of these groups, representing the southeastern corner of a wide belt of Central Sudanic language speakers stretching from Chad to Sudan. The Lugbara live in the highlands, on an almost treeless plateau that marks the watershed between the Congo River and the Nile. The Madi live in the lowlands to the east.

Lugbara and Madi speak closely related languages and bear strong cultural similarities. Both groups raise millet, cassava, sorghum, legumes, and a variety of root crops. Chickens, goats, and, at higher elevations, cattle are also important. Corn is grown for brewing beer, and tobacco is an important cash crop.

This region is densely populated, dotted with small settlements separated from one another by streams or patches of bush. Each settlement consists of a family cluster, with a core of patrilineal relatives and their polygynous families living under the authority of a lineage elder. Membership in a settlement is flexible, however; people leave and rejoin a village on the basis of interpersonal relationships.

The clan leaders adjudicate most disputes. They can order a man to pay compensation for assault or property damage; murder is often avenged by killing. The entire clan shares responsibility in most matters, but the clan segment, or lineage, shares more immediate responsibility for avoiding conflict.

Foreigners

Nubians

Roughly 10,000 Ugandans of Sudanese descent are classified as Nubians, referring to their origin in the area of the Nuba Mountains in Sudan. They are descendants of Sudanese military recruits who entered Uganda in the late nineteenth century as part of the colonial army and were employed to quell popular revolts (see Early Development, ch. 5). Their ethnic identities varied, but some spoke Western Nilotic languages, similar to that of the Acholi people, their closest relatives in Uganda. Many Nubians also spoke a variant of Arabic, and they practiced Islam. Moreover, they believed they were superior to Ugandans because of their mercenary status. Nubian armies raided surrounding villages, capturing slaves and wives. Their villages were organized around their military status. They raised cotton, most of which was used for making uniforms, and they were paid salaries throughout most of the protectorate years.

Both colonial and independent governments attempted to regularize the status of the Nubian community. Many Nubians settled in northern Buganda, near the site of the colonial military headquarters. Others lived among the Acholi in northern Uganda and among other Ugandan Muslim communities in the north. In the late 1980s, they were primarily a dispersed urban population. They generally avoided Western education, opting to send their children to Quranic schools instead. Nubians often worked as unskilled or semi-skilled laborers, or as traders. Most spoke Swahili—a Bantu language with strong Arabic influence. Baganda tolerated, but did not especially welcome, the Nubian population that lived among them, along with other non-Baganda.

Rwandans

Almost 6 percent of the population was of Rwandan descent, comprising Hutu and Tutsi (Watutsi) ethnic groups, in 1969, but at that time, most Rwandans in Uganda were citizens. They were Bantu-speakers, culturally related to the Hima and Iru of the southwestern kingdoms of Bunyoro, Toro, and Ankole. Most Rwandans lived in Buganda, where they worked in agriculture, business, and a variety of service occupations. Most were Roman Catholics. In the early 1980s, as refugees migrated freely across national boundaries throughout East Africa, the government attempted to limit Rwandan influence by restricting those who lacked Ugandan citizenship to refugee camps and by expelling some to Tanzania. In the late 1980s, more than 120,000 Rwandans were recognized as refugees in Uganda by the UNHCR.

Asians

The 1969 census enumerated about 70,000 people of Indian or Pakistani descent—generally referred to as Asians in Uganda. They were officially considered foreigners despite the fact that more than one-half of Uganda's Asians were born in Uganda. Many of their forebears had arrived in Uganda by way of trade networks centered on the Indian Ocean island of Zanzibar (united with Tanganyika in 1964 to form Tanzania), which brought iron, cotton, and other products from India even before the nineteenth century. In the late nineteenth century, many indentured laborers from India remained in Uganda after their service ended, but the government refused to sell them land, and most became traders. Wealthy Baganda traders were almost eliminated as their earliest rivals when the Buganda Agreement of 1900 made land ownership more lucrative than commerce for most Baganda. Indians gained control of retail and wholesale trade, cotton ginning, coffee and sugar processing, and other segments of commerce. After independence, and especially when the Obote government threatened to nationalize many industries in 1969, Asians exported much of their wealth and were accused of large-scale graft and tax evasion. President Amin deported about 70,000 Asians in 1972, and only a few returned to Uganda in the 1980s to claim compensation for their expropriated land, buildings, factories, and estates. In 1989 the Asian population in Uganda was estimated to be about 10,000.

Religion

In the late 1980s, Ugandan officials estimated that 66 percent of the population was Christian—almost equally divided among Protestants and Roman Catholics. Approximately 15 percent of Ugandans were Muslims. Roughly 19 percent of the people professed belief in local religions or denied any religious affiliation. The basic tenets of all religions—that a spiritual realm exists and that spiritual and physical beings can influence one another—permeated much of Ugandan society. World religions and local religions had coexisted for more than a century, and many people established a coherent set of beliefs about the nature of the universe by combining elements of the two. Except in a few teachings, world religions were seldom viewed as incompatible with local religions.

Throughout Uganda's colonial and postcolonial history, religious identity has had economic and political implications. Church

Anglican Cathedral on Namirembe Hill in Kampala Courtesy Carl Fleischhauer

Wedding at a mosque in Kampala Courtesy Carl Fleischhauer

membership has influenced opportunities for education, employment, and social advancement. As a result, the distinction between
material and spiritual benefits of religion has not been considered
very important, nor have the rewards of religious participation been
expected to arrive only in an afterlife.

World Religions

Christianity

One of the largest denominations is Anglican (Episcopal). In 1990
about 4 million Ugandans, or roughly 22 percent of the population, belonged to the nineteen dioceses of the Anglican Church of
Uganda. Protestant churches, including Methodist, Lutheran, Bap-
tist, and Presbyterian, together had fewer than 1 million members.
About 5 million Roman Catholics (roughly 28 percent of the population) were members of the thirteen Catholic dioceses in Uganda.
The Catholic and Anglican archbishops and other church leaders
were Ugandans.

The first Christian missionaries represented the Anglican Church
Missionary Society (CMS) and arrived in Buganda in 1877 (see
Long-Distance Trade and Foreign Contact, ch. 1). Roman Catholic
priests from the Society of Missionaries of Africa (White Fathers),
a French religious order, arrived two years later. These and later
Catholic and Protestant missions competed for converts in southern
Uganda and became embroiled in local politics. British and German military commanders organized Protestant and Catholic converts to defend imperial interests against each other and against
Muslim armies. Many early converts to Christianity were persecut-
ed by local rulers, and nineteenth-century martyrs were commemo-
rated in shrines in several places in southern Uganda.

After the victories of Protestant armies in the conflicts of the 1890s
in southern Uganda, membership in the Anglican church was a
requirement for each *kabaka* of Buganda. The Anglican Cathedral
on Namirembe Hill in Kampala became the site of the *kabaka*'s
coronation. (A Roman Catholic cathedral was built on nearby
Rubaga Hill in 1925.) When Protestant Baganda formed the
political party Kabaka Yekka (KY) to press for autonomy for
Buganda at independence, Catholics formed the Democratic Party
(DP) to oppose the parochial interests of the KY. The DP also won
support in areas where opposition to Buganda was high, and other
political parties organized in reaction to KY and DP demands.
Religion continued to be a factor in national politics through the
first three decades of independence.

Islam

In 1990 Islam was practiced by an estimated 2.6 million Ugandans, representing roughly 15 percent of the population. Islam had arrived in Uganda from the north and through inland networks of the East African coastal trade by the mid-nineteenth century. Some Baganda Muslims trace their family's conversion to the period in which the *kabaka,* Mutesa I, converted to Islam in the nineteenth century.

Islam is a monotheistic religion based on revelations received in seventh-century Arabia by the prophet Muhammad. His life is recounted as the early history of the religion, beginning with his travels from the Arabian town of Mecca about A.D. 610. Muhammad denounced the polytheistic religions of his homeland, preaching a series of divine revelations. He became an outcast, and in A.D. 622, he was forced to flee to the town of Yathrib, which became known as Medina (the city) through its association with Muhammad. The flight (hijra) marked the beginning of the Islamic era and of Islam as a powerful force in history. It also marked the year A.D. 622 as the beginning of the Islamic calendar. Muhammad ultimately defeated his detractors in battle and consolidated his influence as both temporal and spiritual leader of many Arabs before his death in A.D. 632.

After Muhammad's death, his followers compiled his words that they believed were direct from God (Allah) and produced the Quran, the holy scripture of Islam. Muhammad's teachings and his actions as recalled by those who knew him became the *hadith* (sayings). From these sources, the faithful constructed the Prophet's customary practice, or sunna, which they emulate. The Quran, *hadith,* and sunna form a comprehensive guide to the spiritual, ethical, and social life of the faithful in most Muslim countries.

The central requirement of Islam is submission to the will of God, and, accordingly, a Muslim is a person who has submitted his will to God. The most important demonstration of faith is the *shahada* (profession of faith), which states, ''There is no God but God (Allah), and Muhammad is his prophet.'' *Salat* (daily prayer), *zakat* (almsgiving), *sawm* (fasting), and hajj (pilgrimage to Mecca) are also required of the faithful.

When Idi Amin, a Ugandan Muslim, became president in 1971, his presidency seemed to be a victory for Uganda's Muslim community. Then in 1972, Amin's expulsion of Asians from Uganda reduced the Muslim population significantly. As his administration deteriorated into a brutal and unsuccessful regime, Uganda's Muslims began to distance themselves from those in power. After

Amin's overthrow in 1979, Muslims became the victims of the backlash that was directed primarily against the Kakwa and Nubian ethnic groups who had supported Amin. Yusuf Lule, who served a brief term as president from 1979 to 1980, was also a Muslim (and a Muganda). He was not a skillful politician, but he was successful in reducing the public stigma attached to Islam. In 1989 President Yoweri Kaguta Museveni appealed to Uganda's Muslim community to contribute to national reconstruction, and he warned other Ugandans not to discriminate against Muslims. But at the same time, Museveni admonished Ugandans to avoid "sectarian" allegiances, and this warning was directed at the Islamic community as well as other ethnic and religious groups.

Local Religions

Roughly 19 percent of Ugandans professed belief in local religions in the late 1980s. In Uganda as in other countries, religion serves social and political purposes, as well as individual needs. An important social function of religion is reinforcing group solidarity by providing elements necessary for society's survival—remembrances of the ancestors, means of settling disputes, and recognition of individual achievement. Another social function of religion is helping people cope with negative aspects of life—pain, suffering, and defeat—by providing an explanation of their causes. Religious beliefs and practices also serve political aims, especially by bolstering the authority of temporal rulers and at other times by allowing new leaders to mobilize political opposition and implement political change.

Among Bantu-speaking societies in southern Uganda, many local religions include beliefs in a creator God, usually known as Ntu or a variant of that term (e.g., Muntu). Most religions involve beliefs in ancestral and other spirits, and people offer prayers and sacrifices to symbolize respect for the dead and to maintain proper relationships among the living. An important example of this religious attitude is found in western Uganda among members of the Mbandwa religion and related belief systems throughout the region. Mbandwa mediators act on behalf of other believers, using trance or hypnosis and offering sacrifice and prayer to beseech the spirit world on behalf of the living. In Bunyoro, for example, the ancestral spirits, who protect those who pray to them, are believed to be the early mythical rulers, the Chwezi. As a result, the Mbandwa religion in these areas is sometimes called the Chwezi religion.

Ancestors are also important in the lives of the Lugbara people of northwestern Uganda. Ancestors communicate with the living, influence their luck, and can be appeased by those in authority.

A lineage elder is said to "own" an ancestral shrine, and this ownership serves to reinforce his power to communicate with the ancestors. The elder can invoke a curse on a relative, and people with illnesses often consult diviners to interpret the conditions of their lives and determine which elder might have caused the illness.

More secular functions of religion are evident in the Ganda belief system, which reinforces the institution of kingship. The *kabaka* is not considered to be the descendant of gods, but his skill as a leader is judged in part by his ability to defend his people from spiritual danger. Most spiritual beings are considered to be the source of misfortune, rather than good fortune—forces to be placated. A good *kabaka* is one who can defend his kingdom from divine retribution. Important gods in the Ganda pantheon include Kibuka and Nende, the gods of war; Mukasa, the god of children and fertility; a number of gods of the elements—rain, lightning, earthquake, and drought; gods of plague and smallpox; and a god of hunting. Sacrifices to appease these deities include food, animals, and, at times in the past, human beings.

Religion in the Tepeth society in northeastern Uganda also reinforces political values. Authority is concentrated in the hands of a small group of priests and clan elders. They admit men whom they judge to be most capable to a cult known as Sor. Sor initiates make sacrifices to enhance fertility, ensure adequate rainfall, and avoid disease. Men also become members of a society of mediums, who are highly respected, or priests, who are also respected but less so. Women receive spiritual communications regarding social ills, such as crime, but are believed to be incapable of seeing the spirits that communicate with them. Mediums, priests, and others—including women—are allowed to perform rituals that symbolize their spiritual and social prestige.

Religion overlaps with politics in many other areas of life. Ancestors and their agents on earth often support authority systems by punishing transgressions against elders. Killing or striking senior kin is sometimes sufficient to destroy a descent group. The transgressor can avert this tragedy by engaging a spiritual healer and paying the prescribed penalty. Illness is often interpreted as a penalty for flouting the authority of an elder. Illness and a wide variety of misfortunes provide opportunities for individuals to examine their own actions and relationships, admit their weaknesses to a respected leader, and compensate those who otherwise might become their enemies. This pattern of behavior—both political and religious—contributes to stability in many societies.

Millenarian Religions

A number of millenarian religions (promising a "golden age," or millennium) existed in Uganda in the 1980s. They have often arisen in response to rapid culture change or other calamities and have sought to overthrow the political order that allowed the crisis to arise. Many millenarian religions, sometimes called cults, are led by a charismatic prophet who promises followers relief from sufferings. The strength of people's faith sometimes allows a prophet to make extraordinary demands on believers, and a successful prophet can win new converts when political upheaval is compounded by natural disaster, such as epidemics (possibly to include the spread of AIDS in the 1980s and 1990s).

Yakan Religion

One of the most successful millenarian religions in Uganda was the Yakan cult, which arose in Sudan in the late nineteenth century. Leaders from Kakwa society (whose territory extends across the Uganda-Sudan border) traveled south in search of protection against epidemics, Arab slave caravans, and European military forces, all of which were sweeping Kakwa society in the 1890s. They returned home from the neighboring Lugbara territory with spring water they called "the water of Yakan." To those who drank it, they promised restored health, eternal life, and the return of the ancestors and dead cattle. In Kakwa society, Yakan leaders promised protection from bullets, and many Yakan leaders predicted the arrival of wagonloads of rifles to drive out all Europeans.

When sleeping sickness ravaged Lugbara society in 1911, Lugbara leaders sought out the Yakan prophets. One of them— Rembe—traveled to Uganda and dispensed the water of Yakan. He was subsequently deported to Sudan and executed in 1917. With its new martyr, the cult flourished. When the British administration declared the sect illegal, people built shrines inside the walls of their homesteads, and believers used Yakan water to provide what they believed was spiritual protection against British patrols. The ban on the Yakan religion was impossible to enforce, and when it was lifted, Yakan believers felt their faith was vindicated.

As the religion developed, people began to use trance and speaking in tongues to strengthen and demonstrate their faith. In some areas, Yakan leaders appointed their followers to positions of prestige, and, as their power increased, a gradual reorganization of villages began to take place. Religious notables exercised political authority, and eventually they became so oppressive that their followers revolted. Colonial troops came in to restore peace, and the

Yakan religion declined in influence but did not disappear. Promises of a millennium continued to arise in similar form in the 1980s.

Holy Spirit Movement

In the 1980s, the Holy Spirit Movement arose in Acholi territory of northern Uganda, where warfare and political killings had ravaged society for nearly two decades. Alice Lakwena, an Acholi prophet, claimed to bring messages from the spiritual world advising people, even though unarmed, to oppose government intervention in Acholi territory. Lakwena, known locally as "Alice," also advised her followers to protect themselves against bullets by smearing cooking oil on their skin and declared that stones or bottles thrown at government troops would turn into hand grenades. Many of Alice's followers were killed in these confrontations, and many others acquired guns to reinforce their supposed spiritual armor. In 1987, however, Alice fled to Kenya, where she was jailed. A self-proclaimed mystic, Joseph Kony, and Odong Latek succeeded her as leaders of the Holy Spirit Movement.

The appeal of the Holy Spirit Movement continued, and in early 1989, it disrupted the establishment of the grass-roots resistance councils (RCs), which were intended to serve as the base for a people's democracy under the National Resistance Movement (NRM) (see Local Administration, ch. 4). Government officials proclaimed periods of amnesty and sought to weaken the Holy Spirit Movement's appeal by cutting off supplies of weapons (and cooking oil) to the region. As of 1989, the NRM was unable to quell this popular rebellion that clothed itself in religious dogma.

Social Change

Uganda in the 1980s bore the imprint of complex stratification systems that had evolved well before colonial agents arrived in the area. These, in turn, were shaped in part by the Arab slave trade that flourished in the mid-nineteenth century, providing laborers for French sugar and tobacco plantations on several Indian Ocean islands. Tens of thousands of slave captives were taken from northern Uganda, where societies had been organized primarily around descent rules, ritual needs, and cattle. British imperial agents arriving in the north in the late nineteenth century encountered many small village- and lineage-based social units specialized for mobility and warfare.

Karamojong societies in the northeast were highly segmented, allowing people to move away and rejoin a group without disrupting social relations or their pastoral life-style. West of the Karamojong, Acholi and Langi peoples developed a more sedentary economy relying largely on crop cultivation. In most northern societies, status distinctions were based on age, gender, and, in some cases, spiritual prowess. Men with military expertise were also important, but these societies did not develop powerful kingdoms as did those that would dominate southern Uganda. In the south, a more favorable climate contributed to the formation of highly stratified kingdoms, relying in part on labor from the north. Patron-client relationships bound individuals of different strata to one another, and military elites sometimes dominated society, especially in times of war. By the late nineteenth century, British imperial agents saw Buganda as an orderly kingdom with extensive commercial ties throughout the region, ruled by a king who welcomed those who proselytized on behalf of world religions—an ideal environment for establishing a colonial presence.

In 1900 Baganda chiefs agreed to protectorate status for the region in return for title to freehold land, and even in the 1980s, many of Uganda's wealthiest landowners were Baganda who had inherited or purchased that land (still known as *mailo* land because it was measured in square miles) from these early landowners. Similar landowning classes were created in Toro and Ankole, where the British granted freehold tenure to a small group of chiefs, and to a lesser extent in Bunyoro, where the *omukama* followed suit to appease his most important clients. These agreements displaced lineage and clan heads, who became trespassers on ancestral land they had formerly controlled, and the shift from dispersed, temporary power centers to a petite bourgeoisie of African landowners began. Asians, who came to dominate retail and wholesale trade, and a few high-ranking civil servants were also among the new elites.

Tenant farmers began to exercise their political power as the triangular relationship among landlords, tenant farmers, and the state achieved a sort of balance. The state demanded taxes from both landowners and tenant farmers; landlords demanded rent (and a portion of the produce) from their tenants; and farmers threatened to reduce their crop yields if the demands of the other two became too onerous. At times, disgruntled farmers were so successful in withholding production that the state stepped in to impose limits on demands by landlords, thereby protecting the state's ability to tax both landlord and tenant farmer. Successful landowners received government loans at low interest rates, and some of them used the money to purchase facilities for processing cash crops, which would become especially lucrative after independence. Wealthy farmers organized agricultural cooperatives—and eventually, political parties—to implement their demands during the pre-independence

Marketing farm produce in Kampala
Courtesy Carl Fleischhauer

years. They recruited members among their own ethnic or religious groups, however, and therefore most peasant farmers remained poor.

During the years surrounding independence, land ownership was an important factor in the new nation's social organization, but colonial policies also entrenched racial and ethnic differences that hampered the accumulation of wealth by most people. African business people were unable to compete with Asians in many areas of commerce because of discriminatory government licensing regulations and red tape. Urban unskilled workers, lacking both land and political organization, were hampered from organizing nationwide labor actions, and in general the poor found their avenues to middle-class status blocked. Most northerners remained peasants or laborers because agribusiness, commerce, transportation, and educational centers were centered in the south.

Each government after independence altered the identity of the major participants in the national economy without changing the basic nature of that participation. The 1960s government of Milton Obote reduced the privileged status of the southern kingdoms, especially Buganda, and brought northerners into business and politics in increasing numbers. During the 1970s, Amin expelled the Asian commercial bourgeoisie and eliminated many others from the entrenched elite. By expropriating their wealth and nationalizing foreign businesses, Amin's followers acquired substantial resources for patronage purposes, and, as a result, former peripheral groups, such as the Nubian military community, assumed new power and wealth. Many uneducated, untrained military recruits also received important military and political appointments, but by the end of Amin's term in office in 1979, the state's resources for rewarding political clients had begun to dwindle.

Under these conditions of political and economic uncertainty, many skilled workers, even from urban areas, reverted to subsistence cultivation in order to survive. Urban and rural elites fled from state terror tactics and economic destruction, and many who could afford to travel went to other African countries or Britain. Cities and towns stagnated. At the same time, shortages of basic commodities and foodstuffs provided new avenues to wealth through black-market operations and smuggling. For many citizens, the institutions of government became almost irrelevant to social progress.

As the government lost its ability to impose economic and political order, a few people were able to accumulate impressive wealth through open manipulation of illegal economic networks. A specialized vocabulary for black-market activities, termed *magendo,* and its most successful participants, *mafuta mingi* ("dripping in oil"), came to symbolize the importance of this thriving sector of the economy. Local economists estimated that during the early 1980s, *magendo* activities generated as much as one-third of the national output of goods and services, and *mafuta mingi*, both those in government office and "private-sector *magendoists*," constituted the wealthiest class of Ugandans. Together with its lower-class beneficiaries—including those who carried out risky smuggling ventures, ran errands, and stored goods for their superiors, as well as those who were simply thieves (*bayaye*)—*magendo* was thought to provide a living for about 7 percent of the population.

President Amin also embarrassed many Ugandans with his uneducated style as president; his example and tolerance of brutality were viewed with revulsion. Government agents committed much of the violence, provoking violent revenge, and ethnic identity became the basis for much of this revenge. Pervasive violence heightened the destructive impact of widespread corruption. When Museveni seized power in 1986, none of the four administrations that had succeeded Amin had been able to restore order or public confidence in government. The restoration of a viable middle class began, and some urban activity revived, but continuing warfare delayed nationwide social programs. Economic disaster loomed again when international coffee prices plummeted in 1989, and the policy of coopting former rebel opponents produced a burgeoning, expensive military establishment. Museveni's fledgling democratic institutions provided some hope of peace and economic recovery in the 1990s; many members of the small but very wealthy Ugandan elite, however, had accumulated wealth under earlier regimes. Middle-class workers and farmers were struggling just to provide for their families. Government workers were sometimes unpaid, and many civil servants found it necessary to hold more than one job. Urban workers often farmed or had members of their families cultivate rural plots of land for subsistence and profit. Unskilled workers and peasant farmers—i.e., the majority of Ugandans—appeared likely to remain poor.

Women in Society

Women's roles were clearly subordinate to those of men, despite the substantial economic and social responsibilities of women in Uganda's many traditional societies. Women were taught to accede to the wishes of their fathers, brothers, husbands, and sometimes other men as well, and to demonstrate their subordination to men in most areas of public life. Even in the 1980s, women in rural areas of Buganda were expected to kneel when speaking to a man. At the same time, however, women shouldered the primary responsibilities for childcare and subsistence cultivation, and in the twentieth century, women had made substantial contributions to cash-crop agriculture.

Many men claimed that their society revered women, and it was true that Ugandan women had some traditional rights that exceeded those of women in Western societies. Many Ugandans recognized women as important religious leaders, who sometimes had led religious revolts that overthrew the political order dominated by men. In some areas of Uganda, women could own land, influence crucial political decisions made by men, and cultivate crops for their own profit. But when cash-crop agriculture became lucrative, as in southeastern Uganda in the 1920s, men often claimed rights to land owned by their female relatives, and their claims were supported by local councils and protectorate courts.

Polygynous marriage practices, which permit a man to marry more than one woman, have reinforced some aspects of male dominance, but they also have given women an arena for cooperating to oppose male dominance. Moreover, a man sometimes granted his senior wife "male" status, allowing her to behave as an equal toward men and as a superior toward his other wives. But in the twentieth century, polygynous marriages had created bonds that were not legally recognized as marriage, leaving women without legal rights to inheritance or maintenance in the event of divorce or widowhood.

Women began to organize to exercise their political power before independence. In 1960 the Uganda Council of Women passed a resolution urging that laws regarding marriage, divorce, and inheritance should be recorded in written form and publicized nationwide—a first step toward codifying customary and modern practices. During the first decade of independence, this council also pressed for legal reforms that would grant all women the right to own property and retain custody of their children if their marriages ended.

During the 1970s and early 1980s, the violence that swept Uganda inflicted a particularly heavy toll on women. Economic hardships were felt first in the home, where women and children lacked economic choices available to most men. Women's work became more time-consuming than it had been; the erosion of public services and infrastructure reduced access to schools, hospitals, and markets. Even traveling to nearby towns was often impossible. Some Ugandan women believed that the war years strengthened their independence, however, as the disruption of normal family life opened new avenues for acquiring economic independence, and government reports suggested that the number of women employed in commerce increased in the late 1970s and early 1980s.

The Museveni government of the late 1980s pledged to eliminate discrimination against women in official policy and practice. Women are active in the National Resistance Army (NRA), and Museveni appointed a woman, Joan Kakwenzire, to a six-member commission to document abuses by the military (see Human Rights, ch. 5). The government also has decreed that one woman would represent each district on the National Resistance Council (NRC—see The National Resistance Council, ch. 4). In addition, the government-operated Uganda Commercial Bank has launched a rural credit plan to make farm loans more easily available to women (see Banking, ch. 3).

Museveni appointed Joyce Mpanga minister for women and development in 1987, and she proclaimed the government's intention to raise women's wages, increase women's credit and employment opportunities, and improve the lives of women in general. In 1989 there were two women serving as ministers and three serving as deputy ministers in the NRM cabinet. Women civil servants and professionals also formed an organization, Action for Development, to assist women in war-torn areas, especially the devastated Luwero region in central Uganda.

The Uganda Association of Women Lawyers, which was founded in 1976, established a legal-aid clinic in early 1988 to defend women who faced the loss of property or children because of divorce, separation, or widowhood. The association also sought to expand educational opportunities for women, increase child-support payments (equivalent to US$0.50 per month in 1989) in case of divorce, establish common legal grounds for divorce for both men and women, establish common criminal codes for men and women, assist women and children who were victims of AIDS, and implement nationwide education programs to inform women of their legal rights.

Education

Mission schools were established in Uganda in the 1890s, and in 1924 the government established the first secondary school for Africans. By 1950, however, the government operated only three of the fifty-three secondary schools for Africans. Three others were privately funded, and forty-seven were operated by religious organizations. Education was eagerly sought by rural farmers as well as urban elites, and after independence many villages, especially in the south, built schools, hired teachers, and appealed for and received government assistance to operate their own village schools.

Most subjects were taught according to the British syllabus until 1974, and British examinations measured a student's progress through primary and secondary school. In 1975 the government implemented a local curriculum, and for a short time most school materials were published in Uganda. School enrollments continued to climb throughout most of the 1970s and 1980s, but as the economy deteriorated and violence increased, local publishing almost ceased, and examination results deteriorated.

The education system suffered the effects of economic decline and political instability during the 1970s and 1980s. The system continued to function, however, with an administrative structure based on regional offices, a national school inspectorate, and centralized, nationwide school examinations. Enrollments and expenditures increased steadily during this time, reflecting the high priority Ugandans attach to education, but at all levels, the physical infrastructure necessary for education was lacking, and the quality of education declined. School maintenance standards suffered, teachers fled the country, morale and productivity deteriorated along with real incomes, and many facilities were damaged by warfare and vandalism.

In 1990 adult literacy nationwide was estimated at 50 percent. Improving this ratio was important to the Museveni government. In order to reestablish the national priority on education, the Museveni government adopted a two-phase policy—to rehabilitate buildings and establish minimal conditions for instruction, and to improve efficiency and quality of education through teacher training and curriculum upgrading. Important long-term goals included establishing universal primary education, extending the seven-year primary cycle to eight or nine years, and shifting the emphasis in postsecondary education from purely academic to more technical and vocational training.

The School System

Formal education had four levels. The first level consisted of seven primary-school grades (standards one through seven), usually beginning about age six. Based on test scores in seventh grade, pupils could enter one of several types of institutions—a four-year secondary school ("O–level"), a three-year technical training institution, or a four-year teacher training college. About 40 percent of those who passed "O–level" examinations continued their education through one of several options—an advanced two-year secondary course ("A–level"), an advanced two-year teacher training course, a technical institute, or a specialized training program provided by the government. Those who completed "A–level"

Children waiting for a school bus near Kampala
Courtesy Carl Fleischhauer

examinations might study at Makerere University in Kampala or they might study abroad. Other options for "A–level" graduates were the Uganda Technical College, the Institute of Teachers' Education (formerly the National Teachers' College), or National College of Business Studies.

Primary Education

In 1989, the last year for which official figures were available, the government estimated that more than 2.5 million youngsters were enrolled in primary schools; about 45 percent of primary students were female (see table 3, Appendix). This figure represented a four-fold increase from primary enrollment levels of the late 1960s and a near doubling of the almost 1.3 million pupils enrolled in 1980. In that year, just over half of eligible six- to twelve-year-olds were attending government-aided primary schools, while an additional 80,000 pupils were enrolled in private primary schools.

Officials estimated that roughly 61 percent of primary pupils completed seventh grade. Of those, about 25 percent went on to further study. The central government was responsible for training, posting, and promoting primary school teachers, setting salaries and school fees, providing supplies, inspecting schools, and appointing educational committees to deal with local problems. Local school officials, including the headmaster or headmistress, and district education officials were responsible for collecting fees, ordering supplies, and administering the school according to national policy. The District Education Office provided an important intermediary between the school and the Ministry of Education.

Secondary Education

In 1989 secondary school enrollments on all levels totaled 265,000 pupils. Of this number, 238,500 were enrolled in forms one through six in government-aided secondary schools; 35 percent of those enrolled were female. Some 216,000 pupils were enrolled in the first four years (forms one to four) in "O level" studies, while an additional 22,000 were attending teacher training schools or technical institutes on the lower secondary level. Just over 22,000 pupils were enrolled in forms five and six in upper secondary ("A level") studies; at the same time, 4,400 other pupils on this level were enrolled in teacher training colleges or technical institutes.

The most complete breakdown of primary and secondary enrollments was for the year 1980, when about 7 percent of children aged thirteen to sixteen years (about 75,000 pupils) were enrolled in the first four years (forms one to four) of secondary-level education in about 170 government-funded schools. About 70 percent of these pupils were boys. Roughly 66,200 were attending secondary schools in preparation for "O–level" exams, which would qualify them for further academic study, teacher training, or other technical training programs beyond the secondary level. Roughly 6,000 people in the thirteen- to sixteen-year-old age-group were attending teacher training colleges, and about 2,800 were enrolled in technical schools.

Upper secondary education (forms five and six) enrolled about 6,900 pupils in 1980. In addition, about 1,200 students were enrolled in teacher training colleges at this level, and 1,100 in technical training institutes. These 9,200 pupils represented 1.8 percent of the seventeen- and eighteen-year-old age-group. Female students made up roughly 20 percent of the total. In addition to these enrollments, a further 20,000 pupils were attending private secondary schools.

Postsecondary Education

Established in 1922, Makerere University in Kampala was the first college in East Africa. Its primary aim was to train people for government employment, but by the 1980s, it had expanded to include colleges of liberal arts and medicine serving more than 5,000 students from Uganda and other African countries. In 1986 the

College of Commerce separated from Makerere to become the National College of Business Studies, and at the same time, the National Teachers' College became a separate Institute of Teachers' Education. In 1980 these institutions enrolled 5,750 postsecondary students, roughly 23 percent of whom were women. By 1989 enrollments totaled an estimated 8,900 students.

The Organization of the Islamic Conference (OIC) financed the opening of the Islamic University at Mbale in southern Uganda in 1988. This campus provides Islamic educational services primarily to English-speaking students from African nations. In late 1989, a second national university campus opened in Mbarara. Its curriculum is designed to serve Uganda's rural development needs. Development plans for higher education rely largely on international and private donors. In 1989 Makerere University received US$50 million in pledged support from its graduates as part of a US$150-million renovation plan.

In the late 1980s, many other educational opportunities were available. The Ministry of Labour and Social Welfare operated four vocational training centers, providing apprenticeships and classes to upgrade technical skills. The Ministry of Agriculture, Animal Husbandry, and Fisheries conducted training courses at eighteen district farm institutions. Ministry of Community Development personnel also staffed fifteen rural training centers. Other government ministries offered in-service training in agriculture, health, community development, cooperatives, commerce, industry, and public services to satisfy technical labor requirements of these agencies. In addition, the Young Women's Christian Association (YWCA) offered a variety of training courses for women.

Teachers

There was a severe shortage of teachers during the 1980s, made acute by the departure of both Ugandan and expatriate teachers during the 1970s and early 1980s. Aside from shortages of supplies and equipment, high student-teacher ratios, often more than twenty-five to one, made teaching especially difficult. Teacher morale suffered, although the number of teacher training candidates continued to rise during and after the 1970s. The proportion of untrained teachers in primary schools also increased from 14 percent in 1971 to 35 percent in 1981. Although unlicensed teachers continued to teach during the 1980s, teacher training colleges had full enrollments and attempted to train teachers to cope with both the educational and economic problems they would face.

Uganda: A Country Study

Educational Finance

In the mid-1980s, the educational sector was the largest public-sector employer, but after 1986, observers estimated that the defense establishment surpassed education in this regard. The Ministry of Education received about 18 percent of the government's current budget, most of which was used to pay teacher salaries in government schools. Primary and secondary pupils paid school fees ranging from US$5 to US$10 per year, and most schools asked pupils and their parents to contribute labor, food, or materials to the school. "A-level" secondary schools, teacher training institutions, and other postsecondary institutions did not charge fees during the 1980s, but their students were required to bring materials, such as food and bedding, for their own use.

Health and Welfare

In 1989 Uganda's estimated life expectancy, crude death rate, and infant mortality represented significant improvements over those of the 1960s, but local officials also believed the 1980s estimates were optimistic, based on incomplete reports. Health services and record keeping deteriorated during the 1970s and early 1980s, when many deaths resulted from government neglect, violence, and civil war.

In 1989 officials estimated that measles, respiratory tract infections, and gastroenteritis caused one-half of all deaths attributed to illness. Other fatal illnesses included anemia, tetanus, and whooping cough, but some people also died of malnutrition. An estimated 20 percent of all deaths were caused by diseases that were not well known among international health officials. Ugandan health workers were especially concerned about infant mortality, most often caused by low birth weight, premature birth, or neonatal tetanus. Childhood diseases such as measles, gastroenteritis, malaria, and respiratory tract infections also claimed many lives. Malaria and tuberculosis caused an increasing number of deaths among adults during the 1980s.

Certain forms of cancer were common in Uganda before they were first systematically studied in any country. Burkitt's lymphoma, which caused a large number of cancer deaths in children across Africa, was first described in Uganda in 1958. This malignancy was thought to be related to the incidence of malaria and possibly to food storage practices that allowed the growth of carcinogenic strains of bacteria or molds in stored grain or peanuts. Other research, although inconclusive, suggested that the spread of certain cancers might be related to parasites or other insect-borne diseases.

Acquired Immune Deficiency Syndrome (AIDS)

During the 1980s, Uganda developed the highest known incidence of acquired immune deficiency syndrome (AIDS), with an infection rate of over 15 cases per 100,000 population. By mid-1989, the Ministry of Health had reported 7,573 AIDS cases to the World Health Organization (WHO). In mid-1990, local officials reported that at least 17,400 cases had been diagnosed and the number of actual AIDS cases was doubling every six months. In Kampala health officials also reported that more than 790,000 people had positive test results for human immunodeficiency virus (HIV), the infectious agent believed to cause AIDS, a figure estimated at 1.3 million by late 1990. Over 25,000 children under the age of fifteen were HIV-positive, along with 22 percent of all women seeking prenatal medical care at Mulago Hospital, the nation's largest hospital in Kampala. Belgium's Institute of Tropical Medicine reported that an estimated 20 percent of all infant deaths in Kampala were related to HIV infections, and many tuberculosis patients were also infected with HIV.

Uganda's first officially recognized AIDS deaths occurred in 1982, when seventeen traders in the southern district of Rakai died of symptoms that came to be associated with the disease. Within a year, AIDS (then known as "Slim") was diagnosed in Masaka, Rakai, and Kampala, and by 1989, all districts of Uganda were affected. The disease appeared to spread by heterosexual contact, often along main transportation routes. Men and women were equally affected, although the death of a man was more likely to be reported to officials. The majority of AIDS cases occurred in people between sixteen and forty years of age, and by the late 1980s, an increasing number of babies were born HIV-positive. These cases, more than adult deaths, shocked people into changing behavior that risked AIDS infection. Fewer than ten AIDS cases were reported among school-age children, who constituted nearly one-half of the population, prompting intensive efforts to prevent its spread into this age-group.

Government health officials initiated an aggressive nationwide school education program to prevent the spread of the disease among the young, and they implemented nationwide blood screening and public education programs, including television, radio, and local press warnings in English and local languages. By the late 1980s, however, it was clear that the nation's beleaguered health care system could not cope with the increased health needs, and the government intensified efforts to gain international assistance to slow the spread of this deadly disease. The need to combat AIDS was urgent: according to one estimate, Uganda's population in 2015 could total about 20 million, rather than the 32 million that demographers anticipated, because of AIDS, and the number of orphaned children would rise dramatically throughout the 1990s and after.

The transmission of AIDS was complicated by economic decline and problems of national security. In many areas, warfare had destroyed communication systems and health care facilities. At the same time, AIDS slowed the pace of economic development, because skilled workers and young, educated Ugandans had high infection rates. A few people were able to capitalize on the tragedy of AIDS—a small number of local medical practitioners claimed to have cured AIDS victims and became wealthy fairly quickly. A few street vendors in Kampala sold vials of a liquid they identified as Azidothymidine (AZT), a drug being tested for possible AIDS treatment, at prices ranging as high as US$1,000 per vial. They were able to reap fortunes from desperate AIDS victims and their families, despite government warnings that no AZT was available in Uganda.

Health Care

Uganda had a total of seventy-nine hospitals in 1989, providing approximately 20,000 hospital beds. The government operated forty-six of these institutions, while thirty-three were staffed and equipped by religious and other private organizations. In addition, more than 600 smaller health facilities, including community health centers, maternity clinics, dispensaries, subdispensaries, leprosy centers, and aid posts, operated nationwide. At least one hospital was located in each district except the southern district of Rakai; the best-served districts were Mukono and Mpigi, each with five hospitals, and Kampala with seven. In the more sparsely populated northern districts, however, people sometimes traveled long distances to receive medical care, and facilities were generally inferior to those in the south. In 1990 Uganda's entire health care system was served by about 700 doctors.

Uganda's per capita spending on health amounted to less than US$2 per year for most of the 1980s. This rate of spending increased slightly in 1989, when the government allocated US$63 million, roughly 26 percent of its development budget, for social services, and US$24 million of this amount for health services in particular. The amount represented an increase of 50 percent over health spending for the previous year.

The highest priority in government programs was rehabilitating existing facilities and improving supplies. In 1989 funding from

Distribution of food to mothers and children in Kabong
Courtesy World Bank Photo Library

the United Nations Development Programme (UNDP) and the International Development Association (IDA) was earmarked for rehabilitating nineteen of the nation's hospitals, primarily through building repairs and upgrading water and electrical systems. Primary health-care projects, including immunization programs, prescription drugs, clean water supplies, and public hygiene, also received special priority. European Development Fund (EDF) assistance was also used to construct twenty new health centers and one district health office and to train health-care practitioners.

A number of governmental and nongovernmental organizations were involved in health research in the late 1980s, much of this sponsored by the Ministry of Health, the Institute of Public Health, and Makerere University. The nation's largest health-care facility, Mulago Hospital, conducted research on local nutrition and endemic diseases, and researchers there developed child nutrition programs to be implemented through the United Nations Emergency (UNICEF) and the Save the Children Fund.

Several government ministries sponsored research and implemented community programs designed to improve health and nutrition. The Ugandan Red Cross and the Ministry of Health, in cooperation with several international agencies, opened an orthopedic workshop in Kampala for handicapped children and adults, most of whom had suffered from poliomyelitis or severe wounds in outbreaks of violence. Catholic and Protestant missions, the Food and Agriculture Organization (FAO) of the UN, the International Committee of the Red Cross (ICRC), and the Oxford Committee for Famine Relief (Oxfam) were also active in emergency relief projects involving food and nutrition. Many Ugandans criticized their own government for inadequate attention to popular health needs, but they also hoped that government efforts to eliminate violence and warfare would lay the foundation for improved health care.

Social Welfare

Social services were an important factor in government planning in the late 1980s, both to support efforts to improve health care and to upgrade living standards in general. Providing running water in rural areas was a high priority, although even small improvements in water supplies were costly. Projects in the late 1980s focused on drilling wells, protecting springs, replacing and repairing pumps, and training community workers to oversee water systems. The government also recognized that many people had to walk several kilometers to carry water to their homes and declared its intention to extend pipelines into rural areas. Sewage systems, too, were considered an important but expensive improvement. Even so, many urban pipelines and septic tanks were in disrepair, and most rural areas lacked pipelines or sewage treatment facilities. Government workers began installing sewage systems in several small towns, including Rakai, Nebbi, and Bushenyi, in 1988.

Housing was an important symbol of development in Uganda under the NRM government. Providing low-cost urban housing was a high government priority. Projects in Masaka, Mbarara, Arua, and Namuwongo exceeded government spending projections in 1988 and 1989. In 1990 at least three housing projects were underway in Kampala. Estimates were that some 8,000 housing units needed to be built each year throughout the 1990s in urban areas alone to keep pace with population growth. Given the shortage of investment funds and the high cost of imported construction materials, it was unlikely that such a goal would be met. Rural houssing development was also an important goal, but in the late 1980s, most rural residents built their own homes. Although these were often mud-and-wattle huts, they were, nonetheless, a source of pride. Having a well-kept home was important to many Ugandans, even the very poor. People considered deteriorating housing standards a symbol of social disintegration, one that characterized a few poverty-stricken areas and those hardest hit by AIDS. Village cooperative societies in the Luwero region organized brick-making factories in 1988 and 1989, and the government was attempting to organize similar projects in other areas. Other government programs aimed at increasing credit opportunities and improving materials and transportation facilities for rural homebuilders. In the late 1980s, housing assistance was received from Austria, Britain, Finland, and the Netherlands.

One social problem with tragic implications for Uganda's future was the children—more than 1.5 million of them, almost 10 percent of the population—who had been orphaned by the spread of warfare or by AIDS in the late 1970s and early 1980s. By 1990 the number of war orphans alone was estimated at more than half a million. No reliable figures were available for AIDS orphans, but one study predicted that their number would grow over the next twenty years to 4 to 5 million.

Several thousands of these orphans were young boys who had attached themselves to the army. By the late 1980s, the government had established a few schools to provide boarding facilities and primary education for these *kadogos,* or child-soldiers. Others sometimes lived on city streets or in small groups without any regular supervision. Many Ugandans accepted the responsibility for caring for others' children, but this responsibility was generally believed to apply only within the boundaries of the extended family. Many children had lost a large number of relatives, in addition to their parents, and some orphans chose to avoid living with relatives they did not know well. As a result, neither government nor private agencies were able to surmount the economic and social obstacles to programs for immediate care for orphans. One of several ominous implications of this failure was that orphans and *kadogos* could remain on the periphery of society for the rest of their lives.

* * *

Despite the political turmoil of the 1970s and 1980s, publications by several government ministries and the Office of the President testify to the national commitment to disseminating information about Uganda. C. Obbo's research on women in Uganda and G. Ibingira's and D. Mudoola's political analyses are among the many contributions by Ugandan scholars to the growing understanding of their society. Makerere Institute of Social Research also publishes frequent reports by international researchers in Uganda.

Two compilations of essays assessing Uganda's social and political development in the 1980s are *Uganda Now,* edited by H. Hansen and M. Twaddle, and *Conflict Resolution in Uganda,* edited by K. Rupesinghe. Numerous works by N. Kasfir have also contributed an understanding of Uganda's political environment. Volumes in the Ethnographic Survey of Africa series by G. W. B. Huntingford, P. and P. H. Gulliver, and M. Fallers preserve Uganda's rich cultural heritage in the ethnographic present. Field reports and ethnographic analyses from the decades just before and after independence also provide much of the basis for the 1980s' understanding of Ugandan society. These publications include works by J. Beattie, L. Fallers, L. Mair, and A. Richards on Bantu-speaking societies of the south; H. Morris on Uganda's once-thriving Asian community; and A. Southall's publications on Alur society and acculturation in other areas. Works by B. Langlands survey Uganda's social and physical geography.

Several scholars have applied class analysis and dependency theory to Ugandan society without becoming mired in debates over geopolitical alignment. Examples of such works are M. Mamdani's *Politics and Class Formation in Uganda;* S. Bunker's *Double Dependency and Constraints on Class Formation in Bugisu, Uganda* and *Peasants Against the State;* and J. Vincent's *African Elite* and *Teso in Transformation.* S. Heyneman's research on education in the 1970s and early 1980s demonstrates the national commitment to education. Information on AIDS is available in 1988 and 1989 publications by the World Health Organization and the International Committee of the Red Cross. (For further information and complete citations, see Bibliography.)

Chapter 3. The Economy

Women drying coffee berries in the sun

UGANDA WAS ONCE RICH in human and natural resources and possessed a favorable climate for economic development, but in the late 1980s it was still struggling to end a period of political and economic chaos that had destroyed the country's reputation as the "pearl" of Africa. Most of the economic infrastructure, including the power supply system, the transportation system, and industry, operated at only a fraction of capacity. Other than limited segments of the agricultural sector—notably coffee and subsistence production—cultivation was almost at a standstill. And in the wake of the much publicized atrocities of the Idi Amin Dada regime from 1971 to 1979 and the civil war that continued into the 1980s, Uganda's once flourishing tourist industry faced the challenges of reconstruction and restoring international confidence. Successive governments had proclaimed their intention to salvage the economy and attract the foreign assistance necessary for recovery, but none had remained in power long enough to succeed.

Agricultural production based primarily on peasant cultivation has been the mainstay of the economy. In the 1950s, coffee replaced cotton as the primary cash crop. Some plantations produced tea and sugar, but these exports did not alter the importance of coffee in the economy. Similarly, some industries developed before 1970, but most were adjuncts to cotton or sugar production, and they were not major contributors to gross domestic product (GDP—see Glossary). Moreover, Uganda did not possess significant quantities of valuable minerals, such as oil or gold. In sum, although the economy provided a livelihood for the population, it was based largely on agricultural commodities with fluctuating international values. This dependence forced Uganda to import vehicles, machinery, and other major industrial equipment, and it limited development choices. The economy seemed to have the potential to stabilize, but throughout the decade of the 1980s its capacity to generate growth, especially industrial growth, was small.

After 1986 the National Resistance Movement (NRM) succeeded in stabilizing most of the nation and began to diversify agricultural exports away from the near-total dependence on coffee. By 1988 Western donors were beginning to offer cautious support for the three-year-old regime of Yoweri Kaguta Museveni. But in 1989, just as the hard work of economic recovery was beginning to pay off, world coffee prices plummeted, and Uganda's scarce foreign exchange dwindled further. Despite the country's record of economic resilience, it still faced serious obstacles to the goal of economic self-sufficiency.

Historical Background

Peasant agricultural production has been the predominant economic activity since precolonial times. Despite an active trade in ivory and animal hides linking Uganda with the east coast of Africa long before the arrival of Europeans, most Ugandans were subsistence farmers. After declaring Uganda a protectorate in 1893, Britain pursued economic policies that drew Uganda into the world economy primarily to serve Britain's late-nineteenth-century textile industry. Cotton cultivation increased in importance after 1904, and once it became clear that cotton plantations would be too difficult and expensive to maintain, official policy encouraged smallholder farmers to produce and market their cotton through local cooperative associations.

By 1910 cotton had become Uganda's leading export. In the following decades, the government encouraged the growth of sugar and tea plantations. Following World War II, officials introduced coffee cultivation to bolster declining export revenues, and coffee soon earned more than half of Uganda's export earnings.

Uganda enjoyed a strong and stable economy in the years approaching independence. Agriculture was the dominant activity, but the expanding manufacturing sector appeared capable of increasing its contribution to GDP, especially through the production of foodstuffs and textiles. Some valuable minerals, notably copper, had been discovered, and water power resources were substantial. In 1967 Uganda and the neighboring countries of Kenya and Tanzania joined together to form the East African Community (EAC), hoping to create a common market and share the cost of transport and banking facilities, and Uganda registered impressive growth rates for the first eight years after independence.

The economy deteriorated under the rule of President Idi Amin Dada from 1971 to 1979. Amin used nationalist, militarist rhetoric and ill-chosen economic policies to eliminate foreign economic interests and build up the military establishment. In 1972 he expelled holders of British passports, including approximately 70,000 Asians of Indian and Pakistani descent. Many Asians had been active in agribusiness, manufacturing, and commerce. Their mass expulsion and Amin's efforts to expropriate foreign businesses undermined investor confidence in Uganda. Amin also increased public expenditures on military goods, a practice that contributed to escalating foreign and domestic debt during the 1970s. Relations with Uganda's neighbors soured, the EAC disbanded in 1977, and

Tanzanian troops finally led a joint effort to overthrow the unpopular Amin regime in 1979. By 1980 the economy was nearly destroyed.

Following Amin's departure, successive governments attempted to restore international confidence in the economy through a mixture of development plans and austere government budgets. Beginning in 1980, the second government of Milton Obote obtained foreign donor support, primarily from the International Monetary Fund (IMF—see Glossary), by floating the Uganda shilling (USh; for value of the Uganda shilling—see Glossary), removing price controls, increasing agricultural producer prices, and setting strict limits on government expenditures. In addition, Obote tried to persuade foreign companies to return to their former premises, which had been nationalized under Amin. These recovery initiatives created real growth in agriculture between 1980 and 1983. The lack of foreign exchange was a major constraint on government efforts, however, and it became a critical problem in 1984 when the IMF ended its support following a disagreement over budget policy. During the brief regime of Tito Lutwa Okello in 1985, the economy slipped almost out of control as civil war extended across the country.

After seizing power in January 1986, the new NRM government published a political manifesto that had been drawn up when the NRM was an army of antigovernment rebels (see The Ten-Point Program, ch. 4). Several points in the Ten-Point Program emphasized the importance of economic development, declaring that an independent, self-sustaining national economy was vital to protect Uganda's interests. The manifesto also set out specific goals for achieving this self-sufficiency: diversifying agricultural exports and developing industries that used local raw materials to manufacture products necessary for development. The Ten-Point Program also set out other economic goals: to improve basic social services, such as water, health care, and housing; to improve literacy skills nationwide; to eliminate corruption, especially in government; to return expropriated land to its rightful Ugandan owners; to raise public-sector salaries; to strengthen regional ties and develop markets among East African nations; and to maintain a mixed economy combining private ownership with an active government sector.

The NRM government proposed a major Rehabilitation and Development Plan (RDP) for fiscal years (FY—see Glossary) 1987–88 through 1990–91, with IMF support; it then devalued the shilling and committed itself to budgetary restraint. The four-year plan set out primarily to stabilize the economy and promote economic growth. More specific goals were to reduce Uganda's dependence on external assistance, diversify agricultural exports, and encourage the growth of the private sector through new credit policies. Setting these priorities helped improve Uganda's credentials with international aid organizations and donor countries of the West, but in the first three years of Museveni's rule, coffee production remained the only economic activity inside Uganda to display consistent growth and resilience. When coffee-producing nations failed to reach an agreement on prices for coffee exports in 1989, Uganda faced devastating losses in export earnings and sought increased international assistance to stave off economic collapse.

Growth and Structure of the Economy

When coffee replaced cotton as Uganda's principal export in the 1950s, it was still produced in the pattern of small peasant holdings and local marketing associations that had arisen early in the century. The economy registered substantial growth, but almost all real growth was in agriculture, centered in the southern provinces. The fledgling industrial sector, which emphasized food processing for export, also increased its contribution as a result of the expansion of agriculture.

Growth slowed in the late 1950s, as fluctuating world market conditions reduced export earnings and Uganda experienced the political pressures of growing nationalist movements that swept much of Africa. For the first five years following independence in 1962, Uganda's economy resumed rapid growth, with GDP, including subsistence agriculture, expanding approximately 6.7 percent per year. Even with population growth estimated at 2.5 percent per year, net economic growth of more than 4 percent suggested that people's lives were improving. By the end of the 1960s, commercial agriculture accounted for more than one-third of GDP. Industrial output had increased to nearly 9 percent of GDP, primarily the result of new food-processing industries. Tourism, transportation, telecommunications, and wholesale and retail trade still contributed nearly one-half of total output.

Although the government envisioned annual economic growth rates of about 5.6 percent in the early 1970s, civil war and political instability almost destroyed Uganda's once promising economy. GDP declined each year from 1972 to 1976 and registered only slight improvement in 1977 when world coffee prices increased. Negative growth resumed, largely because the government continued to expropriate business assets. Foreign investments, too, declined sharply, as President Idi Amin's erratic policies destroyed almost all but the subsistence sector of the economy.

The economic and political destruction of the Amin years contributed to a record decline in earnings by 14.8 percent between 1978 and 1980. When Amin fled from Uganda in 1979, the nation's GDP measured only 80 percent of the 1970 level. Industrial output declined sharply, as equipment, spare parts, and raw materials became scarce. From 1981 to 1983, the country experienced a welcome 17.3 percent growth rate, but most of this success occurred in the agricultural sector. Little progress was made in manufacturing and other productive sectors. Renewed political crisis led to negative growth rates of 4.2 percent in 1984, 1.5 percent in 1985, and 2.3 percent in 1986.

Throughout these years of political uncertainty, coffee production by smallholders—the pattern developed under British rule—continued to dominate the economy, providing the best hope for national recovery and economic development. As international coffee prices fluctuated, however, Uganda's overall GDP suffered despite consistent production.

The economic decline again seemed to end, and in 1987 GDP rose 4.5 percent above the 1986 level. This rise marked Uganda's first sign of economic growth in four years, as security improved in the south and west and factories increased production after years of stagnation. This modest rate of growth increased in 1988, when GDP expansion measured 7.2 percent, with substantial improvements in the manufacturing sector. In 1989 falling world market prices for coffee reduced growth to 6.6 percent, and a further decline to 3.4 percent growth occurred in 1990, in part because of drought, low coffee prices, and a decline in manufacturing output.

Uganda had escaped widespread famine in the late 1970s and 1980s only because many people, even urban residents, reverted to subsistence cultivation in order to survive. Both commercial and subsistence farming operated in the monetary and nonmonetary (barter) sectors, and the latter presented the government with formidable problems of organization and taxation. By the late 1980s, government reports estimated that approximately 44 percent of GDP originated outside the monetary economy (see fig. 6; table 4, Appendix). Most (over 90 percent) of nonmonetary economic activity was agricultural, and it was the resilience of this sector that ensured survival for most Ugandans.

Role of the Government

In 1986 the newly established Museveni regime committed itself to reversing the economic disintegration of the 1970s and 1980s. Museveni proclaimed the national economic orientation to be toward private enterprise rather than socialist government control.

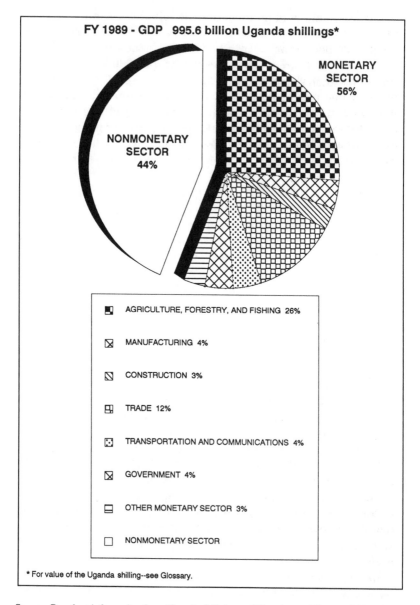

Source: Based on information from Uganda, Ministry of Planning and Economic Development, *Background to the Budget, 1990–1991,* Kampala, 1990, 158; and Economist Intelligence Unit, *Country Report: Uganda, Ethiopia, Somalia, Djibouti,* No. 1, London, 1991, 3.

Figure 6. Gross Domestic Product (GDP) by Sector, Fiscal Year 1989

Many government policies were aimed at restoring the confidence of the private sector. In the absence of private initiatives, however, the government took over many abandoned or formerly expropriated companies and formed new parastatal enterprises. In an effort to bring a measure of financial stability to the country and attract some much-needed foreign assistance in 1987, it also initiated an ambitious RDP aimed at rebuilding the economic and social infrastructure. Officials then offered to sell several of the largest parastatals to private investors, but political and personal rivalries hampered efforts toward privatization throughout 1988 and 1989.

In Museveni's first three years in office, the role of government bureaucrats in economic planning gave rise to charges of official corruption. A 1988 audit accused government ministries and other departments of fraudulently appropriating nearly 20 percent of the national budget. The audit cited the Office of the President, the Ministry of Defence, and the Ministry of Education. Education officials, in particular, were accused of paying salaries for fictitious teachers and paying labor and material costs for nonexistent building projects. In order to set a public example in 1989, Museveni dismissed several high-level officials, including cabinet ministers, who were accused of embezzling or misusing government funds.

Direct Economic Involvement

By 1987 the Ugandan government was directly involved in the economy through four institutions. First, it owned a number of parastatals that had operated as private companies before being abandoned by their owners or expropriated by the government. Second, the government operated marketing boards to monitor sales and regulate prices for agricultural producers. Third, the government owned the country's major banks, including the Bank of Uganda and Uganda Commercial Bank (see Banking and Currency, this ch.). And fourth, the government controlled all imports and exports through licensing procedures (see Foreign Trade and Assistance, this ch.).

In July 1988, officials announced that they would sell twenty-two companies that were entirely or partially government-owned, in an effort to trim government costs and curb runaway inflation. These enterprises included textile mills, vehicle import companies, and iron and gold mines. Officials hoped to sell some of them to private owners and to undertake joint ventures with private companies to continue operating several others. Among the roughly sixty parastatals that would remain in operation after 1989 were several in which the government planned to continue as the sole or majority shareholder. These parastatals included the electric power company, railroads and airlines, and cement and steel manufacturers. Banking and export-import licensing would remain in government hands, along with a substantial number of the nation's hotels. Retail trade would be managed almost entirely by the private sector. By late 1989, however, efforts to privatize parastatal organizations had just begun, as personal and political rivalries delayed the sale of several lucrative corporations. The International Development Association (IDA) awarded Uganda US$16 million to help improve the efficiency of government-owned enterprises. Funds allocated through this Public Enterprise Project would be used to pay for consultancy services and supplies and to commission a study of ways to reform public-sector administration.

By the 1980s, more than 3,500 primary marketing cooperative societies serviced most of Uganda's small-scale farmers. These cooperatives purchased crops for marketing and export, and they distributed consumer goods and agricultural inputs, such as seeds and fertilizers. Prices paid by marketing boards for commodities such as coffee, tea, and cotton were fairly stable but often artificially low, and payments were sometimes delayed until several weeks after purchases. Moreover, farmers sometimes complained that marketing boards applied inconsistent standards of quality and that weights and measurements of produce were sometimes faulty. In 1989 the government was attempting to reduce expensive and inefficient intermediary activity in crop marketing, and Museveni urged producers to report buyers who failed to pay for commodities when they were received.

Budgets

Uganda registered a substantial budget deficit for every year of the 1970s except 1977, when world coffee price increases provided the basis for a surplus. Deficits equivalent to 50 to 60 percent of revenues were not unusual, and the deficit reached 100 percent in 1974. Although declining levels of production and trade, smuggling, and inefficiency all eroded revenues, the Amin government made only modest efforts to restrain expenditures. Amin increased government borrowing from local banks from 50 percent to 70 percent during his eight-year rule.

The budgets of the early 1980s were cautious. They set limits on government borrowing and domestic credit and linked these limits to a realistic exchange policy by allowing the shilling to float in relation to other currencies. Between 1982 and 1989, current revenue increased continuously in nominal terms, in part because of revisions and improvements in the tax system and depreciation of the shilling. In FY 1985 and FY 1986, export taxes—primarily on coffee—contributed about 60 percent of the total current revenue. Export taxes then declined, contributing less than 20 percent of revenues in FY 1989. The share of sales tax remained roughly constant at 20 percent from FY 1983 to FY 1986 but increased to about 38 percent by 1989. Income tax increased its share of the total revenue from about 5 percent in FY 1986 to about 11 percent in FY 1989.

Government expenditures increased during the early 1980s, and the rate of increase rose after 1984. In 1985 civil service salaries were tripled, but in general, the ministries of defence, education, and finance, and the Office of the President were the biggest spenders. In 1988 and 1989, the Ministry of Defence spent roughly 2.9 percent and the Ministry of Education about 15 percent of the current budget. The percentage share of the Ministry of Finance declined from about 30 percent in 1985 to about 22 percent in 1989. The 1987 budget ended with a deficit amounting to 32 percent of total spending. This deficit was reduced to about 19 percent in 1988 and rose slightly in 1989 to just over 20 percent.

The government implemented measures to reform the tax system in FY 1988 and FY 1989. A graduated tax rate, with twenty-five grades, rose from a USh300 minimum to a USh5,000 maximum to account for all classes of income earners. Overall income tax rates were raised in order to gain revenue for local authorities and to allow them greater self-sufficiency in rendering public services. The government also called upon local governing bodies, or resistance councils (RCs) to spearhead the war against tax evaders and defaulters by assuming responsibility for assessing and collecting taxes and monitoring the use of public funds (see Local Administration, ch. 4). Despite all measures to balance the economy, however, the budget deficit in FY 1989 reached USh38.9 million or nearly one-third of total spending, a substantial increase over the government's original target.

The FY 1989 budget sought to reduce current spending in several government departments, including cuts of 25 percent in the Office of the President and 18 percent in the Ministry of Defence, but defense spending in FY 1989 exceeded budget estimates. At the same time, total government expenditures increased to accommodate civil service wage hikes and infrastructural rehabilitation. The government sought to meet these increased expenditures in part through a major revenue collection effort and increased external aid. To help secure this assistance, it implemented reforms, including cuts in executive spending, advocated by the World Bank (see

Glossary) and the IMF. The FY 1989 budget also included agricultural producer price increases ranging from 100 percent to 150 percent. But at the same time, its reduced government subsidies for gasoline and sugar prices resulted in substantial price increases for those products.

In FY 1990, total government expenditures amounted to USh169.3 billion, of which USh105.5 billion was for current expenditures and USh63.7 billion for development expenditures. Total receipts came to USh111.4 billion, of which USh86.5 billion was current revenues—only 82 percent of anticipated receipts—leaving a deficit of USh57.9 billion or about 34 percent of total spending. As in earlier years, the ministries that consumed the bulk of current expenditures were defence (39 percent) and education (14 percent), together with foreign affairs (4 percent) and health (4 percent).

Uganda operated under a separate development budget during the 1980s. This budget consisted of domestic revenues and expenditures on development projects, but it excluded revenues from foreign donors. The development budget increased from FY 1981 to FY 1988, primarily because of inflation, but was trimmed slightly in FY 1989. The Ministry of Finance and Ministry of Defence consumed most of the development budget, however, in part because agricultural and livestock projects were often funded by foreign donors. The Ministry of Housing also received nearly 17.3 percent of FY 1988 development allocations, and much of this amount was earmarked for renovations on government-owned tourist hotels.

Rehabilitation and Development Plan

In June 1987, the government launched a four-year RDP for fiscal years 1988–91 (see table 5, Appendix). It aimed to restore the nation's productive capacity, especially in industry and commercial agriculture; to rehabilitate the social and economic infrastructure; to reduce inflation by 10 percent each year; and to stabilize the balance of payments. The plan targeted industrial and agricultural production, transportation, and electricity and water services for particular improvements. The plan envisioned an annual 5 percent growth rate, requiring US$1,289 million funding over the four-year period. Transportation would receive the major share of funding (29.4 percent), followed by agriculture (24.4 percent), industry and tourism (21.1 percent), social infrastructure (17.2 percent), and mining and energy (6.9 percent). Although the response of the international financial community was encouraging in terms of debt rescheduling and new loans, the initial rate of economic recovery was modest. In its first phase, FY 1988, twenty-six projects were implemented under the RDP, but by late

1989, officials considered the plan's success to be mixed. Improved security and private-sector development contributed to economic growth; however, external shocks, overvalued currency, and high government spending continued to erode investors' and international donors' confidence in Uganda's future.

Labor Force

In the late 1980s, most Ugandans worked outside the monetary economy, in part because the number of jobs in industry was dwindling and the value of Ugandan salaries was declining. Throughout the decade, official wages failed to keep up with the rising cost of living, and most wage earners were able to survive only because they had access to land and raised food crops. By the mid-1980s, typical average wages at the official exchange rate were only US$10 a month for factory workers, US$20 a month for lower-level civil servants, and US$40 a month for university lecturers. In the late 1980s, the converted value of these wages declined even further as the value of the shilling dropped. In addition, the decline in industrial production in the 1970s and 1980s had reduced the proportion of high-paying jobs. As a result, more industrial workers pursued black-market activities in order to support themselves.

Upon seizing power in 1986, the Museveni government tried to improve the status of wage laborers. The 1987 RDP aimed to enhance the country's self-sufficiency by increasing the number of skilled workers in industry. During the late 1980s, the government initiated a number of programs to improve working conditions in industry and provide training for industrial workers as well as government administrators. The Occupational Health and Hygiene Department implemented several projects to minimize occupational hazards in industry and to improve workers' health care. The Directorate of Industrial Training coordinated several vocational training programs, and the Rural Entrepreneurial/Vocational Training Center was established at Bowa. In addition, the government renovated the Institute of Public Administration, which provided training for government employees, and in 1988 it undertook a Public Service Improvement Project to train local administrators. Makerere University also established several training programs in surveying skills, agriculture, environmental studies, pharmacy, and computer science.

A lack of reliable labor statistics hampered the Museveni government's planning efforts in relation to the labor force. To collect reliable data, the government implemented a labor survey in October 1986. The survey concentrated on the formal sector of the economy, assessing available skills, training needs, vacancies in the labor market, and training facilities. In September 1988, the International Labour Office (ILO) surveyed the informal economic sector to assess the potential for growth in this sector.

By the late 1980s, the government, which had become the single major employer in the country, experienced significant problems as a result of almost two decades of economic decline and lax accounting procedures. A major problem was the lack of an accurate count of public wage earners, and to meet this urgent need, the government conducted a census of civil servants in 1987. It discovered 239,528 government employees and a wage bill for the month of May 1987 of USh53.2 million. Teaching and related activities employed 42 percent of all government workers; about 10 percent of civil servants worked in health-related fields. The largest concentration of government workers was in Kampala, although they represented a surprisingly low 15 percent of all government employees. The remaining 85 percent worked in other towns and cities.

Low wage scales led to the second serious problem confronting the government—i.e., corruption and inefficiency in the public sector. Both in government departments and parastatals, charges of corruption were widespread and were often attributed to low earnings. The highest-paid civil servant, the chief justice, received only about USh7,000 a month in 1988 (roughly US$117 at 1988 exchange rates). Gross monthly average pay was USh3,127 (US$52) in government posts, but the lowest-paid civil servants received only USh1,175 (US$20) a month. Workers in parastatal organizations received a monthly wage averaging USh5,786 (US$96), and in the private sector, roughly USh7,312 (US$122). Such income levels explained why a 1989–90 survey showed that more than half of all Ugandans lived below the poverty line, defined by the government as a household income of USh25,000 a month (roughly US$49 at official 1990 exchange rates).

Then in an attempt to streamline the civil service, the government announced plans to eliminate 30 percent of the nation's civil service jobs, leaving about 200,000 people employed by the government. This plan was not implemented, however. A labor survey in 1989 revealed that more than 244,000 people still worked for the national government, in addition to those in parastatal organizations.

Agriculture

Uganda's favorable soil conditions and climate have contributed to the country's agricultural success. Most areas of Uganda usually receive plenty of rain. In some years, small areas of the southeast and southwest have averaged more than 150 millimeters

Terraced fields in eastern Uganda
Houses in northern Uganda
Courtesy Carl Fleischhauer

per month. In the north, there is often a short dry season in December and January. Temperatures vary only a few degrees above or below 20°C but are moderated by differences in altitude. These conditions have allowed continuous cultivation in the south but only annual cropping in the north, and the driest northeastern corner of the country has supported only pastoralism. Although population growth has created pressures for land in a few areas, land shortages have been rare, and only about one-third of the estimated area of arable land was under cultivation by 1989.

Throughout the 1970s, political insecurity, mismanagement, and a lack of adequate resources seriously eroded incomes from commercial agriculture. Production levels in general were lower in the 1980s than in the 1960s. Technological improvements had been delayed by economic stagnation, and agricultural production still used primarily unimproved methods of production on small, widely scattered farms, with low levels of capital outlay. Other problems facing farmers included the disrepair of the nation's roads, the nearly destroyed marketing system, increasing inflation, and low producer prices. These factors contributed to low volumes of export commodity production and a decline in per capita food production and consumption in the late 1980s (see table 6, Appendix).

The decline in agricultural production, if sustained, posed major problems in terms of maintaining export revenues and feeding Uganda's expanding population. Despite these serious problems, agriculture continued to dominate the economy. In the late 1980s, agriculture (in the monetary and nonmonetary economy) contributed about two-thirds of GDP, 95 percent of export revenues, and 40 percent of government revenues. Roughly 20 percent of regular wage earners worked in commercial agricultural enterprises, and an additional 60 percent of the work force earned some income from farming. Agricultural output was generated by about 2.2 million small-scale producers on farms with an average of 2.5 hectares of land. The 1987 RDP called for efforts both to increase production of traditional cash crops, including coffee, cotton, tea, and tobacco, and to promote the production of nontraditional agricultural exports, such as corn, beans, peanuts, soybeans, sesame seeds, and a variety of fruit and fruit products.

Crops

Uganda's main food crops have been plantains, cassava, sweet potatoes, millet, sorghum, corn, beans, and peanuts. Major cash crops have been coffee, cotton, tea, and tobacco, although in the 1980s many farmers sold food crops to meet short-term expenses. The production of cotton, tea, and tobacco virtually collapsed during the late 1970s and early 1980s. In the late 1980s, the government was attempting to encourage diversification in commercial agriculture that would lead to a variety of nontraditional exports. The Uganda Development Bank and several other institutions supplied credit to local farmers, although small farmers also received credit directly from the government through agricultural cooperatives. For most small farmers, the main source of short-term credit was the policy of allowing farmers to delay payments for seeds and other agricultural inputs provided by cooperatives.

Cooperatives also handled most marketing activity, although marketing boards and private companies sometimes dealt directly with producers. Many farmers complained that cooperatives did not pay for produce until long after it had been sold. The generally low producer prices set by the government and the problem of delayed payments for produce prompted many farmers to sell produce at higher prices on illegal markets in neighboring countries. During most of the 1980s, the government steadily raised producer prices for export crops in order to maintain some incentive for farmers to deal with government purchasing agents, but these incentives failed to prevent widespread smuggling.

Coffee

Coffee continued to be Uganda's most important cash crop throughout the 1980s. The government estimated that farmers planted approximately 191,700 hectares of robusta coffee, most of this in southeastern Uganda, and about 33,000 hectares of arabica coffee in high-altitude areas of southeastern and southwestern Uganda. These figures remained almost constant throughout the decade, although a substantial portion of the nation's coffee output was smuggled into neighboring countries to sell at higher prices. Between 1984 and 1986, the European Economic Community (EEC) financed a coffee rehabilitation program that gave improved coffee production a high priority. This program also supported research, extension work, and training programs to upgrade coffee farmers' skills and understanding of their role in the economy. Some funds were also used to rehabilitate coffee factories.

When the NRM seized power in 1986, Museveni set high priorities on improving coffee production, reducing the amount of coffee smuggled into neighboring countries, and diversifying export crops to reduce Uganda's dependence on world coffee prices. To accomplish these goals, in keeping with the second phase of the coffee rehabilitation program, the government raised coffee prices paid to producers in May 1986 and February 1987, claiming that the new prices more accurately reflected world market prices and local factors, such as inflation. The 1987 increase came after the Coffee Marketing Board launched an aggressive program to increase export volumes. Parchment (dried but unhulled) robusta producer prices rose from USh24 to USh29 per kilogram. Clean (hulled) robusta prices rose from USh44.40 to USh53.70 per kilogram. Prices for parchment arabica, grown primarily in the Bugisu district of southeastern Uganda, were USh62.50 a kilogram, up from USh50. Then in July 1988, the government again raised coffee prices from USh50 per kilogram to USh111 per kilogram for robusta, and from USh62 to USh125 per kilogram for arabica.

By December 1988, the Coffee Marketing Board was unable to pay farmers for new deliveries of coffee or to repay loans for previous purchases. The board owed USh1,000 million to its suppliers and USh2,500 million to the commercial banks, and although the government agreed to provide the funds to meet these obligations, some of them remained unpaid for another year.

Uganda was a member of the International Coffee Organization (ICO), a consortium of coffee-producing nations that set international production quotas and prices. The ICO set Uganda's annual export quota at only 4 percent of worldwide coffee exports. During December 1988, a wave of coffee buying pushed the ICO price up and triggered two increases of 1 million (60-kilogram) bags each in worldwide coffee production limits. The rising demand and rising price resulted in a 1989 global quota increase to 58 million bags. Uganda's export quota rose only by about 3,013 bags, however, bringing it to just over 2.3 million bags. Moreover, Uganda's entire quota increase was allocated to arabica coffee, which was grown primarily in the small southeastern region of Bugisu. In revenue terms, Uganda's overall benefit from the world price increase was small, as prices for robusta coffee—the major export—remained depressed.

In 1989 Uganda's coffee production capacity exceeded its quota of 2.3 million bags, but export volumes were still diminished by economic and security problems, and large amounts of coffee were still being smuggled out of Uganda for sale in neighboring countries. Then in July 1989, the ICO agreement collapsed, as its members failed to agree on production quotas and prices, and they decided to allow market conditions to determine world coffee prices for two years. Coffee prices plummeted, and Uganda was unable to make up the lost revenues by increasing export volumes. In October 1989, the government devalued the shilling, making Uganda's coffee exports more competitive worldwide, but Ugandan officials still viewed the collapse of the ICO agreement as a devastating blow to the local economy. Fears that 1989 earnings for coffee exports would be substantially less than the US$264 million earned the previous year proved unfounded. Production in 1990, however, declined more than 20 percent to an estimated 133,000 tons valued at US$142 million because of drought, management problems, low prices, and a shift from coffee production to crops for local consumption.

Some coffee farmers cultivated cacao plants on land already producing robusta coffee. Cocoa production declined in the 1970s and 1980s, however, and market conditions discouraged international investors from viewing it as a potential counterweight to Uganda's reliance on coffee exports. Locally produced cocoa was of high quality, however, and the government continued to seek ways to rehabilitate the industry. Production remained low during the late 1980s, rising from 1,000 tons in 1986 to only 5,000 tons in 1989.

Cotton

In the 1950s, cotton was the second most important traditional cash crop in Uganda, contributing 25 percent of total agricultural exports. By the late 1970s, this figure had dropped to 3 percent, and government officials were pessimistic about reviving this industry in the near future. Farmers had turned to other crops in part because of the labor-intensive nature of cotton cultivation, inadequate crop-finance programs, and a generally poor marketing system. The industry began to recover in the 1980s, and the government rehabilitated ginneries and increased producer prices. In 1985, 199,000 hectares were planted in cotton, and production had risen from 4,000 tons to 16,300 tons in five years. Cotton exports earned US$13.4 million in 1985. Earnings fell to US$5 million in 1986, representing about 4,400 tons of cotton. Production continued to decline after 1986, as violence plagued the major cotton-producing areas of the north, but showed some improvement in 1989.

Cotton provided the raw materials for several local industries, such as textile mills, oil and soap factories, and animal feed factories. And in the late 1980s, it provided another means of diversifying the economy. The government accordingly initiated an emergency cotton production program, which provided extension services, tractors, and other inputs for cotton farmers. At the same time, the government raised cotton prices from USh32 to USh80 for a kilogram of grade A cotton and from USh18 to USh42 for Grade B cotton in 1989. However, prospects for the cotton industry in the 1990s were still uncertain.

Tea

Favorable climate and soil conditions enabled Uganda to develop some of the world's best quality tea. Production almost ceased in the 1970s, however, when the government expelled many owners of tea estates—mostly Asians. Many tea farmers also reduced production as a result of warfare and economic upheaval. Successive governments after Amin encouraged owners of tea estates to intensify their cultivation of existing hectarage. Mitchell Cotts (British) returned to Uganda in the early 1980s and formed the Toro and Mityana Tea Company (Tamteco) in a joint venture with the government. Tea production subsequently increased from 1,700 tons of tea produced in 1981 to 5,600 tons in 1985. These yields did not approach the high of 22,000 tons that had been produced in the peak year of 1974, however, and they declined slightly after 1985.

The government doubled producer prices in 1988, to USh20 per kilogram, as part of an effort to expand tea production and reduce the nation's traditional dependence on coffee exports, but tea production remained well under capacity. Only about one-tenth of the 21,000 hectares under tea cultivation were fully productive, producing about 4,600 tons of tea in 1989. Uganda exported about 90 percent of tea produced nationwide. In 1988 and 1989, the government used slightly more than 10 percent of the total to meet Uganda's commitments in barter exchanges with other countries. In 1990 the tea harvest rose to 6,900 tons, of which 4,700 were exported for earnings of US$3.6 million. The government hoped to produce 10,000 tons in 1991 to meet rising market demand.

Two companies, Tamteco and the Uganda Tea Corporation (a joint venture between the government and the Mehta family), managed most tea production. In 1989 Tamteco owned three large plantations, with a total of 2,300 hectares of land, but only about one-half of Tamteco's land was fully productive. The Uganda Tea Corporation had about 900 hectares in production and was expanding its landholdings in 1989. The state-owned Agricultural Enterprises Limited managed about 3,000 hectares of tea, and an additional 9,000 hectares were farmed by about 11,000 smallholder farmers, who marketed their produce through the parastatal Uganda Tea Growers' Corporation (UTGC). Several thousand hectares of tea estates remained in a "disputed" category because their owners had been forced to abandon them. In 1990 many of these estates were being sold to private individuals by the departed Asians' Property Custodian Board as part of an effort to rehabilitate the industry and improve local management practices.

Both Tamteco and the Uganda Tea Corporation used most of their earnings to cover operational expenses and service corporate debts, so the expansion of Uganda's tea-producing capacity was still just beginning in 1990. The EEC and the World Bank provided

Harvesting grain in Kabong, 1980
Courtesy United Nations (O. Monsen)
Mechanized farming in Buganda
Courtesy United Nations

115

assistance to resuscitate the smallholder segment of the industry, and the UTGC rehabilitated seven tea factories with assistance from the Netherlands. Both Tamteco and the Uganda Tea Corporation were also known among tea growers in Africa for their leading role in mechanization efforts. Both companies purchased tea harvesters from Australian manufacturers, financed in part by the Uganda Development Bank, but mechanized harvesting and processing of tea was still slowed by shortages of operating capital.

Tobacco

For several years after independence, tobacco was one of Uganda's major foreign exchange earners, ranking fourth after coffee, cotton, and tea. Like all other traditional cash crops, tobacco production also suffered from Uganda's political insecurity and economic mismanagement. Most tobacco grew in the northwestern corner of the country, where violence became especially severe in the late 1970s, and rehabilitation of this industry was slow. In 1981, for example, farmers produced only sixty-three tons of tobacco. There was some increase in production after 1981, largely because of the efforts of the British American Tobacco Company, which repossessed its former properties in 1984. Although the National Tobacco Corporation processed and marketed only 900 tons of tobacco in 1986, output had more than quadrupled by 1989.

Sugar

Uganda's once substantial sugar industry, which had produced 152,000 tons in 1968, almost collapsed by the early 1980s. By 1989 Uganda imported large amounts of sugar, despite local industrial capacity that could easily satisfy domestic demand. Achieving local self-sufficiency by the year 1995 was the major government aim in rehabilitating this industry.

The two largest sugar processors were the Kakira and Lugazi estates, which by the late 1980s were joint government ventures with the Mehta and Madhvani families. The government commissioned the rehabilitation of these two estates in 1981, but the spreading civil war delayed the projects. By mid-1986, work on the two estates resumed, and Lugazi resumed production in 1988. The government, together with a number of African and Arab donors, also commissioned the rehabilitation of the Kinyala Sugar Works, and this Masindi estate resumed production in 1989. Rehabilitation of the Kakira estate, delayed by ownership problems, was completed in 1990 at a cost of about US$70 million, giving Uganda a refining capacity of at least 140,000 tons per year (see Manufacturing, this ch.).

Livestock

The country's natural environment provided good grazing for cattle, sheep, and goats, with indigenous breeds dominating most livestock in Uganda. Smallholder farmers owned about 95 percent of all cattle, although several hundred modern commercial ranches were established during the 1960s and early 1970s in areas that had been cleared of tsetse-fly infestation. Ranching was successful in the late 1960s, but during the upheaval of the 1970s many ranches were looted, and most farmers sold off their animals at low prices to minimize their losses. In the 1980s, the government provided substantial aid to farmers, and by 1983 eighty ranches had been restocked with cattle. Nevertheless, by the late 1980s, the livestock sector continued to incur heavy animal losses as a result of disease, especially in the northern and northeastern regions. Civil strife in those areas also led to a complete breakdown in disease control and the spread of tsetse flies. Cattle rustling, especially along the Kenyan border, also depleted herds in some areas of the northeast.

The government hoped to increase the cattle population to 10 million by the year 2000. To do this, it arranged a purchase of cattle from Tanzania in 1988 and implemented a US$10.5 million project supported by Kuwait to rehabilitate the cattle industry. The government also approved an EEC-funded program of artificial insemination, and the Department of Veterinary Services and Animal Industry tried to save existing cattle stock by containing diseases such as bovine pleuro-pneumonia, hoof-and-mouth disease, rinderpest, and trypanosomiasis.

Uganda's dairy farmers have worked to achieve self-sufficiency in the industry but have been hampered by a number of problems. Low producer prices for milk, high costs for animal medicines, and transportation problems were especially severe obstacles to dairy development. The World Food Programme (WFP) undertook an effort to rehabilitate the dairy industry, and the United Nations Children's Fund (UNICEF) and other UN agencies also helped subsidize powdered milk imports, most of it from the United States and Denmark. But the WFP goal of returning domestic milk production to the 1972 level of 400 million liters annually was criticized by local health experts, who cited the nation's population growth since 1972 and urgent health needs in many war-torn areas.

Local economists complained that the dairy industry demonstrated Uganda's continuing dependence on more developed economies. Uganda had ample grazing area and an unrealized capacity for dairy development. Malnutrition from protein deficiency had

Farmers' market in Kampala
Courtesy Carl Fleischhauer

119

not been eliminated, and milk was sometimes unavailable in non-farming areas. Imported powdered milk and butter were expensive and required transportation and marketing, often in areas where local dairy development was possible. School farms, once considered potentially important elements of education and boarding requirements, were not popular with either pupils or teachers, who often considered agricultural training inappropriate for academic institutions. Local economists decried Uganda's poor progress in controlling cattle diseases, and they urged the government to develop industries such as cement and steel, which could be used to build cattle-dips and eliminate tick-borne diseases.

Goat farming also contributed to local consumption. By the late 1980s, the poultry industry was growing rapidly, relying in part on imported baby chicks from Britain and Zambia. Several private companies operated feed mills and incubators. The major constraint to expanding poultry production was the lack of quality feeds, and the government hoped that competition among privately owned feedmills would eventually overcome this problem. In 1987 the Arab Bank for Economic Development in Africa, the Organization of the Petroleum Exporting Countries, the International Development Bank, and the Ugandan government funded a poultry rehabilitation and development project worth US$17.2 million to establish hatchery units and feed mills and to import parent stock and baby chicks.

Uganda's beekeeping industry also suffered throughout the years of civil unrest. In the 1980s, the Cooperative for American Relief Everywhere (CARE) Apiary Development Project assisted in rehabilitating the industry, and by 1987 more than fifty cooperatives and privately owned enterprises had become dealers in apiary products. More than 4,000 hives were in the field. In 1987 an estimated 797 tons of honey and 614 kilograms of beeswax were produced.

Fishing

Lakes, rivers, and swamps covered 44,000 square kilometers, about 20 percent of Uganda's total area. Fishing was therefore an important rural industry. In all areas outside the central Lake Kyoga region, fish production increased throughout the 1980s. The government supported several programs to augment fish production and processing. In 1987 a government-sponsored Integrated Fisheries Development Project established a boat construction and repair workshop at Jinja, a processing plant, several fish collecting centers, and fish marketing centers in several areas of Uganda. They also implemented the use of refrigerated insulated vehicles for

*Herd of cattle showing the effects of the mid-1980s drought
at Ugandan refugee camp in Rwanda
Courtesy International Committee of the Red Cross (Françoise Wolff)*

transporting fish. China had managed the reconstruction of cold storage facilities in Kampala in the early 1980s. Soon after that time, the government established the Sino-Uganda Fisheries Joint Venture Company to exploit fishing opportunities in Lake Victoria.

Uganda's Freshwater Fisheries Research Organization monitored fishing conditions and the balance of flora and fauna in Uganda's lakes. In 1989 this organization warned against overfishing, especially in the Lake Kyoga region, where the combined result of improved security conditions and economic hardship was a 40-percent increase in commercial and domestic fishing activity. A second environmental concern in the fishing industry was the weed infestation that had arisen in lakes suffering from heavy pollution. In late 1989, officials were relatively unsuccessful in restricting the types and levels of pollutants introduced into the nation's numerous lakes.

A few fishermen used explosives obtained from stone quarries to increase their catch, especially in the Victoria Nile region near Jinja. Using byproducts from beer manufacturing to lure fish into a feeding area, they detonated small packs of explosives that killed large numbers of fish and other aquatic life. Several people also drowned in the frantic effort to collect dead fish that floated to the surface of the water. Environmental and health concerns led the

121

government to outlaw this form of fishing, and local officials were seeking ways to ban the sale of fish caught in this manner. Both bans were difficult to enforce, however, and fishing with dynamite continued in 1989 despite the widespread notoriety attached to this activity.

Forestry

In the late 1980s, 7.5 million hectares of land in Uganda consisted of forest and woodland. About 1.5 million hectares, or 7 percent of Uganda's dry land area, were protected forest reserves. Roughly 25,000 hectares of protected reserves were tree farms. The most important forest products were timber, firewood, charcoal, wood pulp, and paper, but other important products included leaves for fodder and fertilizer, medicinal herbs, fruits, and fibers, and a variety of grasses used in weaving and in household applications. Production of most materials increased as much as 100 percent between 1980 and 1988, but the output of timber for construction declined from 1980 to 1985, before increasing slightly to 433 million units in 1987 and continuing to increase in 1988. Paper production also increased substantially in 1988.

Nationwide forest resources were being depleted rapidly, however. Deforestation was especially severe in poverty-stricken areas, where many people placed short-term survival needs ahead of the long-term goal of maintaining the nation's forestry sector. Agricultural encroachment, logging, charcoal making, and harvesting for firewood consumed more wooded area each year. An additional toll on forest reserves resulted from wildfires, often the result of illegal charcoal-making activity in reserves. Neither natural regrowth nor tree-planting projects could keep pace with the demand for forest products.

In 1988 the Ministry of Environmental Protection was responsible for implementing forest policy and management. Ministry officials warned that the loss of productive woodlands would eventually lead to land erosion, environmental degradation, energy shortages, food shortages, and rural poverty in general, and they hoped to change traditional attitudes toward forests and other natural resources. In 1989 the government implemented a six-year forestry rehabilitation project financed by the United Nations Development Programme (UNDP) and the Food and Agriculture Organization of the United Nations (FAO). This project included a nationwide tree-planting campaign and a series of three-year training courses for rural extension agents, leaders of women's groups, educators, and farmers. Britain, the Federal Republic of Germany

(West Germany), and several multilateral donor agencies also provided assistance in the forestry sector.

Economic crises often hampered efforts to conserve natural resources, however. Many people lacked the motivation to plan for future generations when their own survival was at risk. As a result, illegal activities, including logging, charcoal making, and firewood gathering in posted reserves contributed to rapid deforestation. Government forestry agents, who were generally underpaid, sometimes sold firewood for their own profit or permitted illegal activities in return for bribes. In these ways, entrenched poverty and corruption drained public resources from use by present and future generations. In 1989 officials threatened to prosecute trespassers in posted forest areas, but by the end of the year, Uganda had not implemented this policy.

Industry

When the NRM seized power in 1986, Uganda's industrial production was negligible. Manufacturing industries, based primarily on processing agricultural products unavailable in Uganda, operated at approximately one-third of their 1972 level. The mining industry had almost come to a standstill. The rudiments of industrial production existed in the form of power stations, factories, mines, and hotels, but these facilities needed repairs and improved maintenance, and government budgets generally assigned these needs lower priority than security and commercial agricultural development. The city of Jinja, the nation's former industrial hub, was marked by signs of poverty and neglect. The dilapidated road system in and around Jinja provided one of the most serious obstacles to industrial growth.

Industrial growth was a high priority in the late 1980s, however. The government's initial goal was to decrease Uganda's dependence on imported manufactured goods by rehabilitating existing enterprises. These efforts met with some success, and in 1988 and 1989, industrial output grew by more than 25 percent, with much of this increase in the manufacturing sector. Industry's most serious problems were capital shortages and the need for skilled workers and people with management experience. Engineers and repair people, in particular, were in demand, and government planners sought ways to gear vocational training toward these needs.

Energy

In the 1980s, local officials estimated that charcoal and fuel wood met more than 95 percent of Uganda's total energy requirements. These two materials produced 75 percent of the nation's commercial energy, and petroleum products, 21 percent; electricity provided only 3 percent of commercial energy. By the late 1980s, the government sought alternate energy sources to reduce the nation's reliance on forestry resources for fuelwood. Alternative technologies were sought for the tobacco-curing and brick and tile manufacturing industries, in particular, because they both consumed substantial quantities of fuelwood. More than 80 percent of fuelwood consumption was still in the home—primarily for cooking—and to reduce this dependence, the government attempted to promote the manufacture and use of more fuel-efficient stoves. Even this modest effort was difficult and expensive to implement on a nationwide basis, in part because cooking methods were established by long-standing tradition.

Managing the Uganda Electricity Board (UEB) was increasingly difficult during the 1980s. Factors contributing to this problem included increased UEB operating costs and shortages of spare parts, especially conductors and transformers that had been destroyed by vandals during the war years. Supply lines were often vandalized, and oil was even drained from UEB equipment. Despite these problems, the UEB maintained the existing supply system and supplied electricity to a few new coffee factories and corn mills in the late 1980s. The demand for new connections increased, largely as a result of escalating prices of other energy sources, such as kerosene and charcoal. Electricity consumption rose by 21 percent in 1987 despite the upward adjustment of tariffs by 536 percent.

Power generation at Owen Falls dropped from 635.5 million kilowatt-hours in 1986 to 609.9 million kilowatt-hours in 1987. By November 1988, six of the station's ten generators had broken down. Officials hoped that the rehabilitation of Maziba Hydroelectric Power Station at Kabale and the Mubuku Power Scheme at Kasese would ease the pressure on the Owen Falls facilities. As of 1989, planners expected the power generated at the country's existing power station at Owen Falls to be fully used by 1995, so the government rushed to begin a six-year construction project to build a 480-megawatt capacity hydroelectric power station near Murchison (Kabalega) Falls on the Nile River. Officials hoped the new station would meet Uganda's electric power needs up to the year 2020. Environmentalists protested that this project would disrupt the ecosystem of nearby Murchison (Kabalega) National Game Park (one of Uganda's prime tourist attractions), and the government agreed to move the power station two kilometers upstream in response to these complaints.

In the 1980s, Uganda imported all of its petroleum products. The transportation sector consumed about 69 percent of the available supply, whereas the aviation and industrial sectors required 9 percent and 5 percent, respectively. Uganda relied on Kenyan road and rail systems to transport oil imports. When political relations with Kenya worsened in the 1970s, the government tried to expand the country's strategic petroleum product reserves by rehabilitating existing storage facilities and constructing new ones. By late 1989, new tanks at Jinja and Nakasongola were expected to provide a six-month oil supply cushion. Officials also changed procurement procedures for oil from an open general licensing system to the use of letters of credit. An oil board was to be established to import and store petroleum products and to supervise their distribution.

Several international companies were also exploring for oil in western Uganda in 1989. A consortium of four oil companies—Shell, Exxon, Petrofina, and Total—had tendered bids for test drilling to determine if commercial quantities of oil were present. The World Bank provided US$5.2 million to purchase equipment and train Ugandans in drilling procedures. The major areas marked for test drilling were in Masindi, Hoima, Bundibugyo, and Kabarole. Test blocks were also set aside in the southwestern district of Kigezi and portions of Arua and Nebbi districts in the northwest.

In 1989, however, several of these companies appeared to be losing interest in Ugandan oil prospects. Shell withdrew from the consortium, leaving Petrofina operating most oil rigs and Exxon and Total providing most financial backing. Among the reasons for the declining international interest were the slump in crude oil prices worldwide and the high cost of exploring in the relatively remote western region of Uganda. Moreover, uncertain political relations between Uganda and Kenya suggested that prospects for building a trans-Kenya pipeline were becoming more remote, and shipping oil through Tanzania promised to be too costly.

Manufacturing

In the late 1980s, most manufacturing industries relied on agricultural products for raw materials and machinery, and, as a result, the problems plaguing the agriculture sector hampered both production and marketing in manufacturing. Processing cotton, coffee, sugar, and food crops were major industries, but Uganda also produced textiles, tobacco, beverages, wood and paper products, construction materials, and chemicals.

In the late 1980s, the government began to return some nationalized manufacturing firms to the private sector in order to encourage private investment. The primary aim was to promote self-sufficiency in consumer goods and strengthen linkages between agriculture and industry. By 1989 the government estimated manufacturing output to be only about one-third of postindependence peak levels achieved in 1970 and 1971. Only eleven out of eighty-two manufacturing establishments surveyed by the Ministry of Planning and Economic Development were operating at more than 35 percent capacity. Overall industrial output increased between January 1986 and June 1989, and the contribution from manufacturing increased from only 5 percent to more than 11 percent during the same period.

Construction Materials

In the late 1980s, eight companies produced steel products in Uganda, but they were operating at only about 20 percent of capacity, despite increased output after 1986. Their most widely used products were gardening hoes and galvanized corrugated sheets of steel. The production of steel sheets declined dramatically in 1987, leaving some factories operating at only 5 percent of capacity. At the same time, hoe production increased 30 percent over 1986 levels. The government attempted to rejuvenate the industry in 1987 by assessing the availability of scrap iron and the demand for steel products and by providing US$2.7 million in machinery and equipment for use by the government-operated East African Steel Corporation.

The nation's two cement-producing plants at Hoima and Tororo, both operated by the Uganda Cement Industry, also reduced production sharply, from more than 76,000 tons of cement in 1986 to less than 16,000 tons in 1988. Neither plant operated at more than 5 percent of capacity during this time. The government again provided funds, roughly US$3.2 million, for rehabilitating the industry and initiated a study of ways to improve this potentially vital sector of the economy.

Consumer Goods

In 1989 the government estimated that the nation's four textile mills manufactured about 8 million meters of cotton cloth per year, but Uganda's growing population required at least ten times this amount to attain self-sufficiency. The government began rehabilitating three other mills for weaving and spinning operations, and the United Garment Industries commissioned a plant to manufacture knitted apparel, some of it for export, under a US$3 million rehabilitation loan.

The production of beverages, including alcoholic beverages and soft drinks, increased in the late 1980s, and officials believed Uganda could achieve self-sufficiency in this area in the 1990s. In 1987 three breweries increased their production by an average of 100 percent, to more than 16 million liters. In the same year, five soft drink producers increased output by 15 percent to nearly 6 million liters. In addition, Lake Victoria Bottling Company, producers of Pepsi Cola, completed construction of a new plant at Nakawa.

Sugar production was vital to the soft drink industry, so rehabilitating the sugar industry promised to assist in attaining self-sufficiency in beverage production (see Crops, this ch.). The government hoped to reduce sugar imports from Cuba as the Lugazi and Kakira estates resumed production in 1989 and 1990. In 1988 and 1989, Uganda's dairy industry relied on imports of dried milk powder and butter to produce milk for sale to the general public. Processed milk, produced under monopoly by the government-owned Uganda Dairy Corporation, registered an increase of 29.5 percent, from 13 million liters in 1986 to 16.9 million liters in 1987. To improve the local dairy industry, the government rehabilitated milk cooling and collection centers, milk processing plants, and the industry's vehicles. And in the late 1980s, the Ministry of Agriculture, Animal Husbandry, and Fisheries imported 1,500 in-calf frisian heifers to form the nucleus of a restocking effort on private and government farms (see Livestock, this ch.).

Production of wheat and corn flour increased in 1987, 1988, and 1989, despite continuing low-capacity utilization in the industry. Only one establishment, the Uganda Millers, which worked at just over 20 percent of capacity, produced wheat flour. The company nonetheless increased production to 9.5 thousand tons in 1987, 32 percent more than the previous year. At the same time, corn production increased 87.3 percent in 1987, to 4.6 thousand tons.

In 1988 only one cigarette-manufacturing plant, the British American Tobacco Company, operated in Uganda. Its production increased slightly between 1986 and 1987 to 1,434.8 million cigarettes. In 1988 the government provided a loan of US$1.43 million to rehabilitate the company's tobacco redrying plant in Kampala.

In November 1988, President Museveni opened an edible oil mill at Tororo to process cotton, sunflowers, peanuts, and sesame seeds. The plant had the capacity to process fifteen tons of raw oil daily into 4.3 tons of refined cooking oil and to produce an estimated 300 tons of soap annually as a by-product. The mill was built under a barter deal with Schwermaschinen Kombinat Ernst Thaelmann of the German Democratic Republic (East Germany), which received coffee and cotton in exchange. In its first year of production, the plant encountered operating difficulties, but its officers still expected Uganda to achieve self-sufficiency in edible oil manufacturing during the 1990s. Mukwano Industries, Uganda's largest soap-manufacturing company, doubled production in 1988 and 1989.

The Uganda Leather and Tanning Industry was the nation's only leather producer, operating at less than 5 percent of capacity in 1987, when output dropped by nearly 40 percent from the previous year. Although three footwear producers were in operation, the Uganda Bata Shoe Company produced 98 percent of the nation's shoes, and it increased production in 1988 and 1989.

Mining

Although the government recognized the existence of several commercially important mineral deposits, it had not conducted comprehensive exploration surveys for non-oil minerals and, therefore, lacked estimates of their size. In the early 1970s, copper, tin, bismuth, tungsten, rare earths, phosphates, limestone, and beryl were being mined by commercial companies. The mining sector employed 8,000 people and accounted for 9 percent of exports. By 1979 almost all mineral production had ceased, and in 1987 only the mining and quarrying sector recorded any growth. Mining output increased an estimated 20 percent, largely because of the rapid growth in demand for road and housing construction materials, such as sand and gravel. In 1988 the government established the National Mining Commission, intended to encourage investment in the mining sector through joint ventures with the government. This commission also provided some support for small mining operations. In early 1988, the government introduced regulations of gold mining operations that gave the Bank of Uganda monopoly rights to buy gold mined in the country and to market gold at its discretion. In addition, the government initiated projects to rehabilitate the Kilembe copper mine and to extract cobalt from slag heaps at the mine at a combined cost of US$70 million. By late 1990, financing had been secured for preliminary rehabilitation of the mine's facilities, part of it from the Democratic People's Republic of Korea (North Korea). The French were involved in the cobalt venture; plans called for processing and export to France of at least 1,000 tons per year once technology was in place.

Tourism

During the 1960s, revenue from tourism, including restaurants, hotels, and related services, increased faster than any other sector of the economy. In 1971, the peak year for tourist receipts, more than 85,000 foreigners visited Uganda, making tourism the nation's

Local bus stop outside Kampala
Municipal bus station in Kampala
Courtesy Carl Fleischhauer

129

third largest source of foreign exchange, after coffee and cotton. After 1972, however, political instability destroyed the tourist industry. Rebels damaged and looted hotels, decimated wildlife herds, and made many national park roads impassable. Part of the airport at Entebbe was also destroyed.

Recognizing the role tourism could play in economic development, the government assigned high priority to restoring the tourism infrastructure in its RDP. To this end, the government planned to rehabilitate hotels and promote wildlife management. In February 1988, ministry officials announced a plan to build four new hotels worth US$120 million as part of a barter trade agreement with Italy. The Italian company Viginter agreed to construct the 200-room hotels at Masaka, Fort Portal, Jinja, and Mbale. International tourist arrivals gradually increased, from about 32,000 in 1986 to more than 40,000 in each of the next two years. Tourism earned roughly US$4.2 million in 1988. At the same time, continuing unrest in the north halted rehabilitation efforts in Murchison (Kabalega) Falls and Kidepo national parks, and many tourist attractions awaited a reduced climate of violence before maintenance and repairs could be improved.

Transportation and Communications

Like the industrial sector, the transportation and communication infrastructure remained in extreme disrepair during the late 1980s, primarily as a result of more than two decades of continuous warfare. Damaged roads and railroads were accorded high priority in the government's RDP, which allocated 29 percent of planned investment to transportation and communications. The government also hoped to extend Uganda's links with Indian Ocean ports through Tanzania in order to reduce the dependence on Kenya. Air transportation, however, reached a critical state in the late 1980s, with a severe shortage of both aircraft and skilled management personnel.

Rail and Road Systems

Uganda's railroad system extended to 1,240 kilometers in the late 1980s, and about 27,000 kilometers of roads reached all areas of the country (see fig. 7). About 6,000 kilometers of these were all-weather, and 1,800 kilometers were paved. By 1988 many rail sections needed relaying, regrading, or realigning, and the condition of most road surfaces was very poor. Road transport systems also suffered from an acute shortage of vehicles and spare parts for buses, vans, and trucks. Under the RDP, the government resurfaced more than 4,000 kilometers of roads in 1987 and 1988. Road improvement continued to be a high priority, largely because officials viewed transportation infrastructure as the key to stimulating the rural economy.

The government tried to transfer long-distance traffic, particularly bulky freight, from the dilapidated road system to the rail system operated by the Uganda Railways Corporation. The war years of 1985 and 1986, however, followed by ongoing rebel activity in eastern and northern Uganda, undermined rail performance and disrupted service in these areas. In 1987 workers completed construction on the Nalukolongo Diesel Workshop, which repaired locomotives. In addition, the government purchased 700 wagons and 13 locomotives in 1987. The government also bought a fleet of three wagon ferries for operation on Lake Victoria, shortening the transportation time for wagons and facilitating the opening of the Tanzanian route to the coast. In 1987 these ferries carried over 28,000 tons of exports and imports between Jinja and the Lake Victoria ports of Mwanza and Kisumu. In 1990 rehabilitation of the Kampala-Kasese rail line began, with the aim of promoting agriculture, mining, and oil exploration in western Uganda.

Because of strained relations with Kenya, Uganda tried to reduce its overall dependence on the Kenyan road link to the Indian Ocean by promoting an alternative rail route through Tanzania. Moreover, rail traffic between Kampala and the Kenyan border was irregular, so Ugandan officials hoped to build up the Tanzanian link, despite capacity and rolling stock problems. In 1988 Ugandan and Tanzanian officials began exploring this possibility. Ugandan officials indicated they were prepared to invest in Tanzania's railroad if they could plan on three trains a week from Dar es Salaam to Mwanza.

Air Transport

In the late 1980s, Uganda's major international airport at Entebbe was handling about 135,000 passengers annually, a substantial increase over the early and mid-1980s. Six scheduled airlines flew into Entebbe, one of five airports with paved runways. The national airline, Uganda Airlines, suffered several financial setbacks, however, operating a fleet of only four outmoded and unreliable aircraft. British authorities banned the B-707 aircraft from operating in Britain because of noise abatement restrictions. Uganda Airlines also reduced its European service to one flight per week to Italy and West Germany. Uganda then signed a lease agreement with Zambian Airways for a weekly flight to Britain. When this arrangement proved too expensive, a similar agreement was

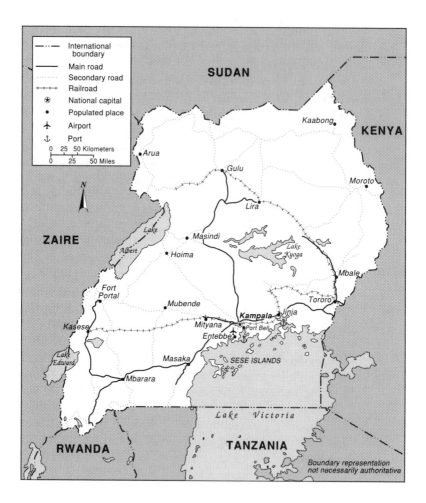

Figure 7. Major Transportation Routes, 1990

signed with Ghana Airways, which began operation of a DC-10 flight between Entebbe and London in April 1988.

The October 1988 crash of a Uganda Airlines Boeing aircraft in Rome seriously crippled the airline's operations. That aircraft was the only one in the fleet fitted with a "hush kit" to reduce noise to European standards. Although Uganda Airlines resumed service with a leased aircraft in December 1988, the financial viability of that service remained questionable. Uganda Airlines continued to operate service to the Middle East and Nairobi in 1988, but these flights, too, were canceled in late 1989. Domestic routes, too, had been reduced to those between Entebbe and the Arua and Kasese airfields. Uganda Airlines was exploring the possibility of merging with Air Tanzania and Zambian Airways, as all three airlines sought to find ways to operate newer, larger aircraft economically but lacked the passenger and freight traffic to do so.

The government contracted with a British consulting firm, Psiair, to conduct a management study of Uganda Airlines Corporation. The 1989 Psiair report urged a complete overhaul of the airlines, citing fiscal and labor mismanagement and safety problems as among the most serious concerns. By late 1989, the government was considering a policy that would require all airline personnel to resign and reapply for their jobs, in an effort to remove ''ghost employees'' from the payroll and reduce nepotism among airline management.

Communications

Uganda's telecommunications system provided fair service for city dwellers, and in 1990 was undergoing improvements after a period of neglect during the early 1980s. Long-distance communications went via a radio-relay system centered in Kampala, and a high-capacity radio-relay link with 960 channels connected the Ugandan capital with Nairobi. A satellite ground station at Mpoma near Kampala had two antennas, one working with the International Telecommunications Satellite Corporation (Intelsat) Atlantic Ocean satellite and the other with the Intelsat Indian Ocean satellite. This ground station provided excellent international telephone and television transmissions and permitted international direct dialing both into and out of the country. At the end of 1990, Uganda counted 61,600 telephones nationwide, or 2.6 telephones per 100 inhabitants.

Radio transmissions originated in Kampala and other large towns, but broadcasts, along with programs from neighboring countries, were received in all areas of the country. Kampala had six of the country's ten amplitude modulation (AM) stations, which broadcast in English, French, Swahili, and several local languages and used both medium and shortwave frequencies. Nine television stations in the larger cities operated in the afternoons and evenings with programs in English, Swahili, and Luganda.

In 1990 several improvements were underway that, when completed, would significantly upgrade the telecommunications system. A new fiber-optic link was being built from the international switching center in the capital to the satellite ground station, and additional telephone exchanges were under construction in Kampala and Kabale.

Uganda: A Country Study

Banking and Currency

Uganda's years of political turmoil left the country with substantial loan repayments, a weak currency, and soaring inflation. During the 1970s and early 1980s, numerous foreign loans were for nonproductive uses, especially military purchases. Even after the Museveni regime seized power, debts climbed while the productive capacity of the country deteriorated. To resolve these problems, the government tapped both external creditors and domestic sources, crowding out private-sector borrowers. The Museveni government then attempted to reduce the percentage of government borrowing from domestic sources and to reschedule payments of foreign loans. The government also implemented successive devaluations of the shilling in order to stabilize the economy.

Banking

Government-owned institutions dominated most banking in Uganda. In 1966 the Bank of Uganda, which issued currency and managed foreign exchange reserves, became the Central Bank. The Uganda Commercial Bank, which had fifty branches throughout the country, dominated commercial banking and was wholly owned by the government. The Uganda Development Bank was a state-owned development finance institution, which channeled loans from international sources into Ugandan enterprises and administered most of the development loans made to Uganda. The East African Development Bank, established in 1967 and jointly owned by Uganda, Kenya, and Tanzania, was also concerned with development finance. It survived the breakup of the East African Community and received a new charter in 1980. Other commercial banks included local operations of Grindlays Bank, Bank of Baroda, Standard Bank, and the Uganda Cooperative Bank.

During the 1970s and early 1980s, the number of commercial bank branches and services contracted significantly. Whereas Uganda had 290 commercial bank branches in 1970, by 1987 there were only 84, of which 58 branches were operated by government-owned banks. This number began to increase slowly the following year, and in 1989 the gradual increase in banking activity signaled growing confidence in Uganda's economic recovery.

Domestic Credit

By 1981 the rate of growth of domestic credit was 100 percent per year, primarily as a result of government borrowing from domestic sources. The 1981 budget attempted to reestablish financial control

134

Central Bank building
in Kampala
Courtesy Nelson Kasfir

by reducing government borrowing and by floating the shilling in relation to world currencies. This measure led to a sharp decline in the growth rate of domestic credit and to a temporary decline in the central government's share of domestic credit from 73 percent to 44 percent in 1986. The following year, however, domestic credit recorded growth of over 100 percent, primarily reflecting credit extended to private-sector owners for crop financing. During 1987 crop financing for private owners again increased, while the government's share of domestic credit fell even further, from 45.3 percent to 30.7 percent. Crop finance accounted for 86 percent of all financing for agriculture, crowding out commercial credit to other areas within agriculture. Commercial lending for trade and commerce also increased during 1987, rising from 15.6 percent to 23.7 percent of total lending in 1986. Commercial lending to manufacturing, building and construction, and transportation rose marginally, while lending to other sectors declined.

The Uganda Commercial Bank introduced a new program, the "rural farmers scheme," to help small farmers through troubled economic times. This program aimed to boost agricultural output by lending small sums directly to farmers, mostly women, on the basis of character references but without requiring loans to be secured. Most of these loans were in the form of inputs such as hoes, wheelbarrows, or machetes, with small amounts of cash provided for labor. The farmers repaid the loans over eighteen months, with interest calculated at 32 percent—marginally lower than commercial rates. Under this program, the bank had loaned USh400 million to approximately 7,000 farmers by 1988. The program attracted more than US$20 million in foreign aid, including US$18 million from the African Development Bank.

Currency and Inflation

Between 1981 and 1988, the government repeatedly devalued the Uganda shilling in order to stabilize the economy. Before 1981 the value of the shilling was linked to the IMF's special drawing right (SDR—see Glossary). In mid-1980 the official exchange rate was USh9.7 per SDR or USh7.3 per United States dollar. When the Obote government floated the shilling in mid-1981, it dropped to only 4 percent of its previous value before settling at a rate of USh78 per US$1. In August 1982, the government introduced a two-tier exchange rate. It lasted until June 1984, when the government merged the two rates at USh299 per US$1. A continuing foreign exchange shortage caused a decline in the value of the shilling to USh600 per US$1 by June 1985 and USh1,450 in 1986. In May 1987, the government introduced a new shilling, worth 100 old shillings, along with an effective 76 percent devaluation. Ugandans complained that inflation quickly eroded the new currency's value. As a result, the revised rate of USh60 per US$1 was soon out of line with the black market rate of USh350 per US$1. Following the May 1987 devaluation, the money supply continued to grow at an annual rate of 500 percent until the end of the year. In July 1988, the government again devalued the shilling by 60 percent, setting it at USh150 per US$1; but at the same time, the parallel rate had already risen to USh450 per US$1. President Museveni regretted this trend, saying, "If we can produce more, the situation will improve, but for the time being we are just putting out fires." The government announced further devaluations in December 1988 to USh165 per US$1; in March 1989, to USh200 per US$1; and in October 1989, to USh340 per US$1. By late 1990, the official exchange rate was USh510 per US$1; the black market rate was USh700 per US$1.

All of the government's efforts to bring the economy under control succeeded in reducing the country's staggering inflation from over 300 percent in 1986 to about 72 percent in 1988. Then the government contributed to rising inflation by increasing the money supply to purchase coffee and other farm produce and to cover increased security costs in early 1989, a year in which inflation was estimated at more than 100 percent. Low rainfall levels in the south contributed to higher prices for bananas, corn, and other foodstuffs.

Shortages of consumer goods and bottlenecks in transportation, distribution, marketing, and production also contributed to rising prices. Moreover, the depreciation of the United States dollar increased the cost of Uganda's imports from Japan and Europe. The government tried to curb inflation by increasing disbursements of import-support funds and tightening controls on credit. These measures helped lower the rate of inflation to 30 percent by mid-1990, but by late 1990, inflation had once again resumed its upward spiral.

Foreign Trade and Assistance

In order to rebuild the economy in the late 1980s, Uganda needed foreign goods, technology, and services, but its chronic shortage of foreign currency and uncertain political climate weakened the nation's standing as a trading partner. The government sought to strengthen Uganda's standing in the world economy, but to meet short-term needs officials turned to foreign donors. Acquiring foreign assistance through direct aid, loans, or grants became an important focus of the government's economic efforts. The nation's balance of trade and payments reflected the fluctuating world value of Uganda's major export, coffee, even though the volume of coffee exports remained almost constant through 1986 and declined only slightly after that. The government encouraged export diversification, and these two important goals—restoring international confidence and reducing the nation's dependence on a single export—dominated external economic planning in the late 1980s.

Foreign Trade

Agricultural products have dominated Uganda's exports throughout its history. Coffee became the most important export after 1950, but cotton, tea, tobacco, and some manufactured goods were also important. During the 1970s, all exports except coffee declined as a result of low producer prices, marketing problems, declining exchange rates, and general economic disruption. Coffee production declined only slightly during these years of political turmoil, but the value of sales was vulnerable to shifts in world market prices.

From 1981 to 1984, general exports steadily increased, but only in 1984 and 1985 were they sufficient to produce a trade surplus. In 1986 a trend of declining exports and increasing imports developed and continued to the end of the decade (see table 7, Appendix). Uganda sent most of its exports to the United States, Britain, the Netherlands, and France. Exports to regional trading partners were less important but increased slightly in the late 1980s.

During the early 1980s, the value of imports remained fairly steady, constrained mainly by the shortage of foreign exchange.

However, in the late 1980s, imports rose dramatically, causing a large deficit in the trade balance. The government normally allocated foreign exchange for the purchase of essential goods such as fuel, vehicles, machinery, medical supplies, and military equipment. Principal imports—mainly construction materials, machinery, and spare parts—came from Kenya, Britain, Malaysia, and Italy.

In November 1988, the government announced a new program to support the expansion of nontraditional exports in an effort to diversify exports and increase foreign exchange earnings. Under this plan, private companies with export licenses granted by the Ministry of Commerce were permitted to retain foreign exchange earned for nontraditional exports, especially including a variety of fruits and vegetables that could be cultivated and transported fairly readily. Under the plan, international traders would be permitted to sell all or part of the foreign exchange received for these exports to the Central Bank. They could then apply for import licenses valued at the equivalent of their foreign exchange earnings in order to finance imports within 180 days.

At the same time, the government established a United States Agency for International Development (AID) export trade promotion credit amounting to US$12.5 million to assist the private sector in expanding production, marketing, and trade in these and other nontraditional exports. Items eligible to be financed under the trade promotion credit included improved seeds, high analysis fertilizers, raw jute for manufacturing gunny sacks, tin for local manufacture of farm tools, and packaging materials.

An important development in Ugandan trade in the late 1980s was the growth of countertrade, or barter, agreements at both government and company levels. Faced with serious foreign exchange shortages, the Ugandan government used this approach to secure essential goods and services, such as petroleum products and technical advice. Between 1986 and 1990, the government transacted more than seventy barter deals valued at an estimated US$534 million. By mid-1989 the turnover from barter trade arrangements was approximately US$60 million a year, or 10 to 15 percent of the value of conventional trade. The Ugandan input was almost always coffee or cotton. These barter deals included some imaginative and innovative schemes, notably hotel and road building projects and plans for technology transfer. They also provided a wider range of imports than would have been possible under conventional trading, especially in view of the continuing shortage of foreign exchange.

Under separate barter agreements in 1988, Uganda received two consignments of petroleum products from Algeria and Libya. The consignment from Libya was part of a US$60 million deal to exchange Libyan oil, cement, and trucks for Ugandan coffee, tobacco, and tea. A similar agreement worth more than US$24 million over three years was signed with Algeria in January 1988.

Uganda declared a temporary moratorium on new barter deals in 1988 because it had insufficient agricultural produce to fulfill existing agreements. Cuba had received only 3,000 tons of the 10,000 tons of beans promised under a 1986 agreement, and other countertrade partners awaited deliveries of agricultural products. Farmers blamed an inadequate round of producer price increases in January 1988 for continuing shortfalls in several crops. Problems were particularly acute surrounding trade in corn. The government promised approximately 10,000 tons of corn to Algeria, Cuba, Egypt, and Libya, plus 12,000 tons to North Korea and 5,000 tons to Yugoslavia. By late 1989, none of these shipments had been delivered, although Uganda had received consignments of industrial goods as part of these barter agreements.

Despite problems in the supply of local products, the government signed two protocol agreements in early 1988 with Rwanda and North Korea. The Rwanda agreement was worth US$10 million over a one-year period; in exchange for exports such as corn, salt, tobacco, wood, and bananas, Uganda was to receive Rwandan goods such as blankets or paint. In June 1988, Uganda and North Korea signed a protocol on barter trade for 1988 and 1989, including Korean cement, machinery, tools, and electrical goods, in return for Ugandan cotton lint, meat, and other agricultural products. The protocol extended over a period of eighteen to twenty-four months and was worth US$14 million to each country. Of this amount, US$8 million was for cement. By late 1990, however, many barter deals were still under suspension and at least some were being renegotiated because of continued shortfalls in Uganda's agricultural production.

In 1988 and 1989, to bring the balance of trade and payments under control, the government imposed new import and export licensing procedures. Imports designated as "foreign exchange required," which included most commercial imports, were processed through a bank. Importers presented their license applications to a bank, together with supporting documentation and a foreign exchange application form. If Ministry of Trade officials approved the application, they issued an import license entitling the bank to open a letter of credit. For imports designated "no foreign exchange required," where the importer already had the foreign exchange or the goods were financed by foreign sources, an import license was required. Imports from other members of the Preferential Trade Area (PTA) for Eastern and Southern Africa enjoyed increasingly favored treatment, while imports from Israel and South Africa were prohibited. The Société Générale de Surveillance of Geneva operated an import contract administration program to ensure contract provisions regarding quantity and quality were met. Each export deal required a Ministry of Trade license stating the agreed price in foreign currency and declaring receipts to the Central Bank. Licenses for nonperishable goods were subject to advance payment to the Central Bank. Some goods could only be exported through official agencies such as the Produce Marketing Board and the Coffee Marketing Board.

Balance of Payments

The economic decline of the 1970s caused a trade deficit, largely the result of a drop in official coffee exports and a steady capital outflow. The government strengthened financial controls in 1981, after Uganda had registered a US$169.2 million trade deficit. By 1984 these controls had enabled Uganda to convert its deficit to a US$65.7 million trade surplus. This improvement, together with declining net imports of services, changed the current account balance from a deficit of US$170.6 million in 1981 to a surplus of US$107.1 million in 1984. During the same three years, however, an outflow of US$120.4 million in short-term capital led to a decrease in reserves of US$56.2 million in 1984. In 1985 the trade balance remained positive, as did the balance on current account.

During the 1980s, the volume of Uganda's major exports maintained a fairly consistent increase, despite the decline in unit value. In particular, the country's major export, coffee, experienced erratic price movements between 1980 and 1987. The price of coffee dropped sharply for two years but recovered to 87 percent of the 1980 level in 1984. It then plummeted to about 74 percent in 1985 and improved to 91 percent in 1986. This recovery was not sustained in 1987, when the index fell sharply to 66 percent. Similarly, the unit values of tea and tobacco, two other traditional exports, also declined, while the price index of cotton, another traditional export crop, recovered from 57 percent in 1986 to 66 percent in 1987. An increase in the volume of exports was not enough to compensate for the loss caused by the sharp fall in unit value. Export income from coffee fell sharply from US$394 million in 1986 to US$264 million in 1989. Cotton suffered a similar fate, dropping from US$5 million to US$4 million during the same period.

While export revenues fell, the value of many imports increased. During 1987 total merchandise imports increased to a record US$635 million. Of this amount, imports financed by official resources were US$249 million on a cash basis, including suppliers' credit, US$34 million received on barter terms, and US$23 million acquired through the EAC Compensation Fund. Private imports using unofficial foreign exchange were estimated at US$98 million. Loans and grants financed imports worth US$228 million. A major part of the rise in the import bill consisted of fully funded capital goods considered necessary inputs for national rehabilitation and development projects.

Reflecting the decline in the overall value of exports and increased import costs, the trade deficit increased sharply in 1987 to US$301 million. The current account (trade balance, net services, and unrequited transfers, taken together) registered a marginal surplus in 1986 but deteriorated substantially during 1987 to register the highest deficit since 1982. At the same time, the capital account balance strengthened in 1987 to register a surplus. This increase resulted in large part from the improvement in medium-term and long-term loans. In sum, the overall balance showed a US$3 million deficit in 1987, a substantial decline from the US$127 million surplus registered in 1986. Domestic (bank and nonbank) sources financed approximately 75 percent of the deficit while external sources financed the remainder.

External Debt

Although Uganda was not one of the largest debtor nations in Africa, by the late 1980s the country had accumulated a significant external debt. By 1980, following eight years of economic decline under President Amin, external liabilities rose to over US$700 million. The Obote government's recovery program produced a further debt increase to US$1.043 billion by 1984. By 1987 Uganda's outstanding external debt stood at US$1.405 billion, representing over half of GDP and nearly three and a half times the level of exports. At the end of 1989, total external debt was US$1.8 billion; by late 1990, it was approaching US$2 billion. At the same time, the cost of servicing the foreign debt rose sharply from US$45 million in 1986 to US$70 million in 1987 and an estimated US$139 million in 1988. With Uganda's foreign earnings sharply down in 1987 and declining further in 1988, the debt service ratio also rose from 11 percent in 1986 to 18.9 percent in 1987 and an estimated 56 percent in 1988. If all debt maturities were to be cleared, payments would still absorb almost 60 percent of export earnings. Arrears due in 1989 were estimated at about US$70 million.

In 1988 more than 95 percent of Uganda's debt was official or officially guaranteed, reflecting the country's weak capacity to borrow from private banks. Nearly 83 percent of the debt was concessional, leading to some improvement in the average grace and maturity periods of the debts. Nevertheless, multilateral debts claimed a significant share of the total, and these debts could not be rescheduled. In FY 1987–88, US$170 million in medium-term and long-term debt reached maturity, comprising US$126.4 million in principal and US$43.6 million in interest. Of this total, US$135.7 million, or about 80 percent, was owed to multilateral creditors, the remainder to bilateral creditors.

The Museveni government tried to counteract these problems with a revised loan program. In particular, the government wanted to obtain grants or project-related loans in agriculture, industry, tourism, and energy to promote local productivity. In addition, terms of the new loans averaged twenty-year maturity periods, with five-year grace periods. Museveni was successful in rescheduling and refinancing some old debt. In June 1987, the Paris Club (see Glossary) rescheduled US$113 million in loans to Uganda, and further Paris Club rescheduling took place in mid-1989.

In September 1988, the IMF approved the second-year structural adjustment program of US$39 million, after the Ugandan government cleared roughly US$18 million in arrears to the agency. Britain, France, the United States, Italy, and Israel expressed satisfaction with Uganda's progress under the IMF program and rescheduled approximately US$25 to 30 million worth of debt.

Aid

Following the political upheavals of the 1970s and early 1980s, Uganda required substantial financial assistance to rebuild its social and economic infrastructure. The recovery program launched by the Obote government in 1982 called for US$1.7 billion in balance of payments and commodity support, but by 1985 many Western donor countries had decided to withhold financial support in protest against the government's poor human rights record. Many agencies again suspended disbursements at the end of 1985, when the short-lived Okello administration failed to end the political chaos. Upon coming to power in January 1986, President Museveni proposed an emergency six-month relief program that would cost US$160 million. Some international support was forthcoming, but most of the major bilateral and multilateral donors preferred to wait until the government had drawn up a more comprehensive plan. In 1987 the government responded with the RDP, which included a US$1.3 billion budget over four years. Approximately US$600 million of this amount was already funded when the plan was launched.

After launching the RDP, the government enjoyed the increasing confidence of Western donor nations (see table 8, Appendix). In 1988 donors pledged over US$377 million in aid, and Uganda received major support and a vote of confidence from both the IMF and the Paris Club. The IMF approved a purchase equivalent to US$33.7 million under the compensatory financing facility to cover an estimated shortfall in export earnings resulting from lower coffee revenues. In October 1988, a consultative group meeting in Paris arranged by the World Bank pledged aid and concessionary loans worth US$550 million. The Ugandan government told potential donors that the government needed a minimum new aid commitment of US$440 million in 1989 in order to meet its development targets and continue disbursements for existing commitments.

Regional Cooperation

In addition to sporadic attempts to revive the defunct East African Community, composed of Uganda, Kenya, and Tanzania, Uganda participated in four regional economic organizations. These included the PTA, the Lomé Convention, the Kagera Basin Organization, and the Intergovernmental Authority on Drought and Development (IGADD). The PTA, with fifteen member states in east, central, and southern Africa, aimed to create a regional common market, liberalize trade, and encourage cooperation in industry, agriculture, transport, and communications. The progressive liberalization of intra-PTA trade began on July 1, 1984, with the adoption of a common list of 209 items of trade. A multilateral clearing facility was established in Harare in February 1984. It handled transactions worth US$10 million in 1985 and twice that amount in 1987. A PTA monetary unit of account (the uapta), was made equivalent to the SDR and used to settle interstate debts every two months. Outstanding balances were payable in United States dollars. The practical effect of the PTA was constrained by rules, known as "rules of origin," which allowed preferential treatment only for goods produced by companies in which citizens of the member state managed their operations and held at least 51 percent of the equity in the company.

The Lomé Convention, a trade and aid agreement between the EEC and sixty-six African, Caribbean, and Pacific nations, including forty-five African countries, guaranteed duty-free entry to the EEC for specific commodities from these countries. Uganda has benefited from this agreement and assistance from the European Development Fund, which disbursed aid to member countries.

In 1981 Uganda joined the Kagera Basin Organization, which was established by Tanzania, Rwanda, and Burundi in 1977. The organization's major goal was to develop 60,000 square kilometers of the Kagera River Basin, which extended into all four countries. Areas of interest to the organization included transport, agriculture, power, mining, hydroelectricity, and external finance, but by the late 1980s its programs were slowed by funding constraints.

Six East African countries established IGADD in 1986. IGADD members included Djibouti, Ethiopia, Kenya, Somalia, Sudan, and Uganda. The organization's aim was to coordinate and channel funding into key regional programs addressing the issues of drought, desertification, and agricultural development. IGADD received approximately US$70 million in aid in 1987 but by 1989 had not yet completed any of its development and environmental projects.

* * *

Authoritative information on the Ugandan economy can be found in the *Background to the Budget,* which is published annually by Uganda's Ministry of Planning and Economic Development. Two Ugandan newspapers are also useful—the government publication, *The New Vision,* and *Financial Times,* which specializes in economic reporting. Economic statistics are available through the publications of the major international financial institutions, including the World Bank and the International Monetary Fund. The best secondary sources on Uganda, widely available in the United States, are the publications of the Economist Intelligence Unit, including the annual *Country Profile: Uganda* and quarterly *Country Report: Uganda, Ethiopia, Somalia, Djibouti,* and monthly reports of *Africa Research Bulletin, Economic Series.* For information on Uganda's early economic development, see the three-volume *History of East Africa* published by Oxford University. (For further information and complete citations, see Bibliography.)

Chapter 4. Government and Politics

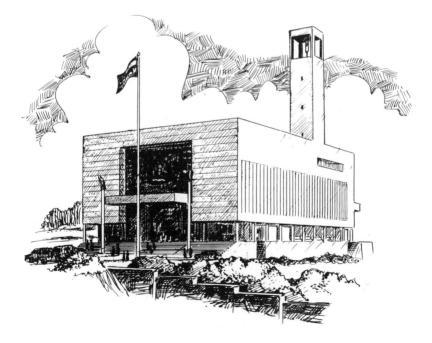

Parliament building in Kampala

THE CENTRAL QUESTION facing Uganda after the National Resistance Movement (NRM) led by Yoweri Kaguta Museveni came to power in January 1986 was whether or not this new government could break the cycle of insecurity and decay that had afflicted the country since independence in 1962. Each new government had made that goal more difficult to achieve. Despite Ugandans' hopes for improvement after the war that ended President Idi Amin Dada's rule in April 1979, national political and economic difficulties worsened in the seven years that followed. A new guerrilla war began in 1981. The National Resistance Army (NRA), military wing of the NRM, seized Kampala and control of the national government in January 1986. The NRM pledged it would establish legitimate and effective political institutions within the next four years. It failed to achieve this goal, however, partly because new civil wars broke out in the north and the east, and in October 1989 the NRM extended its interim rule until 1995.

Few of the basic political questions that confronted Uganda at independence had been settled when the NRM seized power in 1986. Under protectorate rule after 1894, Uganda's various regions had developed along different paths and at different rates. As a result, at independence the most politically divisive issue was the difference in accumulated wealth among these regions. Political tensions centered around the relatively wealthy region of Buganda, which also formed the most cohesive political unit in Uganda, and its relationship to the rest of the country. Adding to these tensions by the late 1960s, northern military domination had been abruptly translated into political domination. Moreover, some political leaders represented the interests of Protestant church organizations in a country that had a Catholic majority and a small but growing Islamic minority. Ugandan officials increasingly harassed citizens, often for their own economic gain, while imprisonment, torture, and violence, although universally deplored as a means of settling political disputes, had become commonplace. All of these factors contributed to political fragmentation.

The NRM government promised fundamental change to establish peace and democracy, to rebuild the economy, and, above all, to end military indiscipline. The new government's political manifesto, the Ten-Point Program, written during the guerrilla war of the 1980s, traced Uganda's problems to the fact that previous political leaders had relied on ethnicity and religion in decision

147

making at the expense of development concerns. The Ten-Point Program argued that resolving these problems required the creation of grass-roots democracy, a politically educated army and police force, and greater national economic independence. It also insisted that the success of Uganda's new political institutions would depend on public servants who would forego self-enrichment at the nation's expense. Political education would be provided to explain the reasons for altering institutions and policies Uganda had used since independence. The new institutions and policies that the NRM announced it intended to put in their place involved drastic changes from the practices of earlier regimes.

At the time that the NRA seized power, however, its organizational life had been brief, its personnel were few, and its political base was narrow. It had few resources to achieve its ambitious proposals for reform. The NRA had been formed in 1981, but its political wing, the NRM, had not been organized as a government until 1985. And because the NRA had been confined primarily to Buganda and western Uganda when it ousted the northern-based Uganda National Liberation Army (UNLA), many Ugandans believed it had simply substituted southern political control for northern domination. Separate civil wars resumed in the north and east only a few months later, and many people in those areas remained deeply skeptical about NRM promises.

In addition, as soon as it came to power, the NRM implemented the policy of broad-based government that Museveni had adopted during the guerrilla war. He appointed leaders of rival political parties and armies to high-level military and cabinet offices. These new leaders generally did not share the NRM's approach to reforms, however. Furthermore, as a government, the NRM had to rely on existing state institutions, particularly government ministries, local administrative offices, and the court system. Government procedures had enjoined public servants working within these institutions from any political activity. Many officials were neither sympathetic to the objectives of the NRM nor convinced that political education for public servants was a legitimate means to accomplish those goals. As a result, Museveni's government was partly led and predominantly staffed by officials who preferred to restore the policies pursued by the Ugandan government in the 1960s. They shared power with a few NRM officials who were committed to radical changes.

Nonetheless, NRM leaders made the most important policy decisions in the regime's first four years, relying on the wave of popular support that accompanied their rise to power and their control over the national army. They introduced several new political bodies, including an inner circle of NRM and NRA officials who had risen to leadership positions during the guerrilla war, a hierarchy of popular assemblies known as resistance councils (RCs), the NRM secretariat, and schools for political education. But the NRM had too few trained cadres or detailed plans to implement the Ten-Point Program during this period. As Museveni himself conceded, the NRM came to power before it was ready to govern.

For these reasons—lack of a nationwide political base, creation of a broad-based government, the absence of sufficient trained cadres of its own, and the necessity of relying on existing government ministries—the new government's leaders chose a path of compromise, blending ideas they had developed during the guerrilla war with existing government institutions on a pragmatic, ad-hoc, day-to-day basis. As a result, during its first four years, the government maintained an uneasy and ambiguous reliance on both old and new procedures and policies. And it was often difficult to determine which official in the government, the NRM, or the NRA possessed either formal or actual responsibility for a particular policy decision.

New civil wars and ill-chosen economic policies diverted the government's energies from many of its ambitious political and economic reforms, but others were begun. In frequent public statements, Museveni returned to the basic themes of the Ten-Point Program, indicating that they had not been abandoned.

The Ten-Point Program

The context in which the NRM's political program was written helps to explain the importance that Museveni and other government leaders who were involved in the guerrilla struggle attached to it. During the interim period after the fall of Amin in April 1979, several small political groups maneuvered to shape the rules for the national parliamentary elections that were held in December 1980 (see Uganda after Amin, ch. 1). Only a few months before the elections, the decision was made to require candidates to run as representatives of parties rather than as individuals. In response, Museveni and other progressives formed a new party, the Uganda People's Movement (UPM), which chose Museveni as its leader. The party nominated candidates in most constituencies, but won only one seat. Museveni ran a close third in Mbarara North constituency.

Following widespread allegations that Milton Obote's Uganda People's Congress (UPC) had manipulated the electoral results to deprive the Democratic Party (DP) of victory, Museveni and a few followers went underground in Luwero District in February 1981,

149

organized the Popular Resistance Army (PRA), and, along with other small bands of fighters, started a guerrilla war. A year later, the PRA broadened its base by negotiating a merger with Yusuf Lule, the first president of Uganda after the fall of Amin, and incorporating the guerrillas Lule had recruited. The new organization was named the NRA; Lule became chair and Museveni became deputy chair and army commander. This arrangement enabled Museveni to recruit and train Baganda (people of Buganda; sing., Muganda) men and women to fight for the NRA, even though he was a Muhima from Mbarara District. When Lule died in 1985, Museveni became chair of the NRA.

Until April 1985, the war was fought exclusively in Buganda, primarily in the Luwero Triangle (named for the area included within the roads between Kampala, Hoima, and Masindi) to oust the UPC government headed by Milton Obote (see The Second Obote Regime: 1981–85, ch. 1). The NRA then left Buganda to open a second front in the west and occupied the entire region following the July 1985 coup d'état in which General Tito Lutwa Okello replaced Milton Obote as head of state. Museveni's NRA undertook a program of political education following classic guerrilla tactics Museveni had learned fifteen years earlier from the liberation movement in Mozambique. NRA soldiers were taught the reasons for their struggle, to respect the villagers among whom they lived, and to pay for food and goods they needed. A political infrastructure to support the NRA was organized through secret, although democratically elected, RCs in villages in Luwero District. The Ten-Point Program, written during the guerrilla campaign, reflects the principles with which the NRA created a disciplined army, organized popular support through RCs, and, in particular, developed a coherent political and economic explanation of why the NRA was fighting against the Ugandan government.

The Ten-Point Program argued that postindependence Ugandan political rulers had greatly exacerbated the problems of economic distortion introduced by British colonial rule. The solution to these problems required a new political and economic strategy that contained ten points. First, real democracy had to be organized at all levels from the village up by elections to "people's committees," by elections to parliament, and on the basis of a decent standard of living so that ordinary people could resist the blandishments of unprincipled politicians. Second, because insecurity in Uganda had been largely the result of "state-inspired violence," it could be eliminated through local democracy, "a politicized army and police, and the absence of corruption at the top." Third, national unity could be consolidated by eliminating sectarianism—that is, through the removal of politics based on religious, linguistic, and ethnic factional issues. Fourth, it was possible to stop the interference of foreign interests in Uganda's domestic concerns since independence, but only if the Ugandan leadership developed independent priorities based on Ugandan interests. Fifth, the most important protection for these interests was to construct an independent, integrated, and self-sustaining national economy that would stop the leakage of Uganda's wealth abroad.

Beyond these goals of the new political strategy were practical steps for achieving these goals. The sixth of the ten points was that basic social services—clean water, health dispensaries, literacy, and housing—had to be restored, particularly in the areas ravaged by the wars that ended the regimes of Amin and Obote. Seventh, because corruption, particularly in the public service, reinforced basic economic distortions, the government had to eliminate it in order to attack economic distortions effectively. Eighth, the problems of victims of past governments should be resolved: land should be returned to thousands of people displaced by mistaken development projects and land seizures; the Karamojong (see Ethnic Diversity and Language, ch. 2) should be settled by providing adequate water; and workers and public servants should receive salaries that would allow them to meet the cost of living. Ninth, Uganda should seek cooperation with other African countries, particularly its neighbors, in order to create larger markets and a more rational use of resources. Nevertheless, Uganda should also defend democratic and human rights of African people against dictators who suppressed them. Finally, Uganda should maintain a mixed economy—combining both capitalist and socialist methods—with small businesses in the hands of private entrepreneurs, and with import-export licensing, monetary policy, ownership of heavy industry, and construction of schools and hospitals under the control of the state.

This analysis of Uganda's problems differed substantially from the general approach taken by previous Ugandan governments. It called for new patterns of organization of Uganda's political economy instead of rehabilitation and restoration of political and economic life as it had existed in the 1960s. Whereas politicians and civil servants from the former regimes had believed the problem was to remove corrupt and ineffectual personnel, the Ten-Point Program called for new structures based on popular control and political education. It claimed that if ordinary citizens understood the basic causes for Uganda's political and economic decay, they would support these basic reforms.

NRM and NRA officials chose to emphasize political education through mass meetings during the latter half of 1985, when, for the first time, they were in open and unchallenged control of part of Uganda. Special district administrators (DAs) were appointed as the most authoritative representatives of the NRM in each district (see Local Administration, this ch.). The largest proportion of their time was spent traveling to villages to explain why ordinary people should become directly involved in politics on the basis of their own economic problems, rather than through the sectarian attachments on which the established political parties were based. Discipline of soldiers who violated the rights of citizens was carried out in front of people in soccer stadiums. A strong change-oriented and populist flavor marked this first effort of the NRM to introduce the Ten-Point Program. But the situation changed significantly when the NRM administration was established in Kampala and became responsible for the government.

Constitutional Development

Uganda has adopted three constitutions since independence. The first was promulgated in 1962 and attempted a quasi-federal arrangement, granting various degrees of autonomy to different local governments established during the protectorate. Of the four kingdoms it recognized, only Buganda received significant federal powers allowing it to raise its own tax revenues, pass laws on specified subjects, enjoy entrenched protection for land tenure and its local courts, and even control through its local legislature the election of the kingdom's representatives to the national parliament. The other three kingdoms—Ankole, Toro, and Bunyoro—and the district of Busoga became "federal states" with fewer powers. The remaining districts, with the exception of Karamoja, retained sufficient autonomy to elect their own councils and pass laws on specified topics but were otherwise governed directly by the national authorities. Because it was the least developed part of the country, Karamoja became a "special district" under central government control.

Nonfederal districts were permitted to elect constitutional heads, who occupied a position equivalent to that of the kings in Buganda, Bunyoro, Toro, and Ankole. The central government held no power to alter the constitutions or form of government in Buganda or the federal states. This complex distribution of powers increased local competition among districts and thus strengthened the bases of power of local leaders. After four years of independence, a struggle for power among local leaders seriously weakened the position of then Prime Minister Milton Obote (see Independence: The Early Years, ch. 1). He responded by suspending the 1962 constitution in April 1966.

At the same time and with a show of military force, Obote ordered members of parliament (MPs) to pass the 1966 constitution without debate. Though understood to be merely an interim constitution, it made sweeping changes that removed all federal provisions in favor of a centralized government. Buganda, the three federal states, and the non-federal districts lost their autonomy; Buganda lost its right to elect its MPs indirectly; and the king of Buganda (the *kabaka*) lost his privileged status. At the national level, the prime minister became an executive president, in place of the preceding ceremonial president. These arrangements strengthened Obote's precarious hold on government while appearing to respect the rule of law. Obote became president in place of the king of Buganda, who had been elected to the position under the 1962 constitution.

A year later, a draft version of the 1967 constitution was introduced in parliament and debated at length. When it was passed three months later, it completed the process of centralization begun the previous year. The 1967 constitution confirmed the president's position as the chief executive. It also continued to sanction multiparty political competition. Each political party had the right to nominate a candidate for president from among its candidates for parliament. Each parliamentary candidate had to declare which candidate for president he or she supported. The elected members of parliament then elected the president. The constitution defined parliament to include members of the National Assembly and the president and made it impossible for MPs to pass a law without the concurrence of the president. The president could also dismiss the National Assembly and legislate by decree in its absence. The 1967 constitution also took the fateful step of abolishing the kings, the kingdoms, and the constitutional heads of the districts. In the case of Buganda, Obote went even further by dividing it into four districts, thus removing official recognition of its cultural unity. Parliament received the authority to change the form of district councils and to allow council members to be appointed rather than elected. The 1967 constitution also empowered the government to employ preventive detention during states of emergency, or as the government deemed necessary.

The 1967 constitution provided for citizenship on the basis of birth in Uganda to a parent (or grandparent) who was a citizen or birth outside Uganda to a father who was a citizen. It also recognized citizenship acquired prior to this constitution, and it gave the right to register for citizenship to women married to Ugandan citizens. According to the 1967 constitution, Ugandan nationals holding dual citizenship who failed to renounce their other citizenship would lose their Ugandan citizenship. The most important purpose of these provisions was to deprive Indians whose applications for Ugandan citizenship had not been approved by 1967, and those who had dual citizenship, of any claim to be Ugandan nationals, and thus it allowed the government to treat them as non-nationals. Citizenship was also the basic criterion for the right to vote, although a voter also had to be twenty-one and a resident in Uganda for six months.

Upon coming to power in January 1986, the NRM government issued a proclamation accepting the authority of the 1967 constitution but suspending portions that granted executive and legislative powers to the president and parliament. Citizenship, most fundamental rights, and government procedures continued on the basis of the 1967 document. With regard to executive and legislative powers, however, the NRM government declared that the National Resistance Council (NRC) "shall have supreme authority of the Government," including the power to pass laws and to choose the national president. Members of the NRC included the chair, representatives of the NRM, and representatives of the NRA. However, the 1986 proclamation noted that the NRC would be increased "from time to time" by adding members from other "political forces" and districts. In addition, the NRC was enjoined "to seek the views of the National Resistance Army Council (NRAC) "on all matters the National Resistance Council considers important." Finally, the proclamation declared the NRM regime an "interim government" to "hold office for a period not exceeding four years."

For the first time in Uganda's history, the national army acquired constitutional standing in the legislative process by virtue of the requirement in the 1986 proclamation that the NRC had to consult the NRAC on any matter the NRC thought important. In 1989 amendments to the original proclamation expanded this principle by declaring that both the NRC and the NRAC "shall participate in the discussion, adoption, and promulgation of the Constitution." These amendments also gave the NRC and NRAC the power to "assemble together and jointly elect or remove the President from office," or "approve a declaration of a state of emergency or insurgency." The effect of the changes in the 1967 constitution created by the 1986 proclamation, and reinforced by the 1989 amendments, was to give the NRM—although only for a four-year period—a monopoly of constitutional authority, even while it brought members of other political forces into the government.

In October 1989, the NRC extended the interim period for five more years until January 1995 in order to allow time to draft, debate, and adopt a permanent constitution, and to complete the political, economic, and rehabilitation programs that had been interrupted by the civil wars in the north and east. Thus, by the end of 1989, the membership of the NRC had been greatly expanded beyond the trusted followers of the NRM and NRA. The government retained the authority to legislate its own program over the objections of any other political forces and extended that authority for an additional five years.

The NRM government had also declared its intention to introduce a new constitution democratically. In November 1988, the NRC passed the Constitutional Commission Act of 1988, which established a body to hear public testimony and draft a new constitution. The government also set guidelines, or minimum requirements, for the commission that included guarantees of fundamental individual rights; separation of the three powers of government, with checks and balances among them; an independent judiciary; a democratic, free, and fair electoral system; and popular accountability. These guidelines conformed to conventional constitutional virtues, though the separation of powers and the imposition of checks and balances represented a change from the notion of parliamentary supremacy in the British Westminster tradition as well as in the original NRM proclamation of 1986.

The guidelines for the constitutional commission did not suggest the creation of a vanguard organization made up of NRM figures who had waged the guerrilla struggle, nor the continuation of a political role for the army. They were also silent on the question of a single or multiparty system. Many Ugandans believed the old political parties would be likely to regain power in a multiparty system. Consequently, they suspected the NRM would need the shelter of a single party, or a ban on all parties, to remain the government after elections were held. Furthermore, the guidelines did not suggest how members of the constitutional commission would eliminate sectarian politics or ensure the achievement of the strategy for an independent self-sustaining economy proposed in the Ten-Point Program. In May 1989, the newly appointed head of the commission announced that it would be two years before the draft was ready to be debated by the Constituent Assembly. The process of hearing public testimony began a few months later.

System of Government

By the end of 1989, Uganda was in the middle of a transition period in which the structure of government was being defined. President Museveni served as head of state, head of the military, and chair of the highest legislative body, the NRC. Below the NRC

155

was a hierarchy of district, county, subcounty, parish, and village
RCs, each with decision-making authority in that area. RC members at each level were elected by RC members at the next lower
level. Uganda had also developed a complex hierarchy of courts
under British rule, supplemented by Islamic and customary institutions for resolving disputes.

The Executive

Under the 1986 proclamation, the president became head of the
executive branch (head of state) with the power to appoint a cabinet of ministers with NRC approval. He was also empowered, again
with the approval of the NRC, to appoint a prime minister to conduct the business of government. Provisions of the 1967 constitution continuing in force authorized the president to organize the
ministries of the public service. Ministers took responsibility for
the implementation of government policy. A permanent secretary
took responsibility for the organization and operation of each ministry. In addition, the president appointed an inspector general of
police, an auditor general, and a director of public prosecutions.
The president, or a person he authorized, made treaties and agreements between Uganda and other countries and international organizations. Among the chapters of the 1967 constitution that were
suspended was the provision specifying a five-year term for the president, but the 1986 proclamation did not clearly spell out a new
term. Presumably, the president served until dismissed by the NRC
(the NRC made this appointment) or until the end of the interim
period of the NRM government. The power of the NRC, acting
in concert with the NRAC, to dismiss the president was made explicit in the February 1989 amendments to the original proclamation.

The NRM consistently followed the principle of broad-based
government from its days of guerrilla warfare through its first four
years in power. NRM leaders viewed this principle as an NRM
reform intended to reverse political disorder by inviting opponents
of the government to share power, instead of following the previous practice of monopolizing power in the hands of the victors.
The NRM's commitment to broad-based government was most
clearly demonstrated in its first cabinet appointments. By reaching outside its own ranks for appointments at the highest levels,
the NRM acknowledged the importance of this principle for national reconciliation. Because the leadership of the NRM consisted
predominantly of new and untested political figures who originated
primarily from the southern part of the country, these appointments reassured many Ugandans that the NRM did not intend

to monopolize high government positions. Dr. Samson Kisekka, a senior associate of former President Yusuf Lule who had joined the NRM when Museveni and Lule merged their movements, became prime minister. An older Muganda politician and medical doctor, Kisekka held more conservative views than Museveni and thus reassured many Baganda that the NRM would not make too many radical changes.

The number of members of the DP in Museveni's first cabinet surprised many observers because the DP had participated in the Okello government, which the NRA had overthrown. The DP had been formed in 1954 and had briefly formed the national government just before independence. The DP had also become the official opposition when the UPC claimed victory following the 1980 elections, although most observers believed the DP had actually won the elections. DP leaders did not serve in government until the party president, Paul Kawanga Ssemogerere, became minister of internal affairs following the July 1985 coup d'état that removed the UPC government. Under the first NRM government, not only did Ssemogerere continue at internal affairs, but the significant portfolios of finance; agriculture, animal husbandry, and fisheries; commerce; and justice were given to DP politicians as well. The leader of the Conservative Party, Joshua Mayanga-Nkangi, who had been the last prime minister of Buganda (in 1966) and whose party, Kabaka Yekka (KY), stood for the return of the Buganda monarchy, was appointed minister of education. The president took the defense portfolio and appointed an NRM official as minister of foreign affairs, but in general NRM leaders were given responsibility for less important ministries or became deputy ministers in more critical ministries.

Additional cabinet members were recruited through negotiations with other guerrilla groups, after the president stated that he was willing to promote peace by merging rivals into his government through negotiation, instead of fighting with them. Museveni's first cabinet contained several such leaders who had switched sides shortly before the NRA took power. Dr. Andrew Kayiira and Dr. David Lwanga, leaders of other guerrilla groups who had opposed Obote, were appointed to the energy and environmental protection ministries, respectively. In July 1986, Moses Ali, leader of a faction of the Uganda National Rescue Front (UNRF) made up of soldiers originally from Amin's army, became minister of tourism and wildlife. Ali had been Amin's minister of finance, so this was a significant expansion of the principle of broad-based government. By narrowing the government's definition of ''political criminals'' it intended to prosecute, the appointment was a further step toward national reconciliation. The principle of broad-based government also led Museveni to expand the size of his cabinet. Between 1986 and 1990, the number of ministers, ministers of state, and deputy ministers grew from thirty-three to seventy-two, including three deputy prime ministers added to the cabinet in April 1989. By this time, a greater proportion of appointments to key ministries came from NRM and NRA ranks.

The commitment to broad-based government in the cabinet had two important consequences for policy making. First, bringing opponents of the NRM into the highest levels of government diluted the policy approach provided in the Ten-Point Program. Second, introducing different perspectives into the cabinet led to sudden and unexpected reversals in policy. The most dramatic example of both points was the change in the government's position regarding the conditions of structural adjustment required by the International Monetary Fund (IMF—see Glossary) in return for foreign loans. At first, Museveni and his advisers who had engaged in the guerrilla struggle rejected the IMF as a source of funds because they believed it would force Uganda to become more dependent on foreign capitalist institutions, while the Ten-Point Program called for the creation of an independent economy. Nevertheless, the government's first budget in May 1986 resembled orthodox IMF strategy, particularly by sharply devaluing the Uganda shilling (USh; for value—see Glossary) and restricting spending. In response, opponents of structural adjustment were able to persuade the cabinet to approve an anti-IMF budget only three months later. This version revalued the shilling and greatly expanded spending beyond the revenue base. Then in May 1987, the government, faced with dizzying inflation, reversed itself again and signed an agreement with the IMF. Once again the shilling was greatly devalued, and government spending was cut (see Currency and Inflation, ch. 3).

The National Resistance Council

Since independence Uganda's governments have been ambivalent about the principle of parliamentary supremacy. Subscribing at first to the British model of government, the 1962 constitution made the prime minister and the cabinet collectively responsible to the parliament. The 1967 constitution provided for a far more powerful executive president while continuing to pay lip service to the principle of parliamentary supremacy. Following Idi Amin's graphic demonstration of the dangers of a chief executive who ignores the rule of law, the Moshi Declaration, which created the Uganda National Liberation Front (UNLF) government in 1979 to replace Amin, put supreme power in its parliament. The 1967

Uganda's parliament building was formerly occupied by the National Assembly. Since the advent of the National Resistance Movement (NRM) government in January 1986, all legislative powers have been vested in the National Resistance Council (NRC).
Courtesy Nelson Kasfir

constitution was restored by the UPC when it returned to power in December 1980. In its 1986 proclamation, the NRM government once again placed the supreme authority of government in the NRC, the parliament it had created during the war. But despite its formal importance, the NRC met rarely for the first year of NRM rule and played an insignificant role in directing the government. For example, it did not even debate the budget of May 1986 (although it did debate the August 1986 revision).

At the time the NRM government seized power, the thirty-eight leading cadres in the NRA and the NRM formed the membership of the NRC by virtue of service, not elections. For the first year, they continued to be the only members of the NRC. Meanwhile, applying the principle of broad-based government meant that most senior ministers were appointed from outside the ranks of the NRM. Governance became particularly awkward for two reasons. First, the cabinet, rather than the NRC, was taking most policy initiatives. Second, cabinet members were excluded from the supreme authority of government. The situation was rectified by expanding the NRC in April 1987 to include all ministers and their deputies, enlarging the NRC to more than seventy members. Then as the ranks of ministerial appointments grew in response to negotiations with more opponents of the government, the NRC automatically expanded as well. After that, the NRC met more frequently but often failed to achieve a quorum because so many of its members had official obligations elsewhere. Frustrated by low attendance over the following year, Haji Moses Kigongo, vice chair of the NRM and chair at most of the NRC meetings, warned in May 1988 that he would suspend members who missed three consecutive meetings. The next day only fifteen members showed up, and that session, too, was canceled for lack of a quorum. On occasion the NRC managed to hold meetings with lively debates and passed legislation in many areas, but few Ugandans would have described it as the nerve center of the government.

In February 1989, new legislation recognized the appointments of the original thirty-eight members of the NRC and provided for the enlargement of the NRC through the election and appointment of additional members. Each county and each district would elect one representative (only women could be candidates for district representative). In addition, one or more of the representatives would be elected by municipalities, depending upon the size of their populations. Provision also was made for five representatives elected by a youth organization and three elected by a workers organization. (But the act did not make clear whether the organizations whose members would comprise the electorate would be existing youth and worker organizations or new ones.) The legislation providing for the elections also created thirty new appointed representatives to the NRC, twenty appointed by the president and ten by the NRAC from the ranks of NRA officers.

Thus, in response to widespread criticism that the 1967 constitution had given too much power to the president, the NRM put supreme power entirely in the hands of the new parliament but limited its membership at first to its own trusted followers. The original parliamentary representatives were legitimized by their participation in the guerrilla struggle, not by elections. Though political figures who had not been part of the NRM or NRA during the war were later appointed to the NRC and in 1989 elected to it, the original NRC members continued to occupy a privileged position. They did not have to stand for election to the NRC. In addition, their special status was formalized in February 1989 with the creation of the National Executive Committee (NEC), a standing committee of the NRC, to contain these original members plus one elected member from each district and ten members appointed by the chair of the NRC from among its members. Because the purposes of the NEC were to "determine the policies and political direction" of the NRM and "monitor and oversee the general performance of the Government," it acquired both a formal vanguard role within the NRC and a powerful position to set the political agenda. But in 1990, it remained unclear whether the NEC would exercise this power to press for the implementation of the Ten-Point Program.

Local Administration

In the early protectorate period, the district commissioner (DC), the representative of the governor, was the most important government official in each district. Before the kingdoms were abolished in 1967, each one had a local government made up of chiefs, who reported to the king, and a central government official who was an adviser to the king. The 1919 Native Authority Ordinance gave the DC responsibility for a hierarchy of appointed chiefs at village, parish, subcounty, and county levels. Councils, originally consisting of these chiefs, were created during the 1930s at each level. After 1949 local administration in Uganda was shared by central and district government officials. The Local Government Ordinance of 1949 established the district as a local government area and as the basis for a separate district administration. During the 1950s, elections to district councils were introduced, and the councils were given responsibility for district administration. Nevertheless, the central government retained the power to control most district council decisions. Chiefs were salaried local government officials but responsible to the central government through the DC for the proper administration of their areas.

At independence Uganda consisted of ten districts, four kingdoms, and one special district (Karamoja). The 1967 constitution abolished the kingdoms and made them districts as well. Because the kingdom of Buganda was separated into four districts, the country was thus divided into eighteen districts. In 1974 President Amin further increased the number of districts to thirty-eight and grouped them into ten provinces. In 1979 after Amin was overthrown, the number of districts was reduced to thirty-three. Moreover, each district was named for its capital in an effort to reduce the significance of ethnicity in politics. In February 1989, however, the addition of Kalangala (the Sese Islands) brought the number of districts back up to thirty-four, and the number of counties increased to 150 (see fig. 1; fig. 2). There were also sixty-five urban authorities, including Kampala City Council, fourteen municipalities, twenty-seven town councils, and twenty-three town boards.

The 1962 constitution had required that nine-tenths of district council members be directly elected. In keeping with its overall emphasis on strengthening central control, the 1967 constitution gave the parliament the right to establish district councils and their offices, to decide whether some or all of their members would be elected or nominated, and to empower a national minister to suspend a district council or to undertake any of its duties. The 1967 Local Administrations Act and the 1964 Urban Authorities Act created a uniform set of regulations that gave the central government direct control over local administration in each district. District councils were limited to specified areas of responsibility— particularly primary education, road construction, land allocation, community development, law and order, and local tax collection. When district councils were revived in 1981, their members were again nominated by the central government. Chiefs and local officials continued to be appointed on the basis of the 1967 act until 1986.

The NRM government significantly altered local administration by introducing elected resistance councils (RCs) in villages, parishes, subcounties, and districts throughout the nation. The original RCs had been created during the early 1980s to support the NRA during its guerrilla war. But after 1986, the introduction of these new assemblies sharply curtailed the powers of chiefs and provided an indirect channel for popular influence at the district level and above. Creation of the RCs was in response to the first point of the Ten-Point Program, which insisted on democracy at all levels of government. In no other respect during its first four years did the NRM government achieve as much progress in implementing the political program it had adopted before taking power.

By September 1987, the NRC had established both district administrations and a hierarchy of RCs (see fig. 8). All adults automatically became members of their village resistance council, known as an RC–I, and came together to elect a nine-person resistance committee, which administered the affairs of the village. An RC was given the right to remove any of its elected resistance committee officers who broke the law or lost the confidence of two-thirds of the council. The nine officials on the resistance committee elected by the RC–I joined with all other village resistance committees to form the parish resistance council, the RC–II, and elected the nine officials who formed the parish resistance committee. The members of this committee assembled with the other parish committee members in the subcounty to form the subcounty resistance council (RC–III) and elected the nine officials who formed the subcounty resistance committee. County resistance councils (RC–IVs) were established in the statute but functioned only intermittently as governing bodies, principally for election purposes. The district resistance council (RC–V) contained two representatives elected from each RC–III and one representative for women elected from each RC–IV and from each municipal RC. At all RC levels, heads of government departments serving that council, including chiefs, were made ex officio members of their respective RCs but without the right to vote. In 1989 the NRC determined that each RC–III would choose one representative for the NRC, and each district resistance council (RC–V) would choose a woman as its representative on the NRC. Thus, direct RC elections and popular recall existed at the village level only. The term of each RC was two years, and the RC could be suspended by the minister of local government for disrupting public security, participating in sectarian politics, engaging in smuggling, obstructing national plans, or diverting commodities to its members' private use. However, the NRC was given the power to overrule the minister.

The NRC also replaced the DC with a new official, the district administrator (DA), appointed by the president as the political head of the district. In addition to providing political direction to the district, the DAs were responsible for overseeing the implementation of central government policy, chairing the security and development committees, and organizing RCs. Providing political direction included organizing courses in political education for officials and ordinary citizens. A second new post, that of district executive secretary (DES), was filled by former DCs. The DES was required to supervise all government departments in the district, integrate district and central administration, supervise the implementation of district resistance council policies, and serve as the accounting officer for the district.

The formal change from the officially neutral DC to the explicitly political DA suggests the importance that the NRM government placed on political education in order to gain support for basic political and economic reforms. The addition of a new bureaucratic level of assistant district administrators, with responsibilities for administration at the county and subcounty levels, and reporting through the DA to the president, further entrenched the central government at the expense of the RCs. The creation of this position further reduced the direct popular control that was contemplated in the Ten-Point Program and that had been enthusiastically supported by NRM officials.

In 1990 the exact duties of the RCs and their relation to the chiefs had not been fully determined. The purpose of RCs during the

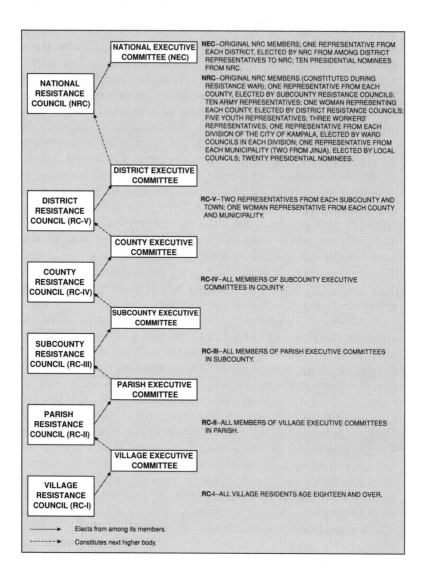

NATIONAL EXECUTIVE COMMITTEE (NEC)

NEC--ORIGINAL NRC MEMBERS; ONE REPRESENTATIVE FROM EACH DISTRICT, ELECTED BY NRC FROM AMONG DISTRICT REPRESENTATIVES TO NRC; TEN PRESIDENTIAL NOMINEES FROM NRC.

NATIONAL RESISTANCE COUNCIL (NRC)

NRC--ORIGINAL NRC MEMBERS (CONSTITUTED DURING RESISTANCE WAR); ONE REPRESENTATIVE FROM EACH COUNTY, ELECTED BY SUBCOUNTY RESISTANCE COUNCILS; TEN ARMY REPRESENTATIVES; ONE WOMAN REPRESENTING EACH COUNTY, ELECTED BY DISTRICT RESISTANCE COUNCILS; FIVE YOUTH REPRESENTATIVES; THREE WORKERS' REPRESENTATIVES; ONE REPRESENTATIVE FROM EACH DIVISION OF THE CITY OF KAMPALA, ELECTED BY WARD COUNCILS IN EACH DIVISION; ONE REPRESENTATIVE FROM EACH MUNICIPALITY (TWO FROM JINJA), ELECTED BY LOCAL COUNCILS; TWENTY PRESIDENTIAL NOMINEES.

DISTRICT EXECUTIVE COMMITTEE

DISTRICT RESISTANCE COUNCIL (RC-V)

RC-V--TWO REPRESENTATIVES FROM EACH SUBCOUNTY AND TOWN; ONE WOMAN REPRESENTATIVE FROM EACH COUNTY AND MUNICIPALITY.

COUNTY EXECUTIVE COMMITTEE

COUNTY RESISTANCE COUNCIL (RC-IV)

RC-IV--ALL MEMBERS OF SUBCOUNTY EXECUTIVE COMMITTEES IN COUNTY.

SUBCOUNTY EXECUTIVE COMMITTEE

SUBCOUNTY RESISTANCE COUNCIL (RC-III)

RC-III--ALL MEMBERS OF PARISH EXECUTIVE COMMITTEES IN SUBCOUNTY.

PARISH EXECUTIVE COMMITTEE

PARISH RESISTANCE COUNCIL (RC-II)

RC-II--ALL MEMBERS OF VILLAGE EXECUTIVE COMMITTEES IN PARISH.

VILLAGE EXECUTIVE COMMITTEE

VILLAGE RESISTANCE COUNCIL (RC-I)

RC-I--ALL VILLAGE RESIDENTS AGE EIGHTEEN AND OVER.

———▶ Elects from among its members.
------▶ Constitutes next higher body.

Figure 8. Structure of Resistance Councils and Executive Committees, 1990

guerrilla war had been far easier to establish before the NRM took power. In addition, continuing civil war and the sheer effort of electing RCs in every village, parish, subcounty, and district drew attention away from the business of the RCs. RCs were new to Uganda, and it took people time to understand how to make use of them. In 1987 the NRC had given the RCs the power "to identify local problems and find solutions.'' During times of shortages of basic commodities, such as sugar in June 1986, the RCs were effectively used as distribution centers. But because RC officials below the district level received no compensation, they were reluctant to give too much time to managing local affairs. In addition, the position of the chiefs remained ambiguous. Chiefs still reported to the Ministry of Local Government. Many chiefs were uncertain how much power they had under the new system, or even whom to obey when the Ministry of Local Government and the RC disagreed over the proper course of action a chief should follow.

Judicial System

The legal system that existed in 1990 included customary, and in some cases Islamic, law in addition to statutory law. Statutory law was published in the government *Gazette*. The constitution provided for a High Court with a chief justice and as many other judges as parliament decided to create. It empowered the president to appoint High Court judges, although it allowed him to choose only the chief justice without following the advice of the Judicial Service Commission (JSC), which was headed by the chief justice. The constitution restricted the choice of judges to those already presiding over courts of unlimited jurisdiction or to lawyers who had practiced for five years before such courts. The High Court heard appeals from magistrates' courts located in each district. In addition, the High Court acted as the court of first instance in questions involving elections to or vacancies in parliament. The 1967 constitution also declared that decisions of the High Court could be appealed to the Court of Appeal for East Africa (CAEA), or to a new court of appeal established by parliament.

With the collapse of the East African Community (EAC) in 1977, the Ugandan government withdrew from the CAEA and created a national Court of Appeal. In 1980 the government made the chief justice the head of the High Court only and appointed a separate president of the Court of Appeal. These changes led to problems in the administration of justice during the next several years. The problems stemmed primarily from the anomalous position of a chief justice constitutionally restricted to be head of an inferior court. To eliminate these problems, the NRM government introduced the Constitution (Amendment) Bill, 1987, and the Judicature Act (Amendment) Bill, 1987, which the NRC passed in August 1987. The name of the Court of Appeal was changed to the Supreme Court of Uganda. The chief justice became its head and the chief administrator of the judiciary. Two new positions were created, a deputy chief justice of the Supreme Court and a principal judge, who became head of the High Court. Appeals from any decision of the High Court were to be referred to the Supreme Court. To be appointed judge of the Supreme Court, a person must have qualified and served as judge of the High Court for at least seven years. Power to appoint the justices and chief justice of the Supreme Court was placed in the hands of the president. Following the precedent of the 1967 constitution, the president had to accept the advice of the JSC except in the appointment of the chief justice. The deputy chief justice was to be appointed from among the principal judge and justices of the Supreme Court.

In 1988 the NRM government substantially changed grass-roots adjudication by giving judicial powers over civil disputes, which up until then had been exercised by chiefs, to elected resistance committees in each village, parish, and subcounty (see Local Administration, this ch.). In the past, despite their pretense of neutrality, chiefs had often discriminated against opponents of the ruling party or military government. The new local court system responded to the first point in the Ten-Point Program by placing petty and customary conflicts in the hands of democratically chosen officials. The new system also received broad popular support, according to a commission of inquiry into local government.

Each elected resistance committee was empowered to constitute itself as a court headed by the chair of the committee. If some of the committee members were absent, other members of the resistance council that had elected the committee could be co-opted. Cases involving contracts, debts, or assault and battery could be heard only if they involved less than USh5,000, a relatively small sum. However, other civil disputes concerning conversion or damage to property or trespassing, and customary disputes involving land held by customary tenure, the marital status of women, the paternity of children, customary heirs, impregnation of or elopement with a female under age eighteen, and customary bail procedures could be heard regardless of amount. The orders that these courts had the power to make ranged from apology and reconciliation to compensation or attachment and sale. Appeals went to the next higher resistance committee and eventually to the High Court.

One of the most important stated objectives of the NRM government was to restore the rule of law. Toward that end, three commissions were either revived or created. The Commission for Law Reform, which had been established in the Ministry of Justice during the Amin government but had been ineffective for lack of financial resources and because of instability, was given a fresh start with the appointment of Justice Matthew Opu of the High Court as commissioner in 1986. The Commission for Law Revision, which had the task of clearing the laws of statutes that had been repealed or had become obsolete and of adding consequential amendments, was revived. The Commission of Inquiry into the Violation of Human Rights was created in 1986 to establish the human rights record from independence up to the take-over by the NRM government. A High Court justice, Arthur Oder, and five other commissioners began public hearings on human rights violations in December 1986.

Elections

National parliamentary elections have occurred five times but only twice since independence. In all five cases, the elections failed to give a clear indication of popular feelings, and on two other occasions scheduled elections did not even occur. During the protectorate period, general elections to the Legislative Council were held in 1958, 1961, and 1962. The 1958 elections were flawed by the refusal of several local governments to agree to any voting at all. The DP won the 1961 elections by unexpectedly winning seats in Buganda where a few of its followers voted despite a mass boycott of the polls organized by the kingdom government. The Buganda seats enabled the DP to form Uganda's first party government under the British governor, even though only a minority of the national electorate had voted for it. Consequently, independence was delayed to permit a second general election.

In the final negotiations for independence, the Kingdom of Buganda acquired the right to elect its national representatives indirectly through its local assembly, the Lukiiko. Elections to the Lukiiko were held in February 1962. The newly formed Kabaka Yekka (KY) party, which reflected intense feelings of cultural unity among the predominantly Baganda electorate, won sixty-five of sixty-eight seats (see Power Politics in Buganda, ch. 1). The Lukiiko then elected KY members to all of the Buganda seats in the National Assembly. The UPC and DP split the seats outside Buganda, leaving no party with a clear national mandate. An unlikely coalition between the mildly progressive UPC and the aggressively ethnic-oriented KY formed the first postindependence government under Obote's leadership in October 1962. The coalition unraveled soon after and was dissolved less than two years after independence.

Postindependence elections scheduled for 1967 were "postponed" by Obote because of the crisis of 1966 (see Independence: The Early Years, ch. 1). Elections organized for 1971 were canceled by Idi Amin when he took power through a military coup d'état. The

167

Uganda National Liberation Front (UNLF), an interim government formed when the Tanzanian army overthrew Amin's military regime in 1979, organized the first national elections since independence. These elections were held in December 1980 under conditions that favored the UPC, which was still led by Obote (see The Interim Period: 1979–80, ch. 1). Widespread local opinion regarded these elections as neither free nor fair, despite acceptance of the results by a Commonwealth Observer Group, which monitored them. The UPC was declared the winner, but most Ugandans believed it actually lost the elections to the DP and took power by altering the results. Thus, before the NRM came to power, only one set of national elections had been held since independence, and its results had been hotly disputed.

In February 1989, the NRM government organized local and national elections on the basis of the RC structure that it had created. The government announced in the middle of January that there would be new elections, starting only three weeks later, for all resistance committee positions in RCs at every level, including, for the first time, the NRC. At the village, parish, and subcounty levels, the elections followed procedures the NRM had already introduced to form the RCs out of the combined membership of the resistance committees elected by the councils at each level. The same procedure was followed for the set of successive elections in urban areas, except that the RC–IIIs were named "wards" rather than subcounties and the RC–IVs "divisions" instead of counties. However, the RC–IIIs also gathered as an electoral college representing their counties or urban divisions to elect three representatives to the district RC, one of whom had to be a woman, as well as one representative to the NRC. Unlike other RC elections, nominees for the NRC did not have to win successive elections in the lower RCs in order to be candidates. Each district RC also chose one representative to the NRC. Only women were permitted to run for this position.

Many of the original NRC members, who continued in office without facing an election in 1989, were appointed to be election supervisors. The only restrictions placed on candidates were to require them to be residents of their constituencies and to prohibit former members of Obote's or Amin's intelligence agencies from becoming candidates. The use of county and district boundaries for constituencies removed the possibility of gerrymandering. Nomination required completion of two simple forms and the support of five qualified electors. Candidates did not have to pay a "deposit." There was no registration of voters. No campaigning was allowed, and candidates could not publicly identify themselves

Queuing up to vote in a resistance council election in a village just outside
Kampala, August 1986
Courtesy Nelson Kasfir

with a political party. The rules limited candidates' campaigns to
a brief introductory speech at the time of the elections.

The elections had to be held in sequence because the RCs formed
a pyramid in which the electorate at each higher level (above RC–II)
was composed of elected officials from the next lower level. Elections of resistance committee officials by voters in village and parish RCs were held only three weeks after President Museveni's
announcement in most parts of the country. One week later, elections were held for subcounty resistance committees. The newly
elected subcounty committees immediately traveled to their county
headquarters to choose two representatives to the district RC; the
following week they assembled again to elect both the county's
representative to the NRC and the county's woman representative to the district RC. Finally, at the end of February 1989, each
district RC (except Gulu) elected its woman representative to the
NRC.

Election was determined by public queuing behind the preferred
candidate. Contestants stood facing away from the queues and were
not permitted to turn around to see who was supporting them. The
use of public queuing as a voting procedure was sharply criticized
because it opened the possibility of coercion. The government

agreed that a secret ballot would have been better, but argued that, for the time being, the expense and prospect of misuse of ballot boxes made queuing a more desirable method of voting. All elections were held during February 1989, except in Gulu District and Usuk County, Soroti District, where they were delayed because of security problems. The Usuk elections were held the following month and the Gulu elections in October 1989. The youth and workers elections had not been held by the end of 1990.

In the February 1989 elections, village turnout was reported to be high in most areas other than those where rebels were active. Almost all elected resistance committee members, the only voters permitted in higher elections, participated in electing NRC members and the upper RCs. Fourteen ministers and deputy ministers lost NRC elections. Only two women won elections in contests against men. Four important members of Obote's government between 1980 and 1985 won seats in county constituencies, and their success provided an indication of the absence of government interference in the voting. Most losers conceded that the elections were conducted fairly, although they frequently objected to the rules under which they had to compete. The most vociferous criticism came from party leaders in the DP and the UPC. As a party, the UPC had not been active since the NRM government took office. DP politicians, on the other hand, had run in the earlier RC elections and had won a large number of them. According to the DP's own calculations, in two-thirds of the district RCs its candidates had won 84 percent of the seats in elections before February 1989. DP leaders felt they had a good chance to win national power democratically through the RC system, if the DP were permitted to compete as a party. Officials of both parties regarded the election rules as a step by the NRM government to remove them from competitive political activity. They insisted that elections without participation by competing parties could not be considered democratic. The government response was, in a meeting with the DP in 1989, to question whether or not political parties were necessary for democracy.

Political Dynamics

When the NRM took power in 1986, it added a new element to the unsolved political issues that had bedeviled Uganda since independence. It promised new and fundamental changes, but it also brought old fears to the surface. If this government demonstrated magnanimity toward its opponents and innovative solutions to Uganda's political difficulties, it also contributed significantly to the country's political tensions. This paradox appeared in one political issue after another through the first four years of the interim period. The most serious political question was the deepening division between the north and the south, even though these units were neither administrative regions nor socially or even geographically coherent entities. The relationship of Buganda to the rest of Uganda, an issue forcibly kept off the public agenda for twenty years, re-emerged in public debate. Tension between the NRM and the political parties that had competed for power since independence became a new anxiety. In addition, the government's resort to political maneuvers and surprise tactics in two of its most important initiatives in 1989, national elections and the extension of the interim period of government, illustrated the NRM's difficulties in holding the nation to its political agenda.

Fears of Regional Domination

For the first time since the protectorate was founded, the NRA victory in 1986 gave a predominantly southern cast to both the new political and the new military rulers of Uganda. For reasons of climate, population, and colonial economic policy, parts of the south, particularly Buganda, had developed economically more rapidly than the north (see The Colonial Era, ch. 1). Until the railroad was extended from the south, cotton could not become an established cash crop in the north. Instead, early in the colonial period, northerners established a pattern of earning a cash income through labor on southern farms or through military service. Although there had never been a political coalition that consisted exclusively, or even predominantly, of southerners or northerners, the head of the government had come from the north for all but one of the preceding twenty-three years of independence, and each succeeding army's officers and recruits were predominantly northerners. Northerners feared southern economic domination, while southerners chafed under what they considered northern political and military control. Thus, the military victory of the NRA posed a sobering political question to both northerners and southerners: was the objective of its guerrilla struggle to end sectarianism, as the Ten-Point Program insisted, or to end northern political domination?

In the first few days following the NRA takeover of Kampala in January 1986, there were reports of incidents of mob action against individual northerners in the south, but the new government took decisive steps to prevent their repetition. By the end of March, NRA troops had taken military control of the north. A period of uneasy calm followed, during which northerners considered their options. Incidents of looting and rape of northern civilians by recently recruited southern NRA soldiers, who had replaced better disciplined but battle-weary troops, intensified northerners' belief that southerners would take revenge for earlier atrocities and that the government would not stop them. In this atmosphere, the NRA order in early August 1986 for all soldiers in the former army, the Uganda National Liberation Army (UNLA), to report to local police stations gave rise to panic. These soldiers knew that during the Obote and Amin governments such an order was likely to have been a prelude to execution. Instead of reporting, many soldiers joined rebel movements, and a new round of civil wars began in earnest (see The Rise of the National Resistance Army, ch. 5).

Although the civil wars occurred in parts of the east as well, they sharpened the sense of political cleavage between north and south and substantiated the perception that the NRM was intent on consolidating southern domination. Rebels killed some local RC officials because they were the most vulnerable representatives of the NRM government. Because war made northern economic recovery impossible, new development projects were started only in the south. And because cash crop production in the north was also impossible, the income gap between the two areas widened. Most government officials sent north were southerners because the NRA officer corps and the public service were mostly southern. By mid-1990, the NRA had gained the upper hand in the wars in the north, but the political damage had been done. The NRM government had become embroiled in war because it had failed to persuade northerners that it had a political program that would end regional domination. And its military success meant that for some time to come its response to all political issues would carry that extra burden of suspicion.

Buganda and the Kingship

At independence the kingship controversy was the most important issue in Ugandan politics. Although there were four kingdoms, the real question was how much control over Buganda the central government should have. The power of the king as a uniting symbol for the Baganda became apparent following his deportation by the protectorate government in 1953 (see Power Politics in Buganda, ch. 1). When negotiations for independence threatened the autonomous status of Buganda, leading notables organized a political party to protect the king. The issue was successfully presented as a question of survival of the Baganda as a separate nation because the position of the king had been central to Buganda's precolonial culture. On that basis, defense of the kingship attracted overwhelming support in local Buganda government elections, which were

Downtown Kampala
Courtesy Carl Fleischhauer

held just before independence. To oppose the king in Buganda at that time would have meant political suicide.

After the 1967 constitution abolished all kings, the Ugandan army turned the king's palace into their barracks and the Buganda parliament building into their headquarters. It was difficult to know how many Baganda continued to support the kingship and how intensely they felt about it because no one could express support openly. After a brief flirtation with restoration, Amin also refused to consider it. By the 1980s, more than half of all Baganda had never lived under their king. The Conservative Party, a marginal group led by the last man to serve as Buganda's prime minister under a king, contested the 1980 elections but received little support. NRM leaders could not be sure that the Baganda would accept their government or the Ten-Point Program. The NRA was ambivalent in its response to this issue. On the one hand, until its final year, the guerrilla struggle to remove Obote had been conducted entirely in Buganda, involved a large number of Baganda fighters, and depended heavily on the revulsion most Baganda felt for Obote and the UPC. On the other hand, many Baganda who had joined the NRA and received a political education in the Ten-Point Program rejected ethnic loyalty as the basis of political organization. Nevertheless, though a matter of dispute, many Ugandans reported that Museveni promised in public, near the end of the guerrilla struggle, to restore the kingship and to permit Ronald Mutebi, the heir apparent, to become king. Many other Ugandans opposed the restoration just as strongly, primarily for the political advantages it would give Buganda.

Controversy erupted a few months after the NRM takeover, when the heads of each of the clans in Buganda organized a public campaign for the restoration of the kingship, the return of the Buganda parliament building (which the NRA had continued to use as the army headquarters), and permission for Mutebi to return to Uganda. Over the next month, the government struggled to regain the political initiative from the clan heads. First, in July 1986 the prime minister, Samson Kisekka—a Muganda—told people at a public rally in Buganda to stop this "foolish talk." Without explanation, the government abruptly ordered the cancellation of celebrations to install the heir of another kingdom a week later. Nevertheless, the newspapers reported more demands for the return of Mutebi by Buganda clan elders. The cabinet then issued a statement conceding the intensity of public interest but insisting the question of restoring kings was up to the forthcoming Constitutional Assembly and not within the powers of the interim government. Then, three weeks later, the NRM issued its own carefully worded statement calling supporters of restoration ''disgruntled opportunists purporting to be monarchists'' and threatening to take action against anyone who continued to agitate on this issue. At the same time, the president agreed to meet with the clan elders, even though that gave a fresh public boost to the controversy. Then, in a surprise move, the president convinced Mutebi to return home secretly in mid-August 1986, presenting the clan elders with a fait accompli. Ten days later, the government arrested a number of Baganda, whom it accused of a plot to overthrow the government and restore the king. But while Museveni managed to take the wind from the sails of Buganda nationalism, he was forced to go to inordinate lengths to defuse public feeling, and nothing was settled. The kingship issue was likely to re-emerge with equal intensity and unpredictable consequences when the draft for a new constitution was presented for public discussion.

Political Parties

With the NRM's accession to power, the very existence of the old political parties, particularly the DP and the UPC, became an issue. The Ten-Point Program blamed much of Uganda's previous difficulties on the excessive reliance of the leaders of the old parties upon manipulation of ethnic and religious loyalties for their own benefit. The alternative, though not spelled out, would be politics without parties. Even though the results were rigged, the 1980 general elections had demonstrated that both the DP and the UPC retained a mass following despite their repression by the Amin dictatorship and that the UPM, the predecessor party of many important NRM leaders, did not attract many voters. For its own part, the NRM claimed that it was a political movement, not a party; but the NRM did not have sufficient political support to liquidate the old parties. Instead, in an ambiguous, informal, and often shifting compromise, it restricted the public activities of the old parties but invited several of their political leaders to participate in its cabinet and even to contest RC elections.

The old parties were permitted to maintain their headquarters and to issue statements but could not hold rallies or campaign on behalf of candidates for RC elections. This decision stirred fears among adherents of the old parties that the NRM intended to consolidate its hold on power and eventually eliminate them. Nevertheless, the NRM's adroit use of another of its principles, broad-based government, kept an uneasy peace with the parties, particularly the DP, through the appointment of party leaders to important government positions. The DP was awarded so many important portfolios in the first cabinet in 1986 that it almost seemed to be

175

the senior coalition partner. In addition, the NRM turned a blind eye toward the successful election of many DP party members in RC elections during the first two years of the interim period. According to the DP's own estimates, it had won 84 percent of the seats in RC–Vs, the district resistance councils, in twenty-two of the then thirty-three districts, compared with only 7 percent for the NRM and 7 percent for the UPC.

At the DP's insistence, the NRM met sporadically between 1986 and March 1988 for private discussions over the appropriate party system for Uganda. These meetings ended when the NRM unilaterally insisted that party activities must be suspended for an unspecified period of time, after which a referendum would be held to decide whether the constitution would adopt a system permitting multiparty competitive politics. Northerners in the rebel Uganda People's Democratic Army (UPDA) expressed similar anxieties. In the peace agreement they signed with the NRM in June 1988, they insisted on a national referendum on the party system and on the form of government to replace interim rule. However, the relationship of the referendum to the process of drafting a new constitution, or even if one would be held, remained unclear at the end of 1990.

When the NRM extended its prohibition on parties to prevent them from campaigning and from nominating candidates for new members of the NRC in the elections of February 1989, the issue became considerably more threatening to the officials of the old parties. The UPC promptly responded by denouncing the elections as a charade intended to consolidate the NRM's grip on power and by insisting that no UPC members would participate. Nonetheless, several prominent UPC politicians did contest NRC seats, but without making any public reference to their party identity. Even more DP politicians ran for the NRC while also following the government rules. After the elections, the DP headquarters issued a statement deploring the ban on parties and warning the NRM not to impose its own choice of government on the people. The DP appeared to have lost its pre-eminent position in the lower RC elections in 1989, and it did not do particularly well in the parliamentary contests either, though its members probably won more elections than UPC politicians. However, data to substantiate this point were not available. Leaders of the NRM defended the elections as successful because they were free from overt sectarian influences. But many observers believed that the NRM's chances for continuing in power through elections might depend on not having to compete on an equal footing with the other parties. If that prediction were widely believed by Ugandans, the

Constitutional Assembly, likely to be the next arena to consider this issue, could find it difficult to resolve.

Surprise Political Tactics

The adroit political maneuvering of the NRM disguised its weakness in implementing its political agenda. Two of the more important political initiatives it took during its first four years were the general elections of February 1989 and the extension of interim rule the following October. In both cases, the government designed the initiatives to protect itself. It kept tight control by surprising its opponents and then moving too fast to permit them to take any political advantages. Museveni announced the February elections only three weeks before they began. The rules ensured that the NRM could not lose control over the government, regardless of the outcome. Aspiring candidates had to make an immediate choice to oppose the electoral system or to participate in it.

The NRM's October 1989 extension of the interim period until 1995 broke the most important promise the NRM had made in taking power, though the difficulties created by the war and the economy had made the four-year deadline impractical. The NRM rushed legislation for the five-year extension through the NRC in one week, despite demands from some parliamentarians for time to consult their constituents. The first person in Uganda ever to resign from parliament did so over the government's failure to allow public discussion of this issue. The government undoubtedly feared that a public campaign against the extension would serve as a vehicle for other political issues and so cripple its legitimacy. As in the case of outwitting the Baganda clan heads, the government's clever tactics helped it win the day but only at the expense of attending to its own agenda. In addition, NRM leaders were sufficiently flexible to bring their opponents into office under the umbrella of broad-based government, but that also reduced their political options by forcing them to respond to their opponents' interests in maintaining their own ethnic, religious, and patronage connections.

At the same time, until 1990 the government did not use surprise tactics to set up a new constitution. It allowed the commission appointed for that purpose to take two years to collect public testimony and write a draft. Indeed, completing the constitutional process without a rush was an important reason for extending the interim period. NRM leaders knew the minefield of Ugandan politics. Giving their opponents more time or room for maneuver might have mired each initiative or forced the government into using coercion and losing any chance to build political support. The interconnections of the north-south question, the Buganda question, and the party question made the government's tactical strategy all the more imperative. The NRM's use of tactics, so reminiscent of its surprise attacks during the guerrilla struggle against the Obote government, allowed it to retain the political initiative. But it also indicated that NRM leaders had discovered how difficult and how slow it would be to make any of the fundamental changes they had called for in the Ten-Point Program.

Foreign Relations

Uganda is landlocked and depends on foreign imports for most of its consumer goods and energy requirements. Even before independence, maintaining an open trade route to the Indian Ocean was the primary foreign policy objective of all governments. For this reason, once the railroad from Mombasa to Kampala was completed early in the protectorate period, relations with Kenya became the government's most significant foreign concern. During much of the period of British rule, the most worrying foreign issue for politically conscious Ugandans was the possibility that Kenyan white settlers would gain control over all of East Africa. During the 1950s, when African nationalism gained the upper hand in the four East African territories, the achievement of closer relations among the four also became an important foreign policy objective.

Later, however, economic differences eroded initiatives toward federation and eventually led to hostilities between Uganda and Kenya in the 1980s that would have been unimaginable two decades earlier. After independence, political issues erupting into violence within Uganda or its neighbors also caused serious strains in their bilateral relations, frequently involving rebels, refugees, and even military incursions. Because of its former colonial rule, Britain maintained a close and special relationship with Uganda. But over time, this role slowly diminished as Uganda cultivated new links with other industrialized countries. And, despite its protestations of nonalignment, Uganda remained far more closely linked, both economically and politically, to the capitalist than to the socialist bloc.

Ugandan foreign policy objectives changed considerably after Idi Amin's coup d'état in 1971. For the first decade after independence, policymakers had emphasized cooperation with Uganda's neighbors and the superpowers, participation in international organizations, and nonalignment in order to protect the state's sovereignty and support the African bloc as much as possible without losing opportunities for expanding trade or gaining assistance for development. When Amin seized power, he followed a far more aggressive, though unpredictable, foreign policy. Uganda threatened its neighbors both verbally and militarily. The gratuitous verbal attacks that Amin launched on foreign powers served mainly to isolate Uganda.

The NRM government introduced new radical foreign policy objectives when it first came to power and consequently brought new complications into Uganda's foreign relations. At the outset, President Museveni enthusiastically supported international and especially African cooperation but conditioned it on an ideological evaluation of whether or not other regimes were racist, dictatorial, or corrupt, or violated human rights. On this basis, shortly after taking power the government went to great lengths to enter trade agreements with other developing countries based on barter rather than cash, in order to publicize Uganda's autonomy, even though most of its exports continued to consist of coffee purchased by the United States or by European states, and most of its imports came from Europe. In response, Uganda's neighbors were suspicious of Museveni's radical pronouncements and felt that he was attacking their rule through his denunciations of their human rights policies. They also avoided close ties to Uganda because they suspected that the NRM government, having come to power through a guerrilla struggle, might assist dissidents intending to overthrow them.

During its first four years in power, the NRM government moderated its foreign policy stance to one that more closely reflected the conventional positions of preceding Ugandan governments than the changes proposed in its Ten-Point Program. Uganda maintained friendly relations with Libya, the Soviet Union, the Democratic People's Republic of Korea (North Korea), and Cuba, although most of its trade and development assistance came from the West. In addition, though it consistently maintained its stance of geopolitical nonalignment, the fact that the NRM government accepted an IMF structural adjustment plan made it more politically acceptable to Western leaders. During this period, many African leaders overcame their suspicion of Museveni and the NRM and elected him chair of the Organization of African Unity (OAU) in July 1990.

Postindependence heads of government in Uganda made almost all significant foreign policy-making decisions themselves, leaving their foreign ministers to carry them out or explain them away. In order to shore up their domestic power bases, Obote, Amin, and Museveni often introduced new foreign policies that broke sharply with existing relations. They also used foreign policy symbolically to signal the international posture they wished to cultivate. Amin's pronouncements were the most puzzling because they frequently incurred enormous costs for Uganda's relations with other states. Foreign ministry officials never knew when it was safe to ignore his orders or when they had to take them seriously. All three presidents often used foreign policy as a public gesture in an effort to give the government more autonomy in international affairs, improve its public standing with radical states, or satisfy vocal militants in the government. In such cases, the government usually gave public support to radical states and causes, while continuing privately to maintain its more conservative foreign relationships. Foreign relations with radical countries, however much they irritated United States and British officials, did not play a significant role in shaping Ugandan foreign policy.

Regional Organizations

Even before independence, overlapping cultural, linguistic, and economic ties, as well as common nationalist sentiments, stimulated a desire for East African federation among Ugandans, Kenyans, and Tanzanians. A declaration of intent, signed in 1963, led to the formation of the East African Community (EAC) in 1967. In 1977 the EAC was dissolved, the victim of Ugandan and Tanzanian fears of Kenyan economic dominance, and, for different reasons, Kenyan and Tanzanian government opposition to

Amin. Despite its brief life, the EAC provided Uganda's deepest regional involvement since independence. In the Ten-Point Program, the NRM government bitterly assailed the break-up of the EAC, blaming national leaders in all three countries for their shortsightedness. Nevertheless, the NRM government chose to participate in African organizations that served larger regions, rather than to try to resurrect a union limited to the three East African states.

Given the importance the NRM attached to African cooperation, it was no surprise that its leaders strongly supported initiatives to build closer economic and developmental relations among states in eastern and southern Africa. The Ugandan government set great store by its membership in the Preferential Trade Area (PTA) for Eastern and Southern Africa, which contained sixteen member states in Central, Southern, and East Africa from Djibouti in the northeast to Zimbabwe in the south. The PTA's main purpose was to stimulate regional trade by removing tariffs among its member states and by arranging for direct payment in their own nonconvertible currencies rather than using their reserves of convertible foreign exchange. In December 1987, the Ugandan government hosted the PTA summit of heads of state in Kampala where the decision was taken to eliminate tariffs among members by the year 2000. In his address to the United Nations (UN) in October 1987, Museveni had predicted that the PTA would help to create a single market among member states that could sustain industrial development (see Regional Cooperation, ch. 3).

The NRM government joined with five other states—Djibouti, Ethiopia, Kenya, Sudan, and Somalia—to form the Inter-Governmental Authority on Drought and Development (IGADD) in January 1986. The organization intended to coordinate projects involving drought, desertification, and agriculture in the region and to interest donors in their implementation. In its first few years, it did little to accomplish this goal. But it did serve as an annual occasion for the heads of member states to meet and discuss pressing political issues.

Uganda also joined the Kagera Basin Organization in 1981. The organization, formed by Tanzania, Rwanda, and Burundi in 1977, attempted to promote various development projects in the Kagera River Basin but was unable to secure sufficient financing to make much progress toward its objectives.

Kenya and Tanzania

A general climate of good neighborliness and noninterference in each others' affairs marked relations among the three East African states during the 1960s. But these ties became strained at the end of the decade, as Obote's tentative moves toward more radical domestic and foreign policies caused anxiety among the more conservative Kenyan leadership and drew praise from the socialist-minded Tanzanians. Amin's coup d'état in 1971 created a sharp break in Uganda's ties to Tanzania and upset relations with Kenya. Immediately after the coup, the Kenyan authorities forced Obote to leave Nairobi, and Kenya recognized Amin's government. The Tanzanians welcomed Obote and continued to consider him the Ugandan head of state until shortly before the overthrow of Amin in 1979. Kenyan business people took sufficient advantage of shortages in Uganda during the Amin period that Kenya eventually replaced Britain as Uganda's main trading partner. However, many of Kenya's exports to Uganda were actually goods transshipped from Europe and the United States. Kenyan business people were frequently paid in Ugandan coffee, which they smuggled across the border and sold to the Kenyan government. These ties were temporarily disrupted in 1976 when Amin suddenly claimed for Uganda all Kenyan territory west of Lake Naivasha on the basis of early colonial boundaries. A large number of Ugandan refugees, particularly the highly educated, found jobs in Kenya during the 1970s.

Meanwhile, the Tanzanian government supported an unsuccessful invasion of Uganda organized by Obote in 1972 (see Military Rule under Amin, ch. 1). In 1978 Amin sent the Ugandan army into the Kagera Salient in northwest Tanzania, where it plundered the area. The Tanzanian authorities sent their army to oust the Ugandans but, after meeting little resistance, invaded Uganda with a small contingent of Ugandan irregulars to overthrow Amin and install a Ugandan liberation front as his successor. The Tanzanian army remained in Uganda to maintain peace while the Ugandan liberation front organized elections to return the country to civilian rule. Officially, the Tanzanians were neutral, leaving political decisions to Ugandan officials. However, in early 1980, the Tanzanian army acquiesced in the removal of the interim president by Obote's supporters in the newly formed Ugandan army. After the 1980 election, President Obote discreetly distanced himself from the Tanzanian government and formed amicable relations with Kenyan officials and business people. After Obote was overthrown in 1985, the short-lived military government maintained friendly ties with the Kenyan president, Daniel T. arap Moi.

The Okello government engaged in a war with the NRM that few observers thought it could win. Moi successfully mediated peace negotiations between the NRM and the Okello government in Nairobi in late 1985. However, the agreement for the two sides

Ugandan foreign minister Paul Kawanga Ssemogerere meets in New York with United Nations Secretary General Javier Pérez de Cuellar, October 1988.
Courtesy United Nations (M. Grant)

to share power was never implemented, as war broke out a month later and quickly resulted in the NRM's seizure of Kampala. President Moi, together with the heads of state from Zaire and Rwanda, met with Museveni shortly thereafter in Goma, Zaire, but he remained irritated over the NRM's "betrayal" of the agreement in which he had invested much of his time and prestige. In addition, Moi feared that the example of a guerrilla force taking power from an established African government might give heart to Kenyan dissidents and that the NRM government might even assist them. He also regarded Museveni's government as left-wing and likely to make alliances with radical states, which Kenya shunned. A year later, Moi accused the Ugandans of permitting Kenyan dissidents to arrange for guerrilla training by Libya.

In its first year in office, the NRM government attempted to reduce the cost of transporting its coffee to the Kenyan port of Mombasa by shifting from private Kenyan trucking companies, thought to have connections with Kenyan government figures, to rail delivery. It also announced plans to shift some of its other trade from Kenyan to Tanzanian routes. The Kenyan government and its press reacted strongly by castigating Uganda, disrupting supplies and telephone service, and unilaterally closing the border on several occasions. In response, in the middle of 1987 Uganda closed down its supply of electricity to Kenya and suspended all coffee shipments through Kenya. It also accused Kenya of assisting Ugandan dissidents fighting in eastern and northern Uganda. For three days in mid-December 1987, there was firing across the border, and it appeared that the two countries might go to war. The two high commissioners were harassed and expelled. The two presidents met in the border town of Malaba two weeks later. They reopened the border, pulled their troops back from it, and agreed to ship coffee to Mombasa on Kenya Railways, but similar hostile threats and actions occurred intermittently over the next several years. In March 1989, the Kenyan government claimed that a sizeable contingent of NRA troops had invaded northwest Kenya and that a Ugandan aircraft had bombed a small town in the same area. Uganda denied both allegations, pointing out it had no aircraft capable of carrying out such a raid and that the "soldiers" were probably cattle rustlers who had carried out raids across the border for years. For its part, the Ugandan government claimed that the Kenyans were continuing secretly to assist rebels infiltrating eastern Uganda, and tensions remained high through mid-1990. Both leaders expressed their willingness to improve relations, however, and in mid-August 1990, Museveni and Moi met and agreed to cooperate in ending their longstanding animosity.

Relations between the NRM government and Tanzania were quieter and more correct, if not especially warm. The two governments were suspicious of each other when the NRM took power. On the one hand, NRM leaders believed the Tanzanians had supported Obote's efforts to gain power during the interim period before the 1980 elections and had helped him in his efforts to suppress the NRA during the guerrilla struggle. On the other hand, Museveni had admired Tanzania's progressive policies since his university days in Dar es Salaam. When the Ugandan government had asked a team of British military advisers to leave in November 1986, it replaced them with Tanzanian army trainers. Moreover, both governments strongly supported regional cooperation. Despite all of Uganda's public statements about developing an alternative route for its exports through Tanzania in the late 1980s, there was little it could send by that route until Tanzanian roads were rebuilt and the port of Dar es Salaam functioned more effectively.

Uganda's Other Neighbors—Sudan, Rwanda, and Zaire

Uganda's relations with its other neighbors were dominated by responses to serious domestic political conflicts within Uganda or a neighboring state that spilled over their common borders. After the NRM took power, the threat that it would support like-minded radical guerrilla movements near the border in each of Uganda's neighbors except Tanzania tinged interstate relations with deep suspicion.

Relations with Sudan had been primarily concerned with the consequences of the Sudanese civil war for the first decade after Uganda's independence. The Ugandan government regarded the war as pitting Africans against Arabs and thus tended to be sympathetic to the southern desire for secession. Thousands of southern Sudanese refugees fled to Uganda. Following the assumption of power by a left-wing Sudanese regime in 1969, Obote tilted his loyalties toward the Sudanese government in order to strengthen his own radical credentials. After this war was settled in 1972, Uganda's relations with Sudan became quieter. Many southern Sudanese took advantage of Amin's ethnic ties to southern Sudan to join the Ugandan army and take part in its indiscriminate attacks on Ugandan civilians. When Amin was overthrown, the Sudanese soldiers, along with many Ugandan supporters of Amin, fled to southern Sudan. There they were joined by 200,000 Ugandan refugees, mostly from northwest Uganda, during Obote's second presidency, when the new Ugandan army took revenge on them.

In 1983 a new phase began with the second Sudanese civil war, which was complicated in 1986 by an outbreak of fighting in northern Uganda between remnants of Obote's former Ugandan army and the NRA. Each government accused the other of assisting antigovernment rebels. After 1987 President Museveni became a mediator in an effort to arrange meetings in Kampala between the leaders of the warring Sudanese factions. In support of this policy, the NRM government announced that it would not export revolution and thus would not help the Sudanese rebels or give them sanctuary in Uganda. By 1990 the border had become considerably less significant in disrupting relations between the two countries because Sudanese rebels controlled most of it, because the northern Ugandan rebels who had used Sudan as a sanctuary were largely defeated, and because most of the Ugandan refugees in Sudan had returned home. In early April 1990, Sudanese ruler Lieutenant General Umar Hasan Ahmad al Bashir visited Kampala and signed a nonaggression pact with Museveni.

Rwandans had started to migrate from their overpopulated country to Uganda in search of jobs early in the colonial period. Four years before Uganda became independent, a revolution in Rwanda in which Hutu agriculturalists took power from their Tutsi (Watutsi) overlords resulted in a mass exodus of Tutsi refugees into Uganda. Many remained in camps, hoping eventually to return home, but the Rwandan government refused to accept them, claiming the country was too overcrowded. During Obote's second presidency in the 1980s, the Ugandan government regarded them as supporters of the NRM. A crisis erupted in 1982 when local officials in south-western Uganda forced 80,000 people of Rwandan descent, including many with Ugandan citizenship, to leave their homes and possessions. Refused entry into Rwanda, they were forced to live in refugee camps on the Ugandan side of the border, where they remained through 1990. Relations with Rwanda were again strained in October 1990, when Rwandans in the NRA joined a rebel invasion of northern Rwanda. President Juvénal Habyarimana accused Museveni of supporting the Rwandan Patriotic Front, and relations worsened throughout the rest of 1990.

Uganda's involvement in rebel activity in Zaire almost brought down the Obote government in 1966, although the Ruwenzururu rebellion on the Ugandan side of the border during the 1960s attracted little support from Zaire. During the late 1980s, however, when a radical Zairian group dedicated to the overthrow of President Mobutu Sese Seko, the Congolese Liberation Party (Parti de Libération Congolaise—PLC), became active in the same mountains, Mobutu accused the NRM of supporting it. Remnants of the Ruwenzururu movement established a working relationship with the PLC in 1987, and the NRM became the enemy of both rebel movements. As the PLC increased its attacks in Zaire from its sanctuary in the Ugandan Ruwenzori Mountains, Mobutu responded by helping former UPC politicians with close links to Ruwenzururu leaders establish an exile group in Zaire for the purpose of overthrowing the NRM government. Meanwhile, farther north there were intermittent clashes between Ugandan and Zairian soldiers, both as a result of the NRM's campaign to eliminate cross-border smuggling and over fishing rights in the lakes along the border. Large numbers of Ugandans, who had fled into Zaire as refugees during the Amin and second Obote governments, had begun to return to Uganda. But in June 1987, the United Nations High Commissioner for Refugees (UNHCR) program assisting them was closed. And in a bizarre incident that further soured interstate relations, Amin attempted to return to northern Uganda through Zaire in January 1989 but was recognized and held in the airport at Kinshasa. In the absence of an extradition treaty with Uganda, Zaire allowed Amin to return to his home in exile in Saudi Arabia, despite NRM demands for his return to stand trial. In September 1990, Museveni and Mobutu agreed to cooperate in resolving border security problems, but despite this pledge the border area remained unsettled for the rest of the year.

Britain

By virtue of its former imperial relationship with Uganda, Britain had special economic and political links with its former territory, although these connections eroded over the quarter century of upheaval after Uganda's independence. As British officials struggled to maintain ties, they chose to support the Amin and second Obote regimes long after most Ugandans and most other foreign governments had rejected them. Relations with Britain also depended on the attitude of different Ugandan governments, which balanced their need for loans and technical assistance against their desire to project an image of a nonaligned foreign policy. At independence Britain had been Uganda's chief trading partner and the queen its head of state. Irritated by President Obote's "move to the left" in the 1960s and by his vocal criticism of British arms sales to South Africa, the British government was delighted when Amin overthrew Obote in January 1971. Britain was the first country to recognize the new Ugandan regime and within a few months provided Amin with military assistance. However, relations were strained to the breaking point in 1972 when, without consultation or warning, Amin expelled Uganda's Indian population (about half of whom held British passports), forcing Britain to accept a large number of refugees despite its own restrictive immigration legislation. Britain responded by halting all aid to Uganda and imposing an economic embargo. In January 1973, Amin recalled his high commissioner from London, nationalized British tea estates and other firms (but not British banks), and threatened to expel the 7,000 British residents of Uganda. By March the following year, 6,000 British citizens had left Uganda, and Britain broke diplomatic relations in July 1976 when Amin's soldiers killed a woman hostage holding British and Israeli citizenship in revenge for the Israeli rescue of the other hostages captured by the Palestinians and held at the airport at Entebbe (see Military Rule under Amin, ch. 1). Nevertheless, despite the revelations of atrocities carried out by state officials, the British government allowed private firms to supply Amin with luxury goods paid for with Ugandan coffee until 1979.

Immediately after the Amin regime was overthrown, Britain recognized the interim government and promised aid and technical assistance. Later in the interim period, the British government sent a team to train the police, a controversial initiative that it has continued ever since. British authorities responded cautiously to Obote's claimed success in the 1980 elections, but once he convinced them of his pro-Western economic policies, they supported him to the bitter end. Despite Western governments' criticism of the Obote regime, as the behavior of the army throughout the country—particularly in the Luwero Triangle—became known, British authorities at first either disputed the allegations or kept silent, as they had during the latter years of the Amin regime. Then in 1986, despite their former support for Obote, the British immediately established close relations with the NRM. In November 1987, Museveni visited London, where he held talks with the queen and the prime minister, but at the same time, he continued to criticize their government for its failure to impose trade sanctions on South Africa.

The United States

The United States has had no significant geopolitical, business, or trading interests in Uganda, although a number of United States firms did a profitable business with Uganda, particularly during the Amin period. For the most part, the United States government has maintained a low profile, avoiding involvement in domestic Ugandan political issues, while administering a relatively small economic assistance program and seeking Uganda's support on several issues before the UN. For their part, the Ugandan authorities attempted to adhere to a policy of nonalignment that allowed them to criticize such United States policies as its intervention in Vietnam, while persuading the United States to expand its development assistance and to support an increase in Uganda's international coffee quota. After Uganda's break with Britain in 1973, the United States became Uganda's chief trading partner for a short time, but relations were nonetheless becoming strained. The United States Embassy was closed in November 1973 (although the Ugandan Embassy in Washington remained open), while United States firms supplied the government with security equipment used by the army and the notorious Ugandan intelligence service. In October 1978, the United States Congress ended all trade with Uganda. With Amin's overthrow in 1979, the United States Embassy reopened and provided emergency relief, particularly food, medical supplies, and small farm implements. When the second Obote regime indicated its pro-Western stance in 1980, the United States government responded with additional agricultural assistance.

The guerrilla struggle soon created new strains between the United States and Uganda, however, as the United States Embassy forthrightly reported to its Congress the pattern of growing human rights violations by government and army officials (see Human Rights, ch. 5). This issue came to a head in July 1984, when the

*President Museveni meets with President Ronald Reagan
at the White House, October 1987.
Courtesy Office of Presidential Libraries, National Archives*

United States assistant secretary of state for human rights and humanitarian affairs testified that between 100,000 and 200,000 Ugandans had been killed in the Luwero Triangle and that Obote's forces behaved much like Amin's army. The United States ambassador publicly added that under the Obote regime, human rights were ignored with greater impunity than under Amin. The Ugandan government denied the accusation and withdrew its military officers who had been training in the United States. When the NRM came to power, friendly relations were quickly restored. The United States aid program was reoriented to focus on immediate rehabilitation priorities identified by the Ugandan government, particularly the war-damaged areas in the Luwero Triangle and in the matter of the resettlement of refugees returning from Sudan and Zaire. Museveni visited Washington in October 1987 and February 1989 for consultations with the president and members of Congress.

Israel

Uganda had friendly relations with Israel until the late 1960s, when Obote strengthened ties with Sudan and tried to prevent the Israelis from continuing to use Ugandan territory to supply the southern Sudanese liberation movement. However, Amin, then head of the army and increasingly at odds with Obote, helped keep these supply routes open. Amin, who may have received some help from the Israeli military mission in Uganda in his 1971 coup, immediately restored friendly relations with Israel after he seized power. But in March 1972, after peace was restored in Sudan and Amin's request for military equipment was rebuffed, he expelled resident Israelis from Uganda, broke diplomatic relations, and established ties with Libya and other Arab nations. Israel promptly imposed a trade embargo on Uganda, and in July 1976, the Israeli government mounted a surprise rescue operation of air passengers hijacked to the airport at Entebbe by the Popular Front for the Liberation of Palestine (PFLP). Following Amin's overthrow, Ugandan governments, including Museveni, continued to support the African boycott of Israel.

The Soviet Union

As part of its proclaimed policy of nonalignment, Uganda established friendly relations with the Soviet Union in 1965. But with the exception of a few years in the mid-1970s when the Soviet Union became Amin's main source of military supplies, its involvement with Uganda was relatively minor. During the 1960s, its major aid project in Uganda was a large textile mill located in the town of Lira. The Soviet Union also provided limited military assistance to Uganda, and Amin's 1971 coup was immediately denounced by *Pravda* as reactionary. Soon after taking power, Amin expelled most of the Soviet military team, and relations between the two countries remained correct but mutually suspicious. After 1973— following Amin's break with Israel, the United States, and Britain— the Ugandan-Soviet relationship became far more visible. Hundreds of Ugandan army and air force recruits went to the Soviet Union and Eastern Europe for training. Soviet fighter aircraft, missiles, and armored personnel carriers were delivered to Amin. But the Soviet Union refused Amin's request for assistance to meet the Tanzanian invasion of 1979. The NRM government established cordial relations with Moscow in 1986, and the following year, the Soviet Union agreed to rehabilitate the Lira textile mill and donated US$50,000 worth of medical supplies to Mulago Hospital in Kampala.

Through its first five years in power, the NRM government's foreign policy was a blend of nonaligned diplomacy and a pragmatic search for economic and military assistance from donors across the military spectrum. But domestic problems, more than foreign policy concerns, dominated the political agenda. Establishing democratic structures at the grass-roots level and defining and implementing RC operations had not yet been accomplished by late 1990. Establishing peace nationwide and furthering the economic recovery also promised to challenge the NRM government throughout most of the 1990s.

* * *

The literature on Uganda, particularly on the past two decades, is relatively small but informative. There is no published guide to Ugandan political and administrative institutions, perhaps because the government has been in a state of flux for many years. However, Ugandan government publications are frequently useful in explaining both policy and the purposes of public institutions. The most useful sources of background material are J. Jørgensen's *Uganda: A Modern History;* G. Ibingira's *The Forging of an African Nation;* N. Kasfir's *The Shrinking Political Arena;* and M. Mamdani's *Imperialism and Fascism in Uganda.* O. Furley's "Britain and Uganda from Amin to Museveni" in K. Rupesinghe's *Conflict Resolution in Uganda* is helpful in setting out the changes in Uganda's foreign relations with Britain and the United States during the Amin and second Obote regimes. M. Mamdani's "Uganda in Transition" provides a useful interpretation of politics under the NRM government. Excellent sources for contemporary reportage include the newspapers *The New Vision* and *Weekly Topic,* both published in Kampala; the quarterly *Country Report: Uganda, Ethiopia, Somalia, Djibouti* by the Economist Intelligence Unit; and *Keesing's Record of World Events.* (For further information and complete citations, see Bibliography.)

Chapter 5. National Security

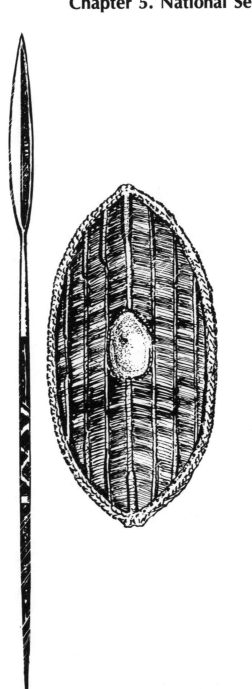

Traditional shield and spear

SINCE INDEPENDENCE IN 1962, Uganda has been plagued by recurring cycles of political upheaval, lawlessness, and civil war. The armed forces have played a significant role in political and social development throughout much of the twentieth century. In the years leading up to independence and for several years after that, military and civilian leaders competed for control. Civilian political institutions were unable to end the regional strife that plagued Uganda, and because they were also unable to address the basic economic and social needs of their citizens, popular support for the idea of military rule increased.

Under Idi Amin Dada's military regime (1971–79), several hundred thousand Ugandans died, many of them as a result of human rights violations by security forces. The violence, together with the practice of using the military to protect presidential wealth and power, destroyed Ugandan society. Amin's aggressive foreign policy also heightened tensions with neighboring states, and in 1979, Tanzanian president Julius Nyerere ordered his troops to invade Uganda. The ensuing conflict led to Amin's downfall.

Milton Obote's second term as president, from 1980 to 1985, followed a period of transition and nationwide elections that renewed hopes for democratic rule. Obote nonetheless failed to restore peace or stability, and as insurgent groups proliferated, the government unleashed another reign of terror against the civilian population. After a succession of short-lived regimes, Yoweri Kaguta Museveni's National Resistance Army (NRA) seized power in 1986 and pledged to end the political upheaval. But the military had changed from a standing force to a loose coalition of former rebel armies, and these groups continued to engage in military and political rivalries. By 1990 it was clear that economic and social reconstruction would be slowed by ethnic-based rivalries and rebel opposition well into the decade.

National Security Environment

Establishing peace and security in Uganda has eluded every government since independence, as each one struggled to create a unified state out of a collection of ethnic groups (see Internal Security Services, this ch.). In 1990 insurgents remained active in northern, eastern, and western Uganda. The government's dual policy of military pacification and offers of unconditional amnesty to recalcitrant rebels failed to end the fighting. Most of the south achieved peace during Museveni's first three years in power, but the government still had to divert scarce national resources to end regional conflicts that kept Uganda weak and divided.

Except for its ties to Tanzania, Uganda's relations with other East African states have deteriorated since Museveni came to power (see External Security Concerns, this ch.). Ugandan and Zairian troops clashed on their common border several times during the 1980s. Relations between the NRA and Sudan, which was experiencing its own civil war, also have been strained, primarily because of Sudanese accusations that Museveni allowed weapons to transit Uganda en route to Sudanese rebels and because each country harbored the other's insurgents and refugees. The Rwandan government has claimed that Uganda allowed Rwandan refugees living in Uganda to form an insurgent group and, with Kampala's help, to launch military operations in Rwanda to overthrow the government of Juvénal Habyarimana. Kenya's President Daniel T. arap Moi protested several times that Uganda was sabotaging the relationship between the two countries by launching attacks on border villages and providing assistance to Kenyan dissidents. These regional strains contributed to instability and drained the nation's resources and energy, but they were overshadowed by the domestic turbulence that plagued Uganda in the post-Amin years.

Military History

Early Development

Uganda has a rich and varied military history. Many of the country's precolonial societies possessed complex military organizations. One of the most powerful traditional leaders, Kabarega, king (*omukama*) of Bunyoro from 1870 to 1899, transformed his personal guard into a standing army (see Early Political Systems, ch. 1). This force used a variety of modern weapons, including Remington rifles, percussion muskets, and breech and muzzle loaders. Mutesa I, king (*kabaka*) of Buganda from 1852 to 1884, also raised a standing army, led by a general and several captains. At the height of its power, Mutesa's army of several thousand warriors had more than 1,500 rifles.

After Britain became interested in Uganda's economic potential in the nineteenth century, a group of British merchants created a small military force to protect their interests. In 1890 the Imperial British East Africa Company (IBEA), which administered the territory that would become Uganda, established an army to defend British investments there. This force of 300 included Sudanese soldiers (most of whom were recruited in Egypt) who were organized into a Zanzibar Levy. The following year, Selim Bey, who commanded a military unit for the German explorer Emin Pasha, agreed to allow about 100 of his Sudanese troops to join the British force in East Africa.

After Britain declared a provisional protectorate over Uganda in 1894, the colonial authorities formed a military unit of 600 regulars and 300 reservists, most of whom were Sudanese. Four Arabic-speaking British officers assumed responsibility for their training. In December 1893, Colonel Henry Colvile led a force of several thousand Baganda (people of Buganda; sing., Muganda) fighters and 420 Sudanese in a campaign against Bunyoro, Buganda's archrival. This "pacification" succeeded in subduing Bunyoro and secured for Buganda a politically dominant role in the protectorate.

Sudanese soldiers provided the mainstay of the Ugandan army, whose task was to preserve British interests and to launch punitive expeditions against those who rebelled against the crown. In 1895 the colonial authorities organized these soldiers into rifle companies, which became known as the Uganda Rifles. Despite the good reputation they achieved at riflery, many Sudanese became disillusioned with the rigors of military service in a foreign country under British command. Their grievances included loneliness, low pay, poor food, bad officers, and frequent reassignments, often to remote areas.

When the colonial government failed to resolve these problems, the Uganda Rifles mutinied in 1897, killing the commander of the force and five other European officers. Discontent spread rapidly through Uganda's Muslim community, which was sympathetic to the Sudanese soldiers, and violence erupted in several regions. Finally, Britain dispatched troops from India to suppress the mutiny.

To prevent another revolt, the colonial government diversified the composition of the military. It reduced the number of Sudanese recruits, increased recruiting among the Indians and Ugandan Africans, and increased the overall ratio of European officers to soldiers. The government also granted a 400 percent military pay raise. But by December 1900, military expenses were eroding the profitability of the colonial enterprise, so Special Commissioner Sir Harry H. Johnston organized a lower-paid constabulary of 1,450 armed Ugandans. The following year, to further reduce costs, British officials consolidated all military forces in East Africa and British Somaliland into the King's African Rifles (KAR). In 1903 the Uganda Armed Constabulary Ordinance and the Uganda Prisons Ordinance separated the police and prisons from the KAR.

The colonial authorities maintained racial separation in the military by assigning Africans to the Fourth Battalion and Indians to the Fifth Battalion. In 1913 the authorities disbanded the Fifth Battalion and supplemented the Ugandan unit with the Uganda Volunteer Reserve and Uganda Rifles Corps, both auxiliary forces that could be used to quell domestic disturbances.

The Fourth Battalion took part in several punitive expeditions and armed patrols in Uganda and neighboring territory. The best documented among these were against the Lumbwa and other peoples of western Kenya between 1902 and 1906; a mission to Lac Kivu, southwest of Uganda, in 1909; the campaign against Shaykh Muhammad Abdullah Hassan (dubbed the "Mad Mullah" by foreigners) in British Somaliland in 1909 and 1910; and patrols against cattle raiders in northeastern Uganda and northwestern Kenya each year from 1910 to 1915.

World War I

World War I transformed Uganda's military establishment. Its personnel grew from 1,058 to 8,190. Emergency legislation upgraded the Fourth Battalion to a regiment. Former Fourth Battalion personnel became part of the new Uganda Regiment, which eventually comprised six battalions. By the end of World War I, 16,000 Africans had served in the KAR and 178,000 had worked as laborers in the carrier corps, primarily in East Africa. The British government awarded decorations to 155 soldiers and mentioned the valor of many others in dispatches to the crown. Casualties in the Uganda Regiment included 225 deaths in battle or as the result of injuries; in addition, 1,164 died from disease and at least 760 were wounded.

Ugandan soldiers saw little action during the interwar years but provided garrison duty on Uganda's northern frontier and at Meru and Lokitaung (both in Kenya). The colonial authorities reorganized the Uganda Regiment several times, however, and reduced its size to about 400. It included two rifle companies, a machine-gun platoon, a marching band, and a battalion headquarters staff at Bombo. In addition, 169 soldiers made up a reserve force.

In 1930 British officials on the Committee of Imperial Defence combined the remnants of the Uganda Regiment with the Third Battalion in Kenya to form the Northern Brigade, headquartered in Nairobi. In the late 1930s, as World War II approached, Uganda's governor, Sir Philip Mitchell, established the Seventh Territorial Battalion to bolster security in Uganda while other troops conducted operations in Kenya. Northern Ugandans dominated the army, although all major ethnic groups were eventually represented in the fighting forces.

World War II

World War II again revolutionized the military. The colonial administration recruited 77,131 Ugandans to serve in nine infantry units, two field artillery batteries, and several auxiliary battalions. Ugandans served outside Africa for the first time, seeing action in the occupation of Madagascar in opposition to the Vichy government in France and the reconquest of Burma from the Japanese. In addition, Ugandans helped defeat the Italians in Ethiopia (then part of Italian East Africa) and worked as part of a military labor force in Egypt and the Middle East. They also garrisoned on Mauritius and at Diégo-Suarez on Madagascar and helped build defenses in Mombasa, Kenya. As in World War I, Ugandan soldiers made important contributions to the war effort and received many awards, including the Distinguished Conduct Medal, the Military Medal, and the Member of the British Empire Medal.

Following the allied victory in 1945, protectorate officials again reduced the army's size, demobilizing 55,595 of the Ugandan troops by March 1948. The remainder belonged to the Fourth Battalion. During the late 1940s, Ugandan troops deployed to British Somaliland and Kenya to contain local uprisings. In the 1950s Mau Mau rebellion in Kenya, Ugandans served in the Kenyan towns of Nakuru, Kinangop, Fort Hall, and Nyeri. As independence approached in both nations in the 1960s, Ugandans participated in joint police-army sweeps against cattle rustlers in northwest Kenya.

In 1948 Britain established the East Africa High Commission to administer its possessions there—Uganda, Kenya, and Tanganyika (which merged with Zanzibar to form Tanzania in 1964)—as one territory. The military arm of the High Commission, the East African Defence Committee, coordinated military policies, but the War Office in London retained ultimate responsibility for military affairs. In 1957 the High Commission assumed all responsibility for administering East Africa's military organizations and changed the name of the King's African Rifles to the East African Land Forces. This unification scheme was shortlived, however, and in 1958 Uganda's Legislative Council created the Military Council to help Uganda's governor administer the army's finances and returned responsibility for the military to London.

As Uganda moved toward independence, the army stepped up recruitment, and the government increased the use of the army to quell domestic unrest. The army was becoming more closely involved in politics, setting a pattern that continued after independence. In January 1960, for example, army troops deployed to

Bugisu and Bukedi districts in the east to quell political violence. In the process, the soldiers killed twelve people, injured several hundred, and arrested more than 1,000. A series of similar clashes occurred between troops and demonstrators, and in March 1962 the government recognized the army's growing domestic importance by transferring control of the military to the Ministry of Home Affairs.

After Uganda achieved independence in October 1962, British officers retained most high-level military commands. Ugandans in the rank and file claimed this policy blocked promotions and kept their salaries disproportionately low. These complaints eventually destabilized the armed forces, already weakened by ethnic divisions. Each postindependence regime expanded the size of the army, usually by recruiting from among people of one region or ethnic group, and each government employed military force to subdue political unrest. These trends often alienated local populations where nationalist sentiment was already low.

National Security since Independence

Despite a relatively peaceful transition to independence in 1962, Uganda became one of the least stable countries in Africa. Internal dissent overshadowed external threats, as seven governments were empowered in just over two decades of independent rule and opposition organized against each regime. The government response to its critics and opponents was often repressive: uncounted instances of officially sanctioned torture, imprisonment, and execution detracted from governmental legitimacy. The violence persisted, and abuses continued to occur in 1990.

The First Obote Regime: The Growth of the Military

In the first year of independence, the KAR was again known as the Uganda Rifles. The armed forces more than doubled, from 700 to 1,500, and the government created a second battalion, stationed at the northeastern town of Moroto. The traditional leader of the Baganda, Edward Mutesa, became president of Uganda and commander in chief of the army. Milton Obote, a northerner and longtime opponent of autonomy for the southern kingdoms including Buganda, was prime minister. Mutesa recognized the seriousness of the rank-and-file demands for Africanizing the officer corps, but he was more concerned about potential northern domination of the military, a concern that reflected the power struggle between Mutesa and Obote. Mutesa used his political power to protect the interests of his Baganda constituency, and he refused to support demands for Africanization of the officer ranks.

In January 1964, following a mutiny by Tanzanian (then Tanganyikan) soldiers in protest over their own Africanization crisis, unrest spread throughout the Ugandan armed forces. On January 22, 1964, soldiers in Jinja mutinied to press their demands for a pay raise and a Ugandan officer corps. They also detained their British officers, several noncommissioned officers, and the minister of interior, Felix Onama, who had arrived in Jinja to represent government views to the rank and file.

Obote appealed for British military support, hoping to prevent the mutiny from spreading to other parts of the country. About 450 British soldiers from the Scots Guards and Staffordshire Regiment responded, surrounded the military barracks at Jinja, seized the armory, and quelled the mutiny. The government responded two days later by dismissing several hundred soldiers from the army, several of whom were subsequently detained.

Although the authorities later released many of the detained soldiers and reinstated some in the army, the mutiny marked a turning point in civil-military relations. The mutiny reinforced the army's political strength. Within weeks of the mutiny, the president's cabinet also approved a military pay raise retroactive to January 1, 1964, more than doubling the salaries of those in private to staff-sergeant ranks. Additionally, the government raised defense allocations by 400 percent. The number of Ugandan officers increased from eighteen to fifty-five. Two northerners, Shaban Opolot and Idi Amin Dada, assumed command positions in the Uganda Rifles and later received promotions to commander in chief and army chief of staff, respectively.

Following the 1964 mutiny, the government remained fearful of internal opposition. Obote moved the army headquarters from Jinja to Kampala and created a secret police force, the General Service Unit (GSU), to bolster security. Most GSU employees guarded government offices in and around Kampala, but some also served in overseas embassies and other locations throughout Uganda. When British training programs ended, Israel started training Uganda's army, air force, and GSU personnel. Several other countries also provided military assistance to Uganda (see Foreign Military Assistance, this ch.).

When Zairian (then Congolese) aircraft bombed the West Nile villages of Paidha and Goli on February 13, 1965, President Obote again increased military recruitment and doubled the army's size to more than 4,500. Further reorganizations included the creation of a third battalion at Mubende, a signals squadron at Jinja, brigade reconnaissance units, an antiaircraft detachment, an army ordnance depot, a brigade signals squadron training wing, a records office, a pay and pensions office, and a Uganda army workshop.

Tensions rose in the power struggle over control of the government and the army and over the relationship between the army and the Baganda people. On May 24, 1966, Obote ousted Mutesa, assumed his offices of president and commander in chief, suspended the 1962 constitution, and consolidated his control over the military by eliminating several rivals. After Mutesa fled to Britain, Obote dismissed twenty-five Baganda officers for disloyalty and again increased recruiting in the north. In July 1967, to further consolidate support within the army, Obote created the Military Police Force under Major General Idi Amin Dada's command. Amin, in turn, recruited forces from his home region of West Nile among Lugbara, Madi, Kakwa, and people of Sudanese descent, who were known by the ethnic label "Nubian." Obote's rivalry with Amin toward the end of the 1960s replaced his earlier power struggle with Mutesa. These tensions helped polarize the rank and file in the military.

Throughout most of the 1960s, military expeditions often contributed to regional antipathy toward centralized control. Army patrols in northeastern Uganda often responded to accusations of cattle rustling and other problems, which, in earlier decades, would have been dealt with locally. Then when the government allowed Sudanese rebels of the Anya Nya movement to operate from bases in the northwest, army detachments deployed to that region to prevent an incursion by Sudanese government troops. Many Ugandans in the area who were of Sudanese descent remained skeptical about Ugandan nationhood and viewed the army presence as a military occupation rather than a security measure.

Idi Amin and Military Rule

On January 25, 1971, Idi Amin Dada took advantage of the turmoil in the military, the weakened popular support for the government, and Obote's absence while attending the Commonwealth Conference of Heads of Government at Singapore to seize control of the government. Claiming to be a professional soldier, not a politician, Amin promoted many of his staunchest supporters, both enlisted personnel and officers, to command positions. His favoritism received widespread publicity, as a number of laborers, drivers, and bodyguards became high-ranking officers, although they had little or no military training. Army recruiters suspended educational requirements for military service, sometimes forcing groups of urban unemployed to volunteer. After the army had established control over the civilian population, Amin unleashed a reign of terror against Ugandans that lasted almost until the end of the decade.

The army changed composition under Amin's rule. By 1977 it had grown to 21,000 personnel, almost twice the 1971 level. Amin killed many of its more experienced officers and imprisoned others for plotting to weaken or overthrow his regime. A few fled the country rather than face the mounting danger. Amin also increased the number of military recruits from other countries, especially Sudan, Zaire, and Rwanda. By 1979 foreigners accounted for nearly 75 percent of the army, exacerbating problems of communication, training, and discipline. The government barely controlled some army units. A few became quasi-independent occupation garrisons, headed by violence-prone warlords who lived off the land by brutalizing the local population.

Amin established several powerful internal security forces, including the State Research Bureau (SRB) and Public Safety Unit (PSU). Both terrorized local populations. By 1979 they had expanded to include about 15,000 people, many of whom acted as informers on fellow citizens. The SRB and PSU were responsible for as many as 250,000 deaths. Their victims included people from all segments of society and were accused of speaking or acting against the regime. One official observer estimated that two-thirds of Uganda's technocrats died or fled into exile during the 1970s. Amin also ordered the expulsion of the country's Asian community, which numbered approximately 70,000. These and other excesses drained the nation's human and financial resources; cash crop cultivation dwindled, most manufacturing ceased, and the economy collapsed. Social services, local government, and public works activities were almost non-existent.

By late 1978, Amin had laid the groundwork for his downfall by eliminating many moderate political and military leaders. His actions intensified rivalries within the army, which destroyed the alliance among factions from the northwest who had remained loyal to Amin. Sudanese and Kakwa soldiers then sought to weaken each other's influence, leading to violent disputes and mutinies within commands. To defuse these tensions, Amin deployed the rebellious Suicide Battalion from Masaka and the Simba Battalion from Mbarara to annex an 1,800-square-kilometer strip of Tanzanian territory north of the Kagera River, known as the Kagera Salient. Tanzania's president, Julius Nyerere, responded with force, and within two months the Tanzanian People's Defence Force (TPDF) had expelled the Ugandans from the salient.

On November 14, 1978, Nyerere ordered the TPDF to invade Uganda and oust Amin. About 1,000 Ugandans who had been in exile in Tanzania and had organized themselves into the Uganda National Liberation Army (UNLA) accompanied the TPDF invasion force. The TPDF–UNLA force numbered about 45,000. They launched a two-pronged attack supported by long-range artillery. One group captured the southern town of Masaka near Lake Victoria; the other advanced to the west of Masaka, moving northward through Mbarara and then east to Kampala.

By mid-March 1979, about 2,000 Libyan troops and several hundred Palestine Liberation Organization (PLO) fighters had joined in the fight to save Amin's regime; however, this intervention failed to stop the TPDF–UNLA force. Entire garrisons of government troops mutinied or deserted when they realized that Amin would lose his hold on the government. Finally, on April 10, 1979, Kampala fell. Amin went into exile in Tripoli, Libya, and approximately 8,000 of his soldiers retreated into Sudan and Zaire. The TPDF eventually withdrew from Uganda, and the victorious UNLA established an unstable government to restore peace and stability.

The Second Obote Regime: Repression Continues

Yusuf Lule, chair of the UNLA's political arm, formed the new government. He called for law and order and outlined a strategy to rehabilitate Uganda. To improve the military's reputation, he set new standards of literacy and political education for army and police recruits. To reduce the army's political role and build a truly national force, he proclaimed his intention to draw military recruits from all ethnic groups in proportion to their population. In achieving this goal, Lule hoped to authorize increased military recruitment among the Baganda, Uganda's largest ethnic group. Non-Baganda government officials opposed this policy. The National Consultative Council (NCC), which became the new legislature, and the Military Commission, which oversaw the army's operation, refused to support Lule's policies, and they voted him out of office after only sixty-eight days as president.

In late 1979, the NCC elected Godfrey Binaisa, who had served as attorney general under Obote and Amin, to form a new government. Binaisa, an ineffective president, failed to consolidate support within the military. His failure to do so allowed senior army officers to operate almost independently of the government. Rather than authorizing military recruiting among all ethnic groups, Binaisa allowed then Minister of Defence Yoweri Kaguta Museveni to enlist a disproportionate number of volunteers from his home region in the southwest. The use of regional and ethnic affiliation as a political lever prompted a power struggle with Chief of Staff David Oyite

Ojok, a northerner. Binaisa tried to resolve this dispute by dismissing Ojok. The Military Commission rejected this action, ousted Binaisa and the NCC, assumed control of the government, and called for national elections in December 1980. Milton Obote, who had been ousted by Amin's 1971 military coup, returned to the presidency. Obote called on the army to restore peace, but instead several ethnic-based military forces emerged to challenge his authority.

Among the groups opposing Obote were Museveni's National Resistance Movement (NRM) and its military wing, the National Resistance Army (NRA), both of which attracted members from western Uganda. Also working to oust Obote were the Former Uganda National Army (FUNA), most of whose members had served in the army under Amin, and the Uganda National Rescue Front (UNRF), which drew members from Amin's home territory in the northwest. In addition, the Uganda Freedom Movement (UFM) and the Federal Democratic Movement of Uganda (FEDEMU), both based primarily in Buganda, opposed Obote. To suppress these groups, the Ministry of Defence spent one-fourth of the government's recurrent expenditures in 1983 and 1984; nevertheless, these groups remained active against the government.

The UNLA mounted counterinsurgency operations in numerous areas, including Arua and Moyo in the northwest, Karamoja in the northeast, and Luwero north of Kampala. The army, whose ranks were filled with poorly trained, poorly clothed, poorly fed, and irregularly paid foot soldiers, had almost no ability to sustain counterinsurgency operations. The government's inability to maintain discipline over the armed forces allowed many units to degenerate into unruly gangs. The military perpetrated numerous human rights violations and engaged in several illegal activities, including theft, looting, assault, and holding civilians for ransom.

In pursuit of remnants of Amin's army in the northwest, UNLA troops entered the area and killed thousands of civilians, many of whom were women, children, and old people. According to a 1983 United Nations (UN) report, this reign of terror forced an estimated 260,000 refugees to flee to Sudan and Zaire. In the northeast, cattle rustlers acquired an army arsenal of automatic weapons and ammunition, which they used on raids in neighboring districts as well as southern Sudan and Kenya. In response to these raids, the UNLA and Kenyan authorities mounted a pacification campaign, which resulted in the eradication or displacement of most of southern Karamoja's population by mid-1984.

Despite its many illegal activities, the UNLA's atrocities in the Luwero Triangle attracted the most international attention. In 1980 the inhabitants of this region had rejected Obote's rule and welcomed opposition guerrillas, including Museveni's NRA. Until the end of the Obote regime in 1985, the UNLA waged war against rebels and civilians in the area, and the Luwero Triangle became known for its devastation. Several local officials estimated that the UNLA killed between 100,000 and 200,000 civilians and that it detained, tortured, and assaulted several thousand others. The International Committee of the Red Cross (ICRC) reported that 150,000 people displaced from Luwero had taken refuge in its camps.

By mid-1985 the demoralized UNLA began to disintegrate. Obote's promotion of Opon Acak, a junior officer from Obote's home region of Lango, to army chief of staff alienated much of the Acholi-dominated officer corps. The UNLA's failure to defeat the NRA, which had emerged as the strongest antigovernment guerrilla group, widened the gulf between the army and the Obote regime. On July 27, 1985, Brigadier (later Lieutenant General) Basilio Olara Okello and a small group of UNLA soldiers overthrew the Obote regime. According to Okello, he launched the coup ''to stop the bloodshed; to create conditions for viable peace, unity, development, and the promotion of human rights.''

Under the new government, which ruled through a Military Council, General Tito Lutwa Okello became head of state, and Brigadier Basilio Olara Okello served as the chief of defense forces. To establish a coalition government, Tito Okello invited all political parties and guerrilla organizations to cooperate with the new regime. In August 1985, members of FEDEMU, FUNA, UFM, and UNRF agreed to this proposal, thereby gaining representation on the Military Council. However, this alliance of former enemies proved unable to govern Uganda. The NRA took advantage of the weak coalition government, established control over rural areas of southwestern Uganda, and overran several military garrisons west of Kampala. The NRA also established an independent administration in former president Amin's home territory in the northwest.

The Rise of the National Resistance Army

On December 17, 1985, after more than four months of negotiations, the NRA and the Military Council signed a peace accord in Nairobi. But then, on January 26, 1986, using Swedish and Libyan military assistance, the NRA abandoned the accord and seized control of the government. The new regime won some popular

A Ugandan army Czech-made armored personnel carrier on parade
A Ugandan army military convoy
Courtesy Thomas Ofcansky

support by pledging it would end human rights violations, improve military discipline, and restore stability. Many UNLA personnel retreated into Sudan, regrouped, and reentered Uganda in August 1986, and Uganda was once again gripped by civil war.

From 1986 to 1990, the Museveni regime tried to end various insurgencies and to establish control over the army. Despite repeated government claims that the NRA had defeated the UNLA and other rebel groups, insurgent activity continued, especially in the northern, eastern, and western regions. In April 1988, 3,000 former Uganda People's Army (UPA) fighters and members of several other small rebel groups accepted a government amnesty by surrendering and declaring their support for Museveni's regime. In June 1988, the president concluded a peace agreement with Uganda People's Democratic Army (UPDA) commander Lieutenant Colonel John Angelo Okello. Although the NRA subsequently integrated many UPA and UPDA personnel into its ranks, thousands of others rejected the peace accord and continued to fight against the NRA.

Throughout most of the late 1980s, Museveni pursued a dual policy of offering rebels unconditional amnesties and intensifying military operations. In 1988 the government promised to pardon rebels who lacked criminal records if they surrendered; those who refused would be tried as "bandits" before special courts designated to deal with insurgents.

In February 1989, Museveni declared a three-month moratorium on military operations against rebels near Gulu. Army officers sought to improve political communication with the regime's opponents; as a result, a few rebels relinquished their arms. Once the moratorium expired, however, the NRA intensified assaults on rebel bases, and in mid-1989 the NRA implemented a "scorched earth" policy in the area. Troops moved several thousand civilians to government-run camps, and they burned houses, crops, and granaries in these depopulated areas. In early February 1990, the NRA tried to isolate rebel forces by rounding up some 200,000 civilians and placing them in guarded camps in eastern and western Uganda. This counterinsurgency strategy enabled the NRA to establish control over some areas, but it also eroded the government's domestic and international support, largely because of the high number of deaths resulting from inadequate food, water, shelter, and medical care in the camps. By late 1990, despite these harsh measures, a large number of rebels remained committed to the war against the NRM regime.

In the late 1980s and early 1990s, one of the most active antigovernment rebel groups was the Holy Spirit Movement (HSM) in north-central Uganda. Alice Lakwena, a self-proclaimed mystic who persuaded her followers that she could turn bullets into water, led the HSM from its formation in April 1987 until mid-1988, when she fled to Kenya. Her successor was Joseph Kony, also a mystic, who claimed to be in communication with a number of spiritual forces. The government-owned newspaper, *The New Vision,* reported that three HSM brigades operated around the northern town of Kitgum and that a mobile brigade of 700 soldiers operated southwest of Kitgum, near Gulu. In mid-1989, government sources reported that an NRA preemptive strike against the HSM–UPA alliance near Soroti resulted in one of the largest confrontations the NRA had encountered since 1985. More than 400 people died, about 180 were captured, and more than 500 HSM–UPA fighters surrendered; the government did not report NRA losses. HSM tactics then switched from battlefield confrontations to kidnapping citizens, attacking hospitals, and ambushing vehicles to erode popular support for Museveni. By January 1990, however, the HSM, which then called itself the United Democratic Christian Movement (UDCM), had reverted to traditional insurgent tactics by launching a series of attacks in Kitgum, Lira, and Apac districts. Later in the year, the HSM mounted operations in Gulu and Soroti districts. Although it enjoyed some local battlefield successes, the NRA failed to destroy the HSM.

An NRA counterinsurgency campaign in eastern Uganda had similarly mixed results. Shortly after coming to power, Museveni disarmed and disbanded local militias that had been organized to protect the region against cattle rustlers. The NRA also absorbed militia units, such as the FUNA and former members of the UNLA, into its ranks. Museveni deployed some of these fighters in the east, and although this tactic succeeded in extending government control into some unsettled areas, in many cases it also left these groups outside government control and weakened discipline within NRA ranks. As a result of the presence of these loosely affiliated NRA troops and other groups that remained outside government control, crimes against the civilian population increased. Much of the subsequent "insurgent" activity in eastern Uganda was little more than organized banditry as many former members of the militia— nearly all of whom lacked a credible political agenda—had decided that life in the bush was preferable to joining the NRA. Continued rebel activity, largely by the UPA, and well-established patterns of cattle raiding prevented the NRA from pacifying eastern Uganda in its first five years in power.

Museveni established good relations with Buganda by offering to reinstitute the office of the *kabaka.* Instead of taking this step, however, he referred the question to a constitutional commission, which, by the end of 1990, had failed to rule on the matter. Meanwhile, a number of Baganda reportedly took up arms to press the regime on this issue. By mid-1989, most rebel operations in Buganda supposedly had been confined to Mpigi, the district that surrounds Kampala, and Entebbe, the site of the nation's largest airport. The government deployed only small numbers of troops to confront the Baganda rebels, confirming the view held by many Western observers that the opposition in Buganda was more political than military.

Museveni tried to consolidate support within the army by filling key NRA positions with his supporters and by punishing soldiers found guilty of committing crimes against the civilian population (see Human Rights, this ch.). Nevertheless, there have been several coup attempts against Museveni. The government has suppressed information about these incidents; however, on February 17, 1989, *The Guide* published reports of five coup attempts since 1986. Among these was an incident in April 1988, when the NRA detained a senior army officer and more than seventy of his personnel for conspiring against the government. Other reports indicated that in September 1988 the NRA arrested and charged twenty-four people suspected of subversion and inciting soldiers to mutiny. Reports of factional opposition to Museveni within the NRA continued into the early 1990s.

The Armed Forces in Society

The armed forces have played a significant role in Uganda's political and social development throughout much of the twentieth century. In the years leading up to independence, however, and for the first few years after independence, the army and civilian leaders competed for control of state decision making. In the 1970s, this power struggle culminated in a military government, and President Amin used the increasingly ill-disciplined army and other security forces to secure his own power and wealth. Then in the early 1980s, the army changed from a standing force to a coalition of rebel armies. As these groups engaged in their own military and political rivalries, military discipline declined even further. Some Ugandans described the military as little more than a rabble preying on the civilian population.

In part because of the army's reputation for poor discipline, many Ugandans viewed Museveni's 1986 accession to power with skepticism. Although he promised to restore stability, end human rights violations, and use the armed forces to implement social, political, and economic reforms, opposition to the regime persisted.

The NRA nonetheless ushered in several important political changes, the most significant of which was the introduction of grass-roots political organizations, or resistance councils (RCs; see Local Administration, ch. 4). RC members, elected at the village level and several administrative levels above the village, were ultimately responsible to the National Resistance Council (NRC). Officials claimed this move marked the beginning of an effort to build democratic institutions and the end of state terrorism.

For many people, the most optimistic development under NRA rule was the promise to end the military's abuse of civilians. Museveni implemented the Code of Military Conduct, which required soldiers to respect civilians' personal and property rights, and directed army units to assist farmers in civic-action programs. Museveni also directed NRA officers to reduce the army's dependence on the civilian economy and to increase NRA self-sufficiency by raising cattle and cultivating cotton and corn on farmland set aside for army use at Kasese and Kiryandongo. These directives have increased popular support for the government, but have not restored the army's tarnished image in most areas of Uganda.

Constitutional Authority

Portions of Uganda's 1967 constitution remained in effect in 1990, especially those providing for a centralized government that vests strong executive powers in the office of the president. The president retains responsibility for maintaining national sovereignty and territorial integrity and overseeing military affairs. Article 78 designates the president as commander in chief of the armed forces and grants him the power to declare war in consultation with the legislature. Article 21 empowers the president to declare a national state of emergency after consultation with his appointed ministers.

Defense Spending

From 1975 to 1985, Uganda's reported military expenditures averaged less than 3 percent of gross national product (GNP—see Glossary) and ranged between 14 and 30 percent of government spending. Arms imports multiplied eightfold between 1977 and 1982, however, from about US$8 million to US$65 million, measured in constant United States dollars. Expenditures then declined to an annual average of US$11 million between 1983 and 1986 and increased slightly in 1987. In 1988–89, the government allocated US$40.7 million to the military. This figure represented a larger portion of government spending than in other East African countries but substantially less in absolute terms than defense spending by those governments (see Budgets, ch. 3).

Military Strength

By 1990 information regarding military organization and composition had not been published. As president, Museveni held the defense portfolio and controlled all military decision making. Western reports of military strength estimated 70,000 men and women. Budgetary problems apparently had prevented Museveni from achieving his promise of increasing the NRA's size to 100,000. No information was available on military organization; Western sources cited only six brigades, several battalions, and a Police Air Wing.

Military Service

Recruitment and Training

Both before and after independence, Uganda relied on voluntary recruitment to the military, although the government forced some people to enlist during the 1970s. Minimum age for recruits was seventeen, and the maximum age, twenty-five. Military service required the equivalent of a seventh-grade education, although this requirement, too, was suspended at times during the 1970s and 1980s. There was no fixed tour of duty. Army regulations requiring either five-year or nine-year contracts for recruits were largely ignored. Soldiers who sought to leave military service applied to their commanding officer, who could reject or grant the request. In 1990 military officials claimed that women served in the military in the same capacity as men, but the number of women in the NRA and their contribution to combat were unknown.

Northerners dominated the military well before independence. Their dominance was in part the result of British economic policies that treated the northern region as a vast labor pool for cash-crop agriculture in the south. Many northerners joined the army as an alternative to agricultural wage labor. Protectorate officials also recruited more intensely in the north. They posted most military recruits away from their home areas and among people of different ethnic, linguistic, and religious backgrounds. This practice was intended to ensure loyalty to military commanders and reduce military sympathies for local citizens.

Before independence professional standards for military training were high. During World War I and World War II, the protectorate fielded an impressive force, and Ugandan soldiers earned international admiration. Then during the 1960s, training standards declined amid the nation's political and economic crises, and military service attracted fewer educated recruits. Morale plummeted when British officers retained most commands, despite the fact that the government had tried to increase the number of Ugandan officers by granting some commissions after the officers had been given a crash course in military affairs. An increasing number of Ugandans found jobs more easily in the civilian economy.

In the 1970s and 1980s, most training facilities were located across the south. Many recruits also trained in other countries (see Foreign Military Assistance, this ch.). In 1986 Museveni pledged to upgrade educational requirements for military recruits, improve training standards and discipline, and override regional and ethnic loyalties that slowed the pace of military development. By late 1990, he had made only limited progress toward these goals.

Conditions of Service

After independence, several national leaders relied on ethnic quotas or preferences to fill the security services with those they believed could be trusted. Thus, during the 1960s, President Obote recruited many Langi soldiers from his home area in the north. During the 1970s, recruits from Idi Amin Dada's home region of the northwest dominated the rank and file at the expense of Acholi and Langi soldiers, many of whom were purged. In 1980 President Yusuf Lule, a Muganda, adopted a quota system to increase recruits from the south and allowed soldiers from Amin's home area to be harassed or expelled from the army. In the late 1980s, President Museveni attempted to halt this cycle of ethnic-based recruitment. He sought to recruit personnel from all regions, reduce the army's political role, and strengthen its image as a national security force. However, even this program of eliminating preferences created a backlash against attempts to achieve equitable regional and ethnic representation in the military.

Military pay, living conditions, and benefits varied widely under Uganda's diverse regimes. Under the British, military pay usually paralleled private-sector wages. After independence, however, life for the common soldier became desperate, and increasingly so in the 1970s and 1980s. Soldiers sometimes mutinied because of nondelivery of food and pay. Officers and enlisted personnel sometimes survived by relying on theft, extortion, or bribery.

In 1986 the government vowed to improve living conditions for military personnel. Museveni instituted pay reforms and punished soldiers found guilty of theft or bribery, but in the late 1980s, the common soldier's life remained difficult. Despite claims of high professional standards among government officials and military officers, many soldiers were not being paid regularly, and discontent in the military was growing.

Uganda's military justice system deteriorated during the 1970s. The Code of Service Discipline, which was incorporated into the Armed Services Act of 1964, had defined offenses and punishments and upheld military standards. It also laid down regulations governing trial and court-martial procedures in military courts. During the 1970s, however, military justice became subject to the whims of the authorities. Military personnel were often imprisoned or executed for poor performance or disloyalty, but in perhaps as many cases, military misconduct went unpunished. Conditions failed to improve during the Lule and Binaisa regimes of 1979 and 1980, respectively, nor did they improve during the second Obote regime from 1980 to 1985. In the late 1980s, Museveni tried to restore confidence in the military justice system among soldiers and civilians. Military tribunals tried members of the armed forces for crimes against civilians, and the government arrested and tried soldiers for thefts and assaults on civilians. In a few cases, soldiers were executed for these crimes.

Veterans

Before 1962 Uganda had a history of helping veterans reenter civilian society, but postindependence governments discontinued these programs. Following World War II, the government had paid veterans pensions and granted them a one-year exemption from poll taxes. It also had created a committee to help veterans readjust to civilian life. The Civil Reabsorption and Rehabilitation Committee provided teacher training programs and instruction in a variety of trades. The government also helped veterans start small businesses by providing subsidies for initial purchases of merchandise. In addition, volunteer members of the Uganda War Memorial Committee and the British Legion helped pay school fees for children of veterans. Old soldiers' homes provided nursing facilities for some aged and disabled veterans.

Veterans did not play an organized role in Uganda's independence movement or in the country's social and political life after independence, and veterans lost most of their former privileges. Economic development needs, political instability, and continuing insurgencies in northern and eastern Uganda prevented the organization of veterans groups in the late 1980s, but President Museveni promised to improve veterans' benefits once stability had been restored.

Kadogos

During the late 1980s, Uganda's most tragic military-related problem was the large number of children, mostly orphans, who

Ugandan soldiers, seven and ten
years old, on patrol, 1986
Courtesy UNICEF
(Yann Gamblin)

Twelve-year-old Ugandan
soldier on a march between
Kampala and Luwero, 1986
Courtesy UNICEF
(Yann Gamblin)

215

had attached themselves to the army. The government estimated that there were several thousand *kadogos* (child soldiers), most of whom were under the age of sixteen (see Social Welfare, ch. 2). Within days of Museveni's seizing control of the government, his press office announced that *kadogos* would be disarmed and enrolled in schools designated for that purpose. The first of these, the Mbarara Kadogo School, opened in February 1988, enrolling about 800 pupils between ages five and eighteen, according to the school's commander. An important government aim was to deter these pupils from joining anti-NRA rebel groups still fighting against government control. By 1990 *kadogos* were no longer evident in regular army units.

Foreign Military Assistance

Foreign Assistance in the 1960s and 1970s

During the years immediately after independence, Ugandan ties with Britain remained strong. Uganda was a member of the Commonwealth of Nations and maintained civil service, judiciary, and educational systems organized according to British institutions. A number of British military personnel remained in Uganda, including the commander of the Ugandan army, and each year two Ugandan students were admitted to the Royal Military Academy at Sandhurst. In 1964 Uganda called on British troops to help suppress a mutiny staged primarily by Baganda soldiers, but Ugandans soon objected to the continued British military presence, and the troops were withdrawn later that year.

Although relations with Britain remained important, Uganda broadened its foreign military relations during the 1960s. Israel, China, and the Soviet Union substantially increased military assistance. Israel and Uganda established diplomatic ties in 1962, and the two nations soon concluded agreements to train Ugandan intelligence, police, military, and paramilitary personnel. In August 1963, four Ugandans qualified as pilots on a Piper Super Cub in Israel. By 1965 Israel was equipping Uganda's security services, supplying small arms, light artillery pieces, and other equipment, and providing Israeli military instructors in Uganda. Israel also helped establish the Ugandan air force and equipped it with Piper Super Cub and Piaggio aircraft. After Congolese (Zairian) aircraft bombed western Ugandan villages in 1965, Israel furnished Uganda with six armed Fouga Magister jet trainers and three DC-3 Dakota transport aircraft. Tel Aviv also established training schools for Ugandan pilots, artillery officers, and paratroopers. By early 1967, Israel had seconded approximately fifty instructors to support this training effort, supplementing nonmilitary assistance for agricultural development and a variety of construction projects.

The government of China hoped to block Israel's efforts to gain a foothold in Africa because of Israel's pro-Western orientation. To neutralize Israeli influence, Beijing supplied a range of economic and military assistance to Kampala, but this effort was short-lived. In 1965 the Chinese granted Uganda US$1 million and provided a US$4 million interest-free loan. Beijing also sent some small arms and a military aid mission to Uganda. In late 1967, after Ugandan officers complained that the Chinese mission was "engaging in revolutionary activity" and distributing lapel buttons displaying the picture of Mao Zedong, President Obote asked the mission to leave the country.

In contrast to China's relatively minor role in Uganda, the Soviet Union eventually became one of Kampala's closest allies. Soviet weapons deliveries to Uganda began after the two countries signed a military agreement in July 1965. Under the terms of this agreement, Moscow trained more than 250 Ugandan army personnel, 20 pilots, and 50 air force technicians and mechanics. In addition, the Soviet Union supplied a squadron of two MiG–15 and four MiG–17F fighter-interceptors, airport ground support and military maintenance facilities, ground-to-ground and ground-to-air radio communication equipment, artillery pieces, and military trucks. All this matériel was free of charge, but Uganda had to pay for spare parts and ammunition purchased after that. By the end of 1967, twenty-five Soviet advisers were in Uganda helping to integrate this equipment into the Ugandan security services.

During the 1970s, the Soviet Union expanded its influence by increasing military assistance. In July 1972, a Ugandan military delegation visited Moscow and arranged to take delivery of a variety of weapon systems, including tanks, armored personnel carriers, missiles, transport aircraft, helicopters, marine patrol boats, field engineering equipment, MiG–21s, and radar. The next major Soviet arms deliveries were in 1974 and 1975, when Uganda obtained more than US$500 million in equipment. Significant items included 12 MiG-21s, 8 MiG-17s, 60 T/34/T/54 tanks, 100 armored personnel carriers, 50 antiaircraft guns, 200 antitank missiles, 850 bombs and rockets, 9 radar units, 2 Mi-8 helicopters, 250 surface-to-air missiles, 6 patrol boats, 6 mobile bridges, an unknown number of trucks and jeeps, and quantities of ammunition, spare parts, and test equipment. In addition, between 1973 and 1975, more than 700 Ugandan military personnel received training in the Soviet Union, while more than 100 Soviet instructors managed a variety of training programs in Uganda.

Ugandan-Soviet relations cooled in 1975, when Amin expelled the Soviet ambassador because of a disagreement over Moscow's intervention in Angola. In July 1976, Israel launched a raid on the airport at Entebbe that freed passengers who had been taken hostage by Palestinian terrorists. Embarrassed and threatened, Amin improved relations with the Soviet Union. Moscow resumed arms shipments and signed a series of technical and cultural protocols with Kampala, but ties became strained once again as the Amin regime began to deteriorate in the late 1970s.

When Tanzania invaded Uganda in 1979, a decline in Soviet military assistance forced Amin to look to Libya and, to a lesser extent, the PLO for support. Tripoli responded by sending large quantities of arms to Uganda, including three BM-21 "Stalin organ" rocket launchers and a Soviet-built Tu-22 bomber, which were used to bomb Tanzanian positions throughout southern Uganda. In addition, Libyan leader Muammar Qadhafi sent approximately 2,000 poorly trained members of the Libyan militia to Uganda. Several hundred PLO guerrillas also took part in the unsuccessful fight to save the Amin regime, which fell in April 1979.

Foreign Assistance in the 1980s

Tanzanian influence increased after Amin's departure. The TPDF maintained about 20,000 troops in Uganda to help restore peace. In addition, Tanzanian soldiers managed a large-scale army training program at Mbarara. By mid-1980, however, tension between TPDF personnel and southern Ugandans, especially Baganda, prompted Dar es Salaam to withdraw about one-half of its troops. Despite this decision and continuing clashes between Tanzanian troops and Ugandan citizens, President Nyerere then agreed to deploy a 1,000-man police unit to Uganda. By mid-1982, Nyerere had further reduced Tanzania's military presence, citing the high cost of maintaining troops in Uganda. When the training missions of the remaining 800 troops were hampered by misunderstandings and delays, they, too, were withdrawn.

Relations with Britain gradually improved after 1980, when Milton Obote began his second term as president, this time emphasizing private-sector development in Uganda's shattered economy. From 1982 until 1984, British soldiers in the Commonwealth Military Training Mission trained approximately 4,000 Ugandan army recruits. On August 19, 1984, Kampala and London signed a military training agreement that increased the British presence from thirteen to twenty men.

After a goodwill visit to the Democratic People's Republic of Korea (North Korea) in 1981, Obote signed a cooperation agreement covering a variety of technical, economic, and cultural areas. P'yŏng-yang agreed to deploy a military team of thirty officers to Uganda, primarily to manage maintenance projects and infantry training in Gulu. During the 1980s, the North Korean officers often led UNLA combat units in the field against antigovernment guerrillas; such operations reportedly claimed the lives of at least three North Koreans. The North Korean contingent left Uganda in September 1985, a few months after the military coup that deposed Obote.

Ugandan-Tanzanian relations improved after Museveni came to power in 1986, and Tanzanian military assistance resumed. In late 1986, about thirty military advisers replaced a British Military Advisory Training Team that had left Uganda. In January 1987, a British representative returned to Uganda with a small, nonresident training team, and a substantial, although unknown, number of Tanzanians remained to serve as advisers and trainers. Between 1988 and 1990, Tanzanian instructors managed portions of Uganda's basic training program. In addition, many NRA troops studied at Tanzania's National Military Leadership Academy in Monduli and the School of Infantry in Nachingwea.

Libya, which provided weapons to the NRA before it seized power, maintained cordial relations with Kampala after 1986 by furnishing a variety of assistance. In 1986 and 1987, Tripoli was Uganda's main arms supplier, and by early 1988, Libya had delivered an impressive array of weapons, including aircraft, antiaircraft artillery, multiple rocket launchers, and small arms and ammunition. Libyan security assistance declined in late 1988 and 1989, when the extent of Libyan military aid to Uganda was unknown. Estimates of the number of Libyan advisers serving in Uganda in 1989 ranged from several dozen to 3,000; by 1990, however, most Western observers believed that the Libyan military presence in Uganda was minimal. Unconfirmed reports accused some Libyans of racism against Ugandans in the NRA, but some military assistance continued, nonetheless.

After 1986 Moscow's relations with Kampala shifted in emphasis. Between 1986 and 1988, the Soviet Union provided more than US$20 million in weapons to the Museveni regime. In November 1988, the Ugandan Ministry of Defence began talks with a Soviet manufacturer to purchase an An–32 transport aircraft, but a year later, the aircraft had not been delivered. By mid-1989, Moscow had halted military aid to Uganda as part of its commitment to reduce its military role in sub-Saharan Africa. Thereafter, Ugandan-Soviet relations concentrated on economic and cultural cooperation.

In the late 1980s, Museveni asked North Korea to return to Uganda to train NRA fighters in the use of North Korean equipment. North Korean advisers helped train Ugandan military, police, and security personnel. P'yŏngyang also supplied a variety of military assistance. For example, a North Korean consignment of weapons offloaded at Dar es Salaam for transshipment to Uganda in late 1987 included Soviet-built SA–7 surface-to-air missiles, sixty antiaircraft guns, eight truck-mounted rocket launchers, ten armored personnel carriers, and an unknown amount of ammunition. Similar deliveries of military equipment continued into the early 1990s.

United States relations with Uganda lacked any military emphasis, but several private corporations sold military equipment to Uganda in the late 1980s. Museveni sought to improve ties that had been strained for more than a decade, and in response to these efforts, Washington increased economic assistance to Uganda. In 1990 United States officials implemented an International Military Education and Training (IMET) program that brought Ugandans to the United States for command and staff training, infantry officer courses, medical training, and courses in vehicle maintenance.

External Security Concerns

Uganda's relations with neighboring states except Tanzania have been strained since Museveni seized power in 1986. Although overshadowed by internal divisions, clashes have occurred with Zaire, Sudan, Kenya, and Rwanda. Accusations of cross-border smuggling were the most frequent cause of these problems, but in some cases, strains already existed because Uganda and its neighbors harbored each other's antigovernment rebel groups. Museveni generally tried to negotiate settlements to these conflicts.

Zaire

Historically, Ugandan-Zairian relations have been complicated by border problems. Border incidents caused by Zairian rebel groups operating from bases in Uganda have increased the strain between the two countries. Long-standing border tensions appeared to diminish in early 1988, largely because of diplomatic efforts by both nations. In April 1988, Ugandan and Zairian security officials met in Goma, Zaire, to resolve problems caused by the Congolese Liberation Party (Parti de Libération Congo-laise— PLC). PLC rebels, opponents of Zairian president Mobutu Sese Seko, were active in the Ruwenzori Mountains, which stretch from southwestern Uganda into eastern Zaire. Ugandans in the area accused PLC members of stealing vehicles for resale in Zaire. The talks produced an agreement to retrieve stolen property peacefully, when possible, and to deal with PLC rebels through official means.

In June 1988, Ugandan-Zairian relations again deteriorated when PLC forces mounted a series of attacks in northeastern Zaire. The PLC claimed to have killed 120 Zairian Armed Forces (Forces Armées Zaïroises—FAZ) troops and wounded many others. When the FAZ launched a counteroffensive, a PLC commander mistakenly led his forces into Ugandan territory. Ugandan troops arrested nineteen members of the PLC at Kasese, incarcerated them at the local military barracks, and registered a complaint that Zaire was failing to control its own political dissidents.

Tensions escalated in November 1988, when FAZ troops raided territory in northwestern Uganda, setting fire to several dozen houses and destroying property. Museveni's protest prompted Zaire to close the border between the two countries. Another confrontation followed when Zairian soldiers again razed several homes in western Uganda, this time in pursuit of fleeing rebels. A third border incident occurred in December 1988, when a FAZ platoon raided military outposts in northwestern Uganda, killing three Ugandan soldiers.

Relations between the two countries were further strained when former Ugandan president Idi Amin Dada appeared in Zaire in January 1989. Holding a false Zairian passport, Amin arrived in Kinshasa on an Air Zaire flight from Libreville, Gabon. He apparently intended to return to Uganda with an estimated 500 armed supporters who were to meet him in northeastern Zaire. Museveni requested the former president's extradition, intending to try Amin for atrocities committed during his eight-year reign. Kinshasa rejected this request because there was no extradition treaty between Uganda and Zaire. Instead, the Mobutu regime detained Amin in Kinshasa and expelled him from the country nine days later. Thereafter, relations between Uganda and Zaire were cool, leading to the mutual expulsion of ambassadors; on September 8, 1989, the two countries restored full diplomatic ties.

Throughout 1990 Ugandan and Zairian officials worked to stabilize their common border. In April the two countries agreed to deal peacefully with judicial, security, and defense matters and to apprehend and repatriate runaway criminals. Talks in July dealt with a variety of security, trade, poaching, and smuggling problems, but the failure of these meetings to achieve any progress prompted FAZ units to seal off the Zaire-Uganda border in October 1990. In late 1990, the border between the two countries appeared likely to remain unstable for the foreseeable future.

Sudan

Uganda's relations with Sudan have been strained, primarily because of long-standing problems with refugees. According to the United Nations High Commissioner for Refugees (UNHCR), an estimated 500,000 Ugandans fled to Sudan between 1978 and 1988. After Sudan's civil war began to intensify in 1983, several thousand Sudanese—perhaps tens of thousands—fled to northern Uganda. Resolving even basic logistical problems caused by the movement of so many people proved difficult, especially for two governments beset by economic crises. To help ease the situation, Khartoum and Kampala in April 1988 signed a memorandum in which they agreed to repatriate approximately 60,000 Ugandan refugees from Sudan. Those who refused repatriation were to be moved to camps well inside Sudan to prevent them from participating in cross-border raids into Uganda.

In June 1988, Uganda claimed that the Sudanese People's Liberation Army (SPLA), which opposed the government in Khartoum, had intruded into Arua and Moyo districts in the northwest. According to Ugandan officials, SPLA troops assaulted, kidnapped, and murdered civilians. They also burned and looted several villages, apparently in search of food and supplies. To lessen the resulting tensions, the Ugandan-Sudanese Joint Ministerial Commission in September 1988 issued a statement addressing problems of security, trade, customs, health, transport, telecommunications, and wildlife conservation, and the two governments pledged to work toward cooperation.

In November 1988, the UNHCR announced that the UN had repatriated 11,000 Ugandans, and the UNHCR reiterated the understanding that Ugandan refugees still in Sudan would be located well inside the border but could return home in small groups whenever they wished. The UN also carried out a two-month emergency foodlift from Entebbe to Juba in southern Sudan and delivered 5,000 tons of supplies to famine victims. UN aircraft also ferried emergency humanitarian supplies provided by Catholic Relief Services and Norwegian Church Aid.

Despite the substantial efforts of Ugandan and Sudanese governments and international relief agencies, the refugee problem continued to overshadow relations between Uganda and Sudan. In February 1989, the UNHCR determined that about 15,000 Ugandan refugees still in Sudan were waiting to return to Uganda. Almost 18,000 Sudanese refugees remained in northwest Uganda, and that number was increasing rapidly in response to Sudan's continuing civil war. Providing food, shelter, water, medical assistance, and transportation for this growing number of refugees threatened to drain both resources and energy from the Ugandan and Sudanese governments for several more years.

Despite Uganda's attempts to contribute to a peaceful solution to the Sudanese civil war and the conclusion of a barter trade agreement with Sudan in September 1989, tension between the two countries continued to mount. Sudan accused Uganda of aiding the antigovernment SPLA, and in November 1989 Sudanese aircraft bombed the town of Moyo in apparent retaliation.

Relations improved somewhat after Sudanese president Lieutenant General Umar Hasan Ahmad al Bashir visited Kampala in December 1989. The two leaders signed a nonaggression pact that committed each country to refrain from using force against the other and to prevent its territory from being used to launch hostile actions against the other. To enforce this pact, Sudan deployed a military team of nine officials to Uganda to monitor security along the common border. President Museveni also renewed efforts to facilitate the peace process in Sudan. Despite these steps, however, many Western observers remained skeptical about the long-term prospects for good relations between the two countries.

Kenya

Relations between Kenya and Uganda have been strained since Museveni seized power, although for much of 1988 and early 1989 Uganda and Kenya vacillated between cooperation and confrontation. In 1987 Kenya's President Daniel T. arap Moi had accused Museveni of allowing Libya to launch destabilizing attacks on Kenya from bases in Uganda, a charge Museveni steadfastly denied. Kenya nonetheless expelled the Ugandan high commissioner and closed the Libyan People's Bureau in Nairobi, and Uganda retaliated by arresting six Kenyan diplomats, including the acting high commissioner. A flurry of high-level communications succeeded in ending this incident, but each nation's fears of cross-border insurgency were heightened.

The year 1988 had begun on a positive note when the two governments agreed to establish a buffer zone along their common border near Busia. At about the same time, however, the NRM government alarmed Kenyan officials by announcing it was considering shipping imports and exports through Dar es Salaam, Tanzania, rather than Mombasa, Kenya. This plan would have cost Kenya transit fees and several hundred jobs in its transport industry, and suspicions of economic sabotage began to sour relations between the two countries.

A more serious problem occurred in July 1988, when several Ugandan soldiers attacked fishers at Sumba Island in Kenyan territory on Lake Victoria. Kenyan security forces responded and inflicted several casualties. Charges and countercharges were aired throughout the rest of 1988. There were also sporadic outbreaks of violence along the border and accusations that Ugandan vehicles were being detained or delayed at the Kenyan border points near Nakuru and Eldoret.

Despite some progress toward peaceful negotiations, the hopeful atmosphere was disturbed on March 2, 1989, when some 300 armed forces, believed to be Ugandans intent on stealing cattle, killed a Kenyan army officer in Kenya's West Pokot District. Kenyan security forces responded, killing seventy-two of the alleged cattle rustlers, by their count. Five days later, the Kenyan government claimed that a military aircraft from Uganda had dropped two bombs near a police post near Oropoi. According to the International Committee of the Red Cross (ICRC), the bombs killed five people and injured seven others. The Ugandan government denied complicity in the attack and suggested that the aircraft had originated in Sudan, a report that appeared to be confirmed by independent observers. Ugandan minister of foreign affairs Tarsis Kabwegyere sought mediation.

In 1990 the acrimony between Uganda and Kenya continued, especially after Ugandan police officials accused President Moi of helping Ugandan dissidents plan to overthrow Museveni. Relations improved after the two leaders met in August and agreed to restore full diplomatic ties and to strengthen border security. However, by year's end, the two countries again were at loggerheads, in part because of Kenyan press allegations that Uganda intended "to establish a Pax Uganda over central and eastern Africa."

Rwanda

The increasing number of Rwandan refugees in Uganda heightened tensions between Kampala and Kigali throughout the 1980s. The fact that many of these refugees had supported Idi Amin while he was in power provoked official displeasure and retribution during Obote's second presidency. In 1982 Obote, hoping to resolve the refugee problem and prevent challenges to his administration, expelled 60,000 ethnic Rwandans, accusing them of "antigovernment activities." Many of those evicted claimed to be Ugandan citizens whose families had lived in Uganda since the late 1800s.

Museveni, who was of Ankole descent but had relatives in Rwanda, had recruited approximately 1,000 Rwandans into the NRA

Ugandan refugee camps in Rwanda in the mid-1980s
Courtesy International Committee of the Red Cross (Françoise Wolff)

225

during the early and mid-1980s. Several journalists had reported that the Rwandans formed the core of the original NRA, and government critics complained about "foreign influence" over the national army. Rumors of Rwandans serving in the Ugandan military forming the Rwandan Patriotic Front (RPF) in the late 1980s alarmed officials in Kigali who believed that the RPF posed a threat to Rwandan president Juvénal Habyarimana. A few officials in Kigali alleged that Museveni had promised assistance to Rwandan insurgents in exchange for their military support in the early 1980s, when he was leading a guerrilla army in western Uganda.

In 1989 Uganda and Rwanda agreed to resolve their differences. In February, for example, Uganda agreed to naturalize a few Rwandans already living in Uganda, while Rwanda pledged to consider repatriating others on a case-by-case basis. In early May, Museveni and Habyarimana affirmed their commitment to resolve the refugee problem with assistance from the UNHCR.

Despite both governments' optimism that these discussions marked the beginning of improved relations, hostilities between the two countries soon resumed. On October 1, 1990, the RPF invaded Rwanda from bases in Uganda. The initial force, numbering a few thousand, grew to approximately 7,000, including roughly 4,000 deserters from the NRA and a number of Rwandan refugees. The RPF issued its Eight-Point Program calling for economic and political reforms in Rwanda, similar to those espoused by Museveni in Uganda.

As the war spread throughout northern Rwanda in late 1990, relations between the two countries became more strained. President Habyarimana repeatedly accused Uganda of providing military assistance to the RPF and preparing to invade Rwanda, charges that Kampala consistently denied. President Museveni, in turn, accused Rwandan government troops of conducting "hot pursuit" operations into Uganda. Repeated efforts to negotiate an end to the fighting in Rwanda failed.

Internal Security Services

Early Development

Ugandan police history began in 1900 when Special Commissioner Sir Harry Johnston established the Armed Constabulary with 1,450 Africans under the command of British district officers. In 1906 the Protectorate Police replaced the constabulary, and the colonial government appointed an inspector general as the commanding officer of all police detachments.

Although created as a civilian force, the police frequently carried out military duties. In 1907, for example, police detachments participated in internal security operations in the western kingdom of Toro and the eastern district of Bugisu. To support this expanded role, colonial authorities enlarged the Protectorate Police, and in 1908 they opened a fingerprinting bureau in Kampala. By 1912 the police operated fifteen stations and possessed a small criminal investigation division, a countrywide heliograph signal system, and a small bicycle pool for transport. The police continued their paramilitary functions, patrolling border areas between Uganda and German East Africa (later Tanzania) during World War I and patrolling Karamoja District to suppress cattle raiding and border skirmishes.

After 1918 the police became a more traditional internal security force. Most of their work involved homicide investigations; traffic control; and supervision of vehicle, bicycle, and trade licenses. Worldwide economic depression caused the colonial government to reduce the size of the police force from its 1926 level of 33 officers and inspectors with 1,368 in the rank and file to 37 officers and inspectors with 1,087 rank and file.

At the outbreak of World War II, the police again undertook military duties. In 1939 the Protectorate Police dispatched a garrison to Lokitaung, Kenya; arrested German nationals in Uganda; and provided security at key installations. In addition, the police assumed responsibility for operating and guarding camps for detained aliens. Many members of the police force also served in British army units in East Africa and in overseas operations. After World War II, the colonial authorities expanded the police force, and in July 1954, the Legislative Council established new police stations and posts throughout Uganda. The government also formed a specially recruited Internal Security Unit that subsequently became the Special Force Units. By the mid-1960s, there were eighteen Special Force Units, each comprising fifty police trained in commando tactics, normally assigned to crowd-control duties and border patrols.

Postindependence Security Services

Uganda's independence constitution in 1962 reaffirmed the British policy of allowing the kingdoms of Buganda, Bunyoro, Toro, and Ankole to maintain local police forces, which were nominally accountable to Uganda's inspector general of police. When the 1967 constitution abolished the federal states and Buganda's special status, the local police forces merged into the Uganda Police Force or became local constabularies responsible to the district commissioner under the inspector general's authority.

During the 1960s, the Uganda Police Force comprised the Uniform Branch, which was assigned mainly to urban duties; Special Branch and Criminal Investigation Department (CID); Special Constabulary; Special Force Units; Signals Branch; Railway Police; Police Air Wing; Police Tracker Force; Police Band; and Canine Section. Four regional commanders directed police operations and assisted the inspector general. The Police Council—composed of the inspector general, the permanent secretary of the Ministry of Internal Affairs, and four other members appointed by the minister—recommended policies regarding recruitment and conditions of service. The Public Service Commission, in consultation with the inspector general, appointed senior police officers. The Police Training School in Kampala conducted initial training for new recruits. In-service training for noncommissioned officers and constables took place at the Uganda Police College at Naguru, and many officers studied in Australia, Britain, Israel, and the United States.

By 1968 the Uganda Police Force was a multiethnic, nonpolitical, armed constabulary of between 7,000 and 8,000 officers and constables. In addition to regular urban police activities, it undertook extensive paramilitary duties, provided honor guard detachments for visiting dignitaries, and performed most of the public prosecution in the criminal courts.

During the late 1960s, the government increased its use of the police, and, in particular, the CID, to eliminate political dissent. Some politicians complained that this emphasis allowed street crime to flourish. President Obote also created the General Service Department (GSD) outside the police organization to monitor the political climate and report disloyalty. Some GSD agents infiltrated other organizations to observe policies and record discussions. They reported directly to the president on political threats arising from other government agencies and the public. Ugandans both ridiculed and feared GSD agents, whom they described as spies in their midst.

During the 1970s, the police force was practically moribund, but President Amin, like his predecessor, used a number of agencies to root out political dissent. More arrests were made for political crimes than for street crimes or corruption. Amin's government relied on the Military Police, the Public Safety Unit (PSU), and the State Research Bureau (SRB) to detect and eliminate political disloyalty. In 1971 Amin created the SRB as a military intelligence unit directly under the president's control. Its agents, who numbered about 3,000, reportedly kidnapped, tortured, and murdered suspects in their headquarters in Nakasero. Many SRB personnel were non-Ugandans; most had studied in police and military academies in Britain and the United States. Most served one-year tours of duty with the SRB and were then assigned to military duty, government service, or overseas embassy guard duty.

During the early years of the Amin regime, the PSU and the Military Police also acquired reputations as terrorist squads operating against their compatriots. In 1972 the PSU, which was created as an armed robbery investigative unit within the civil police organization, was equipped with submachine guns. Amin ordered PSU agents to shoot robbers on sight, but in practice, he exerted almost no control over them, and PSU agents became known among many Ugandans as roving death squads.

In the early 1980s, the strength of the police force was only about 2,500, many of whom were trained in Britain or North Korea. The heads of the four police departments—administration, criminal investigation, operations, and training—reported to the Ministry of Internal Affairs. The Special Branch of the CID assumed the responsibilities of the SRB. The Police Special Force, a paramilitary riot control unit, engaged in widespread atrocities against people who opposed the regime, especially in Buganda.

Another internal security agency, the National Security Agency (NSA), was formed in 1979. Many of its first recruits were former GSD members. NSA agents testified before human rights investigators later in the 1980s that although they did not wear uniforms, they carried arms, and many believed themselves to be above the law. Their testimony also related instances of torture and murder, as well as frequent robbery and looting. Detainees were sometimes held in military barracks, in keeping with the NSA policy of avoiding police or prison system controls. In the notorious Luwero Triangle in Buganda, NSA agents became known as "computer men," because they often carried computer printouts in their search for reported subversives.

When the NRA seized power in 1986, Museveni inherited a force of 8,000. A screening exercise revealed that out of the 8,000 personnel, only 3,000 qualified to be retained as police officers. The government augmented this force by contracting 2,000 retired police officers. However, at 5,000 this force was too small to maintain law and order. Museveni therefore ordered the NRA to assume responsibility for internal security. He also announced plans to upgrade police training and equipment, increase the force to 30,000 personnel, revive a defunct marine unit to combat smuggling on Uganda's lakes, improve the Police Air Wing's reconnaissance capability by acquiring more aircraft, and form a new paramilitary unit to bolster internal security.

In December 1988, Uganda's inspector general initiated investigations into charges of police abuse, in the hope of improving the force's reputation. In July 1989, he also announced the creation of new departments of political education, legal affairs and loans, and local government, but their authority had not been fully defined.

In December 1989, President Museveni announced that the police, then numbering almost 30,000, and other internal security organs eventually would assume responsibility for law and order in all districts except Lira, Apac, Gulu, Kitgum, Moroto, Kotido, Soroti, and Kumi—where antigovernment rebels remained active. He also announced plans to end the army's internal security mission as the police assumed greater responsibility for law and order. These changes would enable the army to pursue new training programs and, he hoped, improve morale. Museveni also directed the minister of internal affairs to augment police salaries by providing basic rations, such as food, soap, and blankets, and to investigate ways of supplementing educational costs for the police.

During the 1980s, Britain, France, North Korea, and Egypt provided assistance to the Uganda Police Force. British instructors taught courses on criminal investigations and police administration, and they trained future police instructors. British assistance also included equipment, such as high-frequency radio sets and Land Rovers, and Britain had agreed to furnish bicycles, office equipment and supplies, and crime detection kits.

In 1989 French police officials provided three-month training courses in riot control and suppression techniques. The first thirty Ugandans to complete this training became instructors for subsequent courses. In December 1990, another French team of five police officials trained 100 Ugandan police officers in antiriot techniques. Museveni also accepted North Korean offers of equipment and training assistance. By July 1989, P'yŏngyang had trained and equipped Uganda's newly established Mobile Police Patrol Unit (MPPU) of 167 officers. Despite British, French, and North Korean training, the government admitted that the police still needed specialized training programs to improve its investigative capabilities.

Criminal Justice System

When Britain assumed control of Uganda, the judicial system consisted of a number of local authorities, tribal chiefs, and kin group elders, who worked primarily to enforce local customary law. Islamic law was also practiced in areas of northern Uganda. During the twentieth century, British jurisprudence was gradually imposed, spreading more quickly across the south than the north. At independence the resulting legal system consisted of the High Court, which heard cases involving murder, rape, treason, and other crimes punishable by death or life imprisonment; and subordinate magistrates' courts, which tried cases for crimes punishable by shorter terms of imprisonment, fines, or whipping. Magistrates' court decisions could be appealed to the High Court. All courts had the privilege of rendering ''competent verdicts,'' whereby a person accused of one offense could also be convicted of a minor, related offense.

After independence the director of public prosecutions (DPP), appointed by the president, prosecuted criminal cases. Under the attorney general's direction, the DPP initiated and conducted criminal proceedings other than courts-martial. The DPP also could appoint a public prosecutor for a specific case. In some cases, a police official was the prosecutor, and the DPP reviewed and commented on the trial proceedings.

The legal system virtually broke down during the 1970s, in part because Amin undermined the judicial system when it attempted to oppose him. In March 1971, for example, when Amin granted the security forces the right to ''search and arrest,'' they implemented the decree to harass political opponents. The courts were then blocked from rendering verdicts against security agents through a second decree granting government officials immunity from prosecution. By absolving soldiers and police of any legal accountability, Amin unleashed a reign of terror on the civilian population that lasted eight years.

The end of Amin's regime brought no significant improvement in the criminal justice system. In an effort to reassert the rule of law, in June 1984 the government prohibited the army from arresting civilians suspected of opposition to the government, and it allowed prisoners, for the first time in over a decade, to appeal to the government for their release from prison. The army ignored the 1984 law, however, and continued to perpetrate crimes against the civilian population.

When Museveni became president in 1986, he pledged to end the army's tyranny and reform the country's criminal justice system (see Judicial System, ch. 4). He succeeded in granting greater autonomy to the courts, but the NRA also arrested several thousand suspected opponents during counterinsurgency operations in northern and eastern Uganda. In late 1988, the NRC passed a constitutional amendment giving the president the power to declare any region of the country to be in a ''state of insurgency.'' Subsequent legislation allowed the government to establish separate courts in these areas, authorized the military to arrest insurgents, permitted magistrates to suspend the rules of evidence to allow hearsay and uncorroborated evidence in the courtroom, and shifted the burden of proof from the accuser to the accused.

Prison System

During colonial times, the principal penal facility was Luzira Prison near Kampala, although jails were common in larger towns. Prisoners in Luzira were separated according to categories such as long-term convicts, ''recidivists,'' women, children, Asians, and Europeans. Cells for specific punishments and death row were also separate from the regular prison population, and the facility had several workshops and a hospital. The government also maintained smaller prisons for local convicts in Buganda, Bunyoro, Toro, and Ankole. Terms of less than six months were generally served in smaller jails located in each district.

In 1964 the Prison Service operated thirty prisons, many of which were actually industrial or agricultural facilities, intended to rehabilitate prisoners. By mid-1968, the Prison Service had a force of about 3,000 under the command of the commissioner of prisons.

During the 1970s, civilian and military prison conditions deteriorated, and prisoner abuse became common. At Makindye and Mutukula military prisons outside Kampala, for example, Langi and Acholi soldiers suspected of disloyalty to the regime were murdered. The PSU killed several thousand political opponents at the Uganda Police College at Naguru. At the SRB's Nakasero headquarters, some prisoners claimed they had survived through cannibalism.

Prison conditions in the early 1980s were also dismal. According to Amnesty International, the Obote regime imprisoned civilians without charge or for political crimes. Many were held in police stations, military barracks, and NSA detention centers. Almost all penal facilities were overcrowded, sometimes housing ten times the number of inmates intended. Other reports, however, indicated that members of the Uganda Prison Service sometimes treated inmates relatively humanely, allowing them to read, exercise, and attend religious services.

When Museveni seized power, he promised to improve the country's prison system, but this proved to be a difficult task, in part because so many people were arrested. In late 1986, the Uganda Human Rights Activists (UHRA) charged that the authorities had imprisoned as many as 10,000 people at the Murchison Bay Prison in western Uganda, a facility with an 800-inmate capacity. Moreover, the UHRA and Amnesty International claimed that prisoners lived in abominable conditions, which caused a number of deaths from disease.

In 1987 Museveni allowed the ICRC to survey conditions in Uganda's civil prisons. Although some reports suggested that prison conditions improved as a result, there had in fact been little change. In late 1990, for example, Chief Justice Samuel Wako Wambuzi condemned overcrowding in Masaka Central Prison. According to his investigation, the prison contained 456 inmates rather than the authorized 120 people. Similar conditions existed in most of Uganda's other prisons.

Patterns of Crime and the Government's Response

Patterns in criminal behavior and arrests have often reflected Uganda's economic and political setting. During the colonial period, most arrests were for murder, rape, robbery, and, on occasion, treason. People were also imprisoned for failing to pay taxes. After Uganda gained independence, however, crime patterns slowly shifted to involve more violent crimes. Attacks by bands of armed robbers (*kondos*) became common in urban areas. Then in the 1970s, this pattern shifted to emphasize political crimes. Many arrests and executions were not recorded, and statistics were unavailable.

Uganda's parliament tried to stop the rise of organized violent crime in 1968, amending the 1930 Penal Code to mandate the death penalty for those convicted of armed robbery. Parliament also amended the criminal procedure code to require ex-convicts to carry identity cards and to present these cards at police stations at regular intervals. A few months later, the government passed the Public Order and Security Act, authorizing the president, or a delegated minister, to detain indefinitely anyone whose actions were judged prejudicial to national defense or security. After 1970 the government increased its reliance on this act to detain political opponents.

Following the overthrow of the second Obote regime in 1985, the government freed about 1,200 prisoners held under the Public Order and Security Act. Some abuses still continued to be reported in 1990, despite government promises to end abuse by police and prison officials and to respect individual rights before the law.

Human Rights

Uganda's human rights record deteriorated after Idi Amin seized power in 1971. By the end of the 1970s, it was one of the worst in the world. Several hundred thousand civilians died at the hands of local security forces. In 1986 Museveni pledged to improve Uganda's reputation for human rights. To achieve this goal, the NRM arrested and tried soldiers and civilians for such crimes, and the government worked to improve its reputation for respecting human rights.

In May 1986, NRM officials created the Commission of Inquiry into the Violation of Human Rights to investigate these crimes under all governments since independence until the day before the NRM seized power. The commission examined judicial and other records regarding arbitrary arrest and detention, torture, and executions. Its hearings began in December 1986, when an investigation team and the commission's chief counsel, Edward Ssekandi, began selecting witnesses who would testify in public session. One of the most controversial witnesses, a former NRA political instructor, testified that political opponents were considered traitors.

A lack of resources hampered the commission's performance. Financial and transportation problems initially confined its activities to Kampala; later, these difficulties temporarily brought public hearings to an end. Although a February 1988 Ford Foundation grant enabled the public hearings to resume, the commission's final report was unavailable in late 1990.

In 1987 the president also established the post of inspector general of government (IGG) to investigate individual complaints about human rights abuses committed since the NRM came to power. The inspector general answered only to the president and had the authority to seize documents, subpoena witnesses, and question civil servants as high ranking as cabinet ministers, with presidential approval. Government officials had to cooperate with the IGG or face three-year prison terms or fines. Budgetary problems and staff shortages reduced the inspector general's effectiveness, and there were complaints during the 1988–90 period that his investigations were too slow and produced no results, despite lengthy testimony and evidence by international human rights groups and individual witnesses.

Several nongovernmental human rights organizations also worked to improve conditions in Uganda. The UHRA, for example, has monitored developments in Uganda since the early 1980s through its quarterly publication, *The Activist*. Initially, UHRA's relations with the government were tense after the 1989 arrest of UHRA Secretary General Paulo Muwanga for comparing the NRM's human rights record to that of the Amin government. Muwanga was subsequently released, and a UHRA report in 1990 generally approved of Museveni's human rights record.

The Uganda Law Society is one of the most vocal advocates for protection of human rights in Uganda. In 1990 a quarter of the country's 800 lawyers belonged to the Uganda Law Society. Apart from speaking out against human rights violations in northern and eastern Uganda, the Uganda Law Society has called for an independent judiciary, an end to illegal arrests and detentions, legal reform, and constitutionalism. A lack of funds and resources has hampered Uganda Law Society activities.

The Uganda Association of Women Lawyers works to inform rural populations of their legal rights, promote family stability through legal advice and counseling, ensure equal protection under the law for women and children, and promote Ugandan citizens' welfare by emphasizing laws that promote economic development. In March 1988, the association opened a legal clinic to help indigent Ugandans, especially women and children. By August 1990, the clinic had handled more than 1,000 cases dealing with property rights, inheritance, and a variety of family and business concerns.

To counter accusations of human rights abuse, particularly in northern and eastern Uganda, the government has punished members of the NRA convicted of assault or robbery against civilians. Several soldiers have been executed for murder or rape. Military officers even carried out some of these executions in the area where the crimes were committed, inviting local residents to witness the executions. Despite protests by several international organizations, these executions continued in 1990. Uganda's attorney general, George Kanyeihamba, justified the practice, insisting that strict discipline was necessary to maintain order in the military.

Despite these harsh measures, human rights violations continued in parts of northern, eastern, and western Uganda in the late 1980s and early 1990s. In October 1987, for example, witnesses reported that soldiers killed 600 people in Tororo District during an NRA counterinsurgency operation. People in the southwest claimed that the security services killed a number of school children in antigovernment protests and that as many as 200 villagers were shot for refusing to attend a political rally. Murders of people suspected of being rebel sympathizers were also reported.

In early 1989, Dr. H. Benjamin Obonyo, secretary general of the antigovernment Uganda People's Democratic Movement (UPDM), corroborated evidence of atrocities acquired by Amnesty International and other human rights organizations. He also charged that the NRA had "burned or buried civilians alive" in regions of the north and east.

Throughout 1990, according to Amnesty International, the NRA killed a number of unarmed civilians in the districts of Gulu,

Tororo, Kumi, and Soroti. Despite several government inquiries, Amnesty International claimed that no NRA personnel were ever charged with these human rights violations or brought to trial. Moreover, more than 1,300 people remained in detention without charge at the end of 1990. Government officials labeled most of these allegations "exaggerated," but it was clear that they were unable to eliminate abuses by the military forces and that Uganda would face mounting international protests engendered by such abuse.

* * *

Several comprehensive studies deal with the evolution of security issues in Uganda. The colonial era is covered in H. Moyse-Bartlett's *The King's African Rifles* and *Uganda,* by H. Thomas and R. Scott. A. Omara-Otunnu's *Politics and the Military in Uganda, 1890–1985* also assesses the development of the security services. A. Mazrui's *Soldiers and Kinsmen in Uganda* provides insight into the military's role in society. *Conflict Resolution in Uganda,* edited by K. Rupesinghe, is a compilation of papers by Ugandan scholars presented at a 1987 conference in Kampala concerning Uganda's quest for peace and stability.

Uganda's tradition of an open and lively press was being revived in the late 1980s. *The New Vision, The Guide,* and numerous other local newspapers report and comment on current developments. Numerous government publications also provide valuable information on the history of the security forces, conditions of service, and the effects of political and cultural change on them. *Uganda Journal* is useful for information about the historical development of the security services. For more recent information on the Ugandan military, see *African Defence Journal* or the National Resistance Army's journal, *The 6th of February.* Preindependence information on crime and the criminal justice system is available in the *Annual Reports* of the Uganda Police Force and the Prison Service. (For further information and complete citations, see Bibliography.)

Appendix

Table 1. Metric Conversion Coefficients and Factors

When you know	Multiply by	To find
Millimeters	0.04	inches
Centimeters	0.39	inches
Meters	3.3	feet
Kilometers	0.62	miles
Hectares (10,000 m²)	2.47	acres
Square kilometers	0.39	square miles
Cubic meters	35.3	cubic feet
Liters	0.26	gallons
Kilograms	2.2	pounds
Metric tons	0.98	long tons
....	1.1	short tons
....	2,204	pounds
Degrees Celsius	9	degrees Fahrenheit
(Centigrade)	divide by 5 and add 32	

Table 2. Estimated Population and Urban Distribution, Selected Years, 1978-90

	1978	1980	1982	1984	1986	1988	1990 *
Total population (in millions)	12.3	13.2	14.1	15.2	16.2	15.9	16.9
Percentage urban	8.5	8.7	9.0	9.3	9.7	n.a.	10.0

n.a.—not available.

* Official estimate.

239

Table 3. Enrollment in Government-Aided Educational Institutions,
Selected Years, 1965–89
(in thousands)

Institutions	1965	1970	1975	1980	1985	1989 [1]
Primary schools	580	727	918	1,292	2,117	2,532
Secondary schools	16	37	46 [2]	75 [2]	160 [2]	265
Makerere University ..	0.9	2.6	3.4	4.0	5.3	6.3
Other higher institutions [3]	n.a.	n.a.	n.a.	n.a.	1.7 [4]	2.6

n.a.—not available.
[1] Provisional.
[2] O-level and A-level only.
[3] Institute of Teachers' Education, National College of Business Studies, and Uganda Polytechnic.
[4] 1986 figure.

Table 4. Gross Domestic Product (GDP) by Sector, 1984–89
(in millions of [new] Uganda shillings) [1]

Sector	1984	1985	1986	1987	1988	1989
Monetary economy						
Agriculture	1,799	5,384	13,122	44,631	125,604	244,408
Forestry and fishing	136	267	629	3,038	10,442	16,336
Mining	8	14	24	34	35	37
Manufacturing	254	518	1,655	6,734	22,630	40,840
Electricity and water	15	32	37	130	558	1,459
Construction	13	223	378	2,999	12,918	27,422
Retail and wholesale trade	862	2,382	5,830	18,977	61,829	122,680
Transportation and communications	317	620	1,413	5,812	14,700	39,919
Government	1,193	2,090	2,491	7,126	17,963	38,607
Miscellaneous services	17	39	84	512	1,782	3,638
Rents	189	443	1,301	4,588	13,560	25,760
Total monetary economy	4,903	12,012	26,964	94,581	282,021	561,106
Nonmonetary economy						
Agriculture	3,108	8,803	21,766	73,156	189,474	399,282
Forestry and fishing	66	171	438	1,469	4,532	6,191
Construction	9	21	44	262	896	1,788
Owner-occupied dwellings	214	495	1,432	4,975	14,509	27,212
Total nonmonetary economy	3,397	9,490	23,680	79,862	209,411	434,473
TOTAL	8,300	21,502	50,644	174,443	491,432	995,579
GDP per capita [2]	581	1,465	3,355	11,245	30,819	60,711

[1] For value of the (new) Uganda shilling—see Glossary. All figures are quoted in (new) Uganda shillings, created in May 1987.

[2] In thousands of (new) Uganda shillings.

Source: Based on information from Uganda, Ministry of Planning and Economic Development, *Background to the Budget, 1990–1991,* Kampala, 1990, 158.

Table 5. Development Allocations by Sector, Fiscal Years 1988–91
(in millions of United States dollars)

Sector	Planned Spending	Percentage of Total	Funding as of March 1988	Balance
Transportation and communications ...	378.7	29.4	171.0	207.7
Agriculture	314.5	24.4	186.8	127.7
Industry and tourism	271.9	21.1	93.7	178.2
Social infrastructure	221.0	17.2	90.8	130.2
Mining and energy	89.2	6.9	53.4	35.8
Public administration	13.2	1.0	1.2	12.0
TOTAL	1,288.5	100.0	596.9	691.6

Source: Based on information from Economist Intelligence Unit, *Country Profile: Uganda, 1989–90,* London, 1989, 10.

Table 6. Agricultural Production, 1984–89
(in thousands of tons unless otherwise indicated)

	1984	1985	1986	1987	1988	1989
Export crops						
Cocoa	0.3	0.2	0.1	0.1	0.2	0.5
Coffee	138.7	155.0	143.3	159.4	153.6	174.0
Cotton	12.2	16.3	4.4	2.9	1.8	2.6
Sugar (raw)	2.4	0.8	n.a.	n.a.	7.5	15.9
Tea	5.2	5.6	3.3	3.5	3.5	4.6
Tobacco	2.0	1.5	0.9	1.3	2.5	3.8
Food crops						
Cereals	944	1,171	1,058	1,220	1,398	1,619 [1]
Oilseeds	149	134	163	163	184	206 [1]
Plantains	6,250	6,468	6,565	7,039	7,293	7,469 [1]
Pulses	372	338	346	374	430	485 [1]
Root crops	4,731	4,532	4,863	4,960	5,177	5,474 [1]
Fish catch	212.3	160.8	200.9	149.7	214.3	213.5
Livestock [2]						
Cattle	4,993	5,000	5,200	3,905	4,260	4,184
Goats	3,091	3,246	3,300	2,503	2,110	2,280
Pigs	227	238	250	470	452	553
Poultry	1,200	3,000	5,000	8,330	n.a.	n.a.
Sheep	1,602	1,674	1,680	683 [3]	690 [3]	644 [3]

n.a.—not available
[1] Estimate.
[2] In thousands.
[3] As reported.

Source: Based on information from Uganda, Ministry of Planning and Economic Development, *Background to the Budget, 1990–1991,* Kampala, 1990, 194, 195, 197, 198.

Table 7. Foreign Trade, 1984-89
(in millions of United States dollars)

	1984	1985	1986	1987	1988	1989
Exports						
Coffee	359.6	348.5	394.2	311.1	264.3	263.6
Cotton	12.1	13.4	4.9	4.1	3.1	4.0
Corn	8.9	2.9	0.0	0.0	0.3	0.0
Tea	3.3	1.0	3.1	1.9	1.2	3.1
Tobacco	1.5	0.4	0.0	0.0	0.6	1.5
Total exports, including other ...	407.9	379.0	406.7	333.7	272.9	251.5
Imports	342.2	264.1	476.0	634.5	627.4	659.1
Trade balance	65.7	114.9	−69.3	−300.8	−354.5	−407.6

Source: Based on information from Uganda, Ministry of Planning and Economic Development, *Background to the Budget, 1990-1991,* Kampala, 1990, 162-63; and Economist Intelligence Unit, *Country Profile: Uganda, 1989-90,* London, 1989, 26.

Table 8. Official Development Assistance (ODA), 1984-88
(in millions of United States dollars)

	1984	1985	1986	1987	1988
Bilateral	50.1	45.5	88.0	92.7	195.4
Multilateral	119.3	143.0	120.3	193.0	180.9
TOTAL (ODA)	169.4	188.5	208.3	285.7	376.3
Of which, grants	98.5	84.0	131.5	153.5	257.8

Source: Based on information from Organisation for Economic Co-operation and Development, *Geographical Distribution of Financial Flows to Developing Countries,* Paris, 1990, 285.

Bibliography

Chapter 1

Apter, David E. *The Political Kingdom in Uganda*. (2d ed.) Princeton: Princeton University Press, 1967.

Atkinson, R. "Adaptation and Change in Acholi, 1850-1900." (Research paper.) Kampala: Makerere University 1971.

_____. "State Formation and Development in Western Acholi." (Research paper.) Kampala: Makerere University, 1971.

Avirgan, Tony, and Martha Honey. *War in Uganda: The Legacy of Idi Amin*. Westport, Connecticut: Hill, 1982.

Baker, Samuel W. *Ismailia: A Narrative of the Expedition to Central Africa*. London: Macmillan, 1874. Reprint. New York: Negro Universities Press, 1969.

Davidson, Basil. *A History of East and Central Africa to the Late 19th Century*. Garden City, New York: Anchor Books, 1969.

Dunbar, A.R. *A History of Bunyoro-Kitara*. (Rev. ed.) Nairobi: Oxford University Press on behalf of Makerere Institute of Social Research, 1969.

Ehrlich, Cyril. "The Uganda Economy, 1903-1945." Pages 395-475 in Vincent Harlow and E.M. Chilver (eds.), *History of East Africa*, 2. London: Oxford University Press, 1965.

Furley, Oliver W. "Britain and Uganda from Amin to Museveni: Blind Eye Diplomacy." Pages 275-94 in Kumar Rupesinghe (ed.), *Conflict Resolution in Uganda*. Athens: Ohio University Press, 1989.

Gertzel, Cherry. "Kingdoms, Districts, and the Unitary State, Uganda 1945-1962." Pages 65-106 in D.A. Low and Alison Smith (eds.), *History of East Africa*, 3. London: Oxford University Press, 1976.

_____. *Party and Locality in Northern Uganda, 1945-1962*. London: Athlone Press, 1974.

Hansen, Holger Bernt. *Mission, Church, and State in a Colonial Setting: Uganda, 1890-1925*. New York: St. Martin's Press, 1984.

Hansen, Holger Bernt, and Michael Twaddle (eds.). *Uganda Now: Between Decay and Development*. Athens: Ohio University Press, 1988.

Harlow, Vincent, and E.M. Chilver (eds.). *History of East Africa*, 2. London: Oxford University Press, 1965.

Ibingira, G.S.K. *The Forging of an African Nation: The Political and Constitutional Evolution of Uganda from Colonial Rule to Independence, 1894-1962*. New York: Viking Press, 1973.

Ingham, Kenneth. *The Making of Modern Uganda.* Westport, Connecticut: Greenwood Press, 1983.

International Commission of Jurists. *Uganda and Human Rights.* (Report to the United Nations Commission on Human Rights.) Geneva: 1977.

Jørgensen, Jan Jelmert. *Uganda: A Modern History.* New York: St. Martin's Press, 1981.

Karugire, Samwiri Rubaraza. *A Political History of Uganda.* Exeter, New Hampshire: Heinemann Educational Books, 1980.

Kasfir, Nelson. *The Shrinking Political Arena: Participation and Ethnicity in African Politics.* Berkeley: University of California Press, 1976.

Kendall, R.L. "An Ecological History of the Lake Victoria Basin." (Ecological Monograph No. 39.) Nairobi: East African, 1969.

Kiwanuka, M.S.M. Semakula (ed.). *The Kings of Buganda.* Nairobi: East African, 1971.

Kyemba, Henry. *A State of Blood: The Inside Story of Idi Amin.* New York: Grosset and Dunlap, 1977.

Langlands, B.W. *Sleeping Sickness in Uganda, 1900-1920.* (Occasional Paper No. 1.) Kampala: Department of Geography, Makerere University, 1967.

Law of Uganda, 1969: Statutes. Entebbe: Government Printer, 1967.

Low, D.A. *Buganda in Modern History.* Berkeley: University of California Press, 1971.

———. "The Northern Interior, 1840-44." Pages 297-351 in Roland Oliver and Gervase Mathews (eds.), *History of East Africa,* 1. London: Oxford University Press, 1963.

———. "Uganda: The Establishment of the Protectorate, 1894-1919." Pages 57-120 in Vincent Harlow and E.M. Chilver (eds.), *History of East Africa,* 2. London: Oxford University Press, 1965.

Low, D.A., and Robert Cranford Pratt (eds.). *Buganda and British Overrule, 1900-1955.* Nairobi: Oxford University Press, 1960.

Low, D.A., and Alison Smith (eds.). *History of East Africa,* 3. London: Oxford University Press, 1976.

Martin, David. *General Amin.* London: Faber and Faber, 1974.

Mazrui, Ali. *Soldiers and Kinsmen in Uganda.* Beverly Hills: Sage, 1975.

Minority Rights Group. *Uganda and Sudan—North and South.* (Report No. 66.) London: 1984.

Mudoola, Dan. "Communal Conflict in the Military and Its Political Consequences." Pages 116-40 in Kumar Rupesinghe (ed.), *Conflict Resolution in Uganda.* Athens: Ohio University Press, 1989.

Mutesa II, Edward. *Desecration of My Kingdom.* London: Constable, 1967.

Ogot, Bethwell A., and J.A. Kieran (eds.). *Zamani: A Survey of East African History.* New York: Humanities Press, 1968.

Oliver, Roland, and Gervase Mathew (eds.). *History of East Africa,* 1. London: Oxford University Press, 1963.

Omara-Otunnu, Amii. *Politics and the Military in Uganda, 1890–1985.* New York: St. Martin's Press, 1987.

Pratt, C. "The Politics of Indirect Rule: Uganda 1900–1955." Pages 161–366 in D.A. Low and Robert Cranford Pratt (eds.), *Buganda and British Overrule, 1900–1955.* Nairobi: Oxford University Press, 1960.

Roberts, A. "The Sub-Imperialism of the Baganda," *Journal of African History,* 8, No. 3, 1962, 435–50.

Roscoe, J. *The Baganda: Their Customs and Beliefs.* London: Cass, 1965.

Rothchild, Donald, and Michael Rogin. "Uganda." Pages 337–40 in Gwendolyn M. Carter (ed.), *National Unity and Regionalism in Eight African States.* Ithaca: Cornell University Press, 1966.

Rowe, John A. "The Baganda Revolutionaries," *Tarikh* [Ikeja, Nigeria], 3, No. 2, 1970, 34–46.

———. "Islam under Idi Amin: A Case of Déja Vu?" Pages 267–79 in Holger Bernt Hansen and Michael Twaddle (eds.), *Uganda Now: Between Decay and Development.* Athens: Ohio University Press, 1988.

———. *Lugard at Kampala.* Kampala: Longmans of Uganda, 1969.

———. "Revolution in Buganda." (Ph.D. dissertation.) Madison: University of Wisconsin, 1966.

Rupesinghe, Kumar (ed.). *Conflict Resolution in Uganda.* Athens: Ohio University Press, 1989.

Sathyamurthy, T.V. *The Political Development of Uganda, 1900–1986.* Brookfield, Vermont: Gower, 1986.

Smith, George Ivan. *Ghosts of Kampala.* London: Weidenfeld and Nicolson, 1980.

Speke, John Hanning. *Journal of the Discovery of the Source of the Nile.* London: Blackwood, 1863. Reprint. New York: Greenwood Press, 1969.

———. *What Led to the Discovery of the Source of the Nile.* London: Blackwood, 1864. Reprint. London: Cass, 1967.

Stanley, Henry M. *Through the Dark Continent.* New York: Harper, 1879. Reprint. New York: Greenwood Press, 1969.

Twaddle, Michael (ed.). *Expulsion of a Minority: Essays on the Ugandan Asians.* London: Athlone Press, 1975.

United States. Congress. 96th, 1st Session. House of Representatives. Committee on Foreign Affairs. Subcommittee on Africa. *U.S. Policy Toward Uganda.* Washington: GPO, 1979.

van Zwanenberg, R.M.A., and Anne King. *An Economic History of Kenya and Uganda, 1800–1970.* London: Macmillan, 1975.

Welbourn, F.B. *Religion and Politics in Uganda, 1952–1962.* (Historical Series No. 1.) Nairobi: East African, 1965.

Were, Gideon S. "The Western Bantu Peoples from A.D. 1300 to 1800." Pages 177–97 in Bethwell A. Ogot and J.A. Kieran (eds.), *Zamani: A Survey of East African History.* New York: Humanities Press, 1968.

Wiebe, Paul D., and Cole P. Dodge (eds.). *Beyond Crisis: Development Issues in Uganda.* Kampala: Makerere Institute of Social Research, 1987.

Chapter 2

Ade, Adefuye. "The Kakwa of Uganda and the Sudan." Pages 51–69 in A.I. Asiwaju (ed.), *Partitioned Africans.* Lagos, Nigeria: Lagos University Press, 1984.

Akhtar, Rais (ed.). *Health and Disease in Tropical Africa: Geographical and Medical Viewpoints.* New York: Harwood Academic, 1987.

Alnaes, Kirsten. "Songs of the Rwenzururu Rebellion: The Konzo Revolt Against the Toro in Western Uganda." Pages 243–72 in P.H. Gulliver (ed.), *Tradition and Transition in East Africa.* Berkeley: University of California Press, 1969.

Amnesty International. *Memorandum to the Government of Uganda on an Amnesty International Mission to Uganda in January 1982 and Further Exchanges Between the Government and Amnesty International.* New York: 1983.

_____. *Uganda: Evidence of Torture.* New York: 1985.

Apter, David E. *The Political Kingdom in Uganda.* (2d ed.) Princeton: Princeton University Press, 1967.

Avirgan, Tony, and Martha Honey. *War in Uganda: The Legacy of Idi Amin.* Westport, Connecticut: Hill, 1982.

Beattie, John. *Bunyoro: An African Kingdom.* (Case Studies in Cultural Anthropology.) New York: Holt, Rinehart, and Winston, 1960.

_____. "Democratization in Bunyoro: The Impact of Democratic Institutions and Values on a Traditional African Kingdom." Pages 101–10 in John Middleton (ed.), *Black Africa.* New York: Collier-Macmillan, 1970.

Berger, Iris, and Carole A. Buchanan. "The Cwezi Cults and the History of Western Uganda." Pages 43–78 in Joseph T. Gallagher (ed.), *East African Culture History*. Syracuse: Maxwell School of Citizenship and Public Affairs, Syracuse University, 1976.

Bujra, Janet M. "Urging Women to Redouble Their Efforts . . .: Class, Gender, and Capitalist Transformation in Africa." Pages 117–40 in Claire Robertson and Iris Berger (eds.), *Women and Class in Africa*. New York: Africana, 1986.

Bunker, Stephen G. *Double Dependency and Constraints on Class Formation in Bugisu, Uganda*. Urbana: University of Illinois Press, 1983.

_____. *Peasants Against the State: The Politics of Market Control in Bugisu, Uganda, 1900–1983*. Urbana: University of Illinois Press, 1987.

Carlston, Kenneth S. *Social Theory and African Tribal Organization*. Urbana: University of Illinois Press, 1968.

Cohen, Ronald, and John Middleton (eds.). *From Tribe to Nation in Africa*. Scranton: Chandler, 1970.

Commonwealth Regional Health Community of East, Central, and Southern Africa. *Report of the Workshop on Curriculum Development for Health Teachers in Nursing/Midwifery and Allied Professions*. Kampala: 1985.

Cunningham, J.F. *Uganda and Its Peoples*. Chicago: Afro-Am Press, 1969.

Decalo, Samuel. "African Personal Dictatorships," *Journal of Modern African Studies* [Cambridge], 23, No. 2, 1985, 209–37.

_____. "The Politics of the Personalist Coup: Uganda." Pages 173–230 in Samuel Decalo (ed.), *Coups and Army Rule in Africa*. New Haven: Yale University Press, 1976.

Dhadphale, M., and O.E. Omolo. "Psychiatric Morbidity among Khat Chewers," *East African Medical Journal* [Nairobi], 65, No. 6, June 1988, 355–59.

Diamond, Larry, Juan J. Linz, and Seymour Martin Lipset (eds.). *Democracy in Developing Countries, 2: Africa*. Boulder, Colorado: Rienner, 1988.

Dodge, Cole P., and Magne Raundalen (eds.). *War, Violence, and Children in Uganda*. Oslo: Norwegian University Press, 1987.

Dodge, Cole P., and Paul D. Wiebe (eds.). *Crisis in Uganda: The Breakdown of Health Services*. New York: Pergamon Press, 1985.

Doob, Leonard W. "Leaders, Followers, and Attitudes Toward Authority." Pages 336–56 in Lloyd A. Fallers (ed.), *The King's Men: Leadership and Status in Buganda on the Eve of Independence*. London: Oxford University Press, 1964.

Fallers, Lloyd A. *Bantu Bureaucracy.* Chicago: University of Chicago Press, 1965.

————. *The Social Anthropology of the Nation-State.* Chicago: Aldine, 1974.

Fallers, Lloyd A. (ed.). *The King's Men: Leadership and Status in Buganda on the Eve of Independence.* London: Oxford University Press, 1964.

Fallers, Margaret Chase. *The Eastern Lacustrine Bantu (Ganda and Soga).* (Ethnographic Survey of Africa: East Central Africa, Part 11.) London: International African Institute, 1968.

Fortes, M., and G. Dieterlen (eds.). *African Systems of Thought.* London: Oxford University Press for International African Institute, 1965.

Fredland, Richard A. *AIDS in Africa: A Political Overview.* (Universities Field Staff International, UFST Reports, Africa, No. 8.) Indianapolis: January 1989.

Gibbs, Jr., James L. (ed.). *Peoples of Africa.* New York: Holt, Rinehart, and Winston, 1965.

Grillo, R.D. "The Tribal Factor in an East African Trade Union." Pages 297–321 in P.H. Gulliver (ed.), *Tradition and Transition in East Africa.* Berkeley: University of California Press, 1969.

Gulliver, P.H. "The Jie of Uganda." Pages 157–96 in James L. Gibbs, Jr. (ed.), *Peoples of Africa.* New York: Holt, Rinehart, and Winston, 1965.

Gulliver, P.H. (ed.). *Tradition and Transition in East Africa.* Berkeley: University of California Press, 1969.

Gulliver, Pamela, and P.H. Gulliver. *The Central Nilo-Hamites.* (Ethnographic Survey of Africa: East Central Africa, Part 7.) London: International African Institute, 1953.

Hall, S.A., and B.W. Langlands (eds.). *Uganda Atlas of Disease Distribution.* Nairobi: East African, 1975.

Hansen, Holger Bernt, and Michael Twaddle (eds.). *Uganda Now: Between Decay and Development.* Athens: Ohio University Press, 1988.

Heyneman, Stephen P. "Education During a Period of Austerity: Uganda, 1971–1981," *Comparative Education Review,* 27, No. 3, October 1983, 403–13.

————. "Influences on Academic Achievement: A Comparison of Results from Uganda and More Industrialized Societies," *Sociology of Education,* 49, No. 3, July 1976, 200–11.

————. "Why Impoverished Children Do Well in Ugandan Schools," *Comparative Education,* 15, No. 2, June 1979, 175–85.

Hilts, Philip J. "Dispelling Myths about AIDS in Africa," *Africa Report,* 33, No. 6, November–December 1988, 26–31.

Hooper, Ed. "AIDS in Uganda," *African Affairs* [London], 86, No. 345, October 1987, 469–77.

Hopkins, Elizabeth. "The Nyabingi Cult of Southwestern Uganda." Pages 60–132 in Robert I. Rotberg (ed.), *Rebellion in Black Africa*. London: Oxford University Press, 1971.

Huntingford, G.W.B. *The Northern Nilo-Hamites*. (Ethnographic Survey of Africa: East Central Africa, Part 6.) London: International African Institute, 1953.

Ibingira, G.S.K. *The Forging of an African Nation: The Political and Constitutional Evolution of Uganda from Colonial Rule to Independence, 1894–1962*. New York: Viking Press, 1973.

International Committee of the Red Cross. *Africa: Emergency Appeal No. 13*. Geneva: 1987.

Jacobson, David. *Itinerant Townsmen: Friendship and Social Order in Urban Uganda*. (The Kiste and Ogan Social Change Series in Anthropology.) Menlo Park, California: Cummings, 1973.

Karugire, Samwiri Rubaraza. *A Political History of Uganda*. Exeter, New Hampshire: Heinemann Educational Books, 1980.

Kasfir, Nelson. "Land and Peasants in Western Uganda: Bushenyi and Mbarara Districts." Pages 158–74 in Holger Bernt Hansen and Michael Twaddle (eds.), *Uganda Now: Between Decay and Development*. Athens: Ohio University Press, 1988.

_____. *The Shrinking Political Arena: Participation and Ethnicity in African Politics*. Berkeley: University of California Press, 1976.

_____. "State, *Magendo*, and Class Formation in Uganda," *Journal of Commonwealth and Comparative Politics*, 21, November 1983, 84–103.

Kasfir, Nelson (ed.). *State and Class in Africa*. Totowa, New Jersey: Cass, 1984.

Katorobo, James. *Education for Public Service in Uganda*. New York: Vantage Press, 1982.

Kenny, Michael G. "Mutesa's Crime: Hubris and the Control of African Kings," *Comparative Study of Society and History*, 30, No. 4, October 1988, 595–612.

Kokole, Omari H., and Ali A. Mazrui. "Uganda: The Dual Policy and the Plural Society." Pages 259–98 in Larry Diamond, Juan J. Linz, and Seymour Martin Lipset (eds.), *Democracy in Developing Countries, 2: Africa*. Boulder, Colorado: Rienner, 1988.

La Fontaine, J.S. "Tribalism among the Gisu." Pages 177–92 in P.H. Gulliver (ed.), *Tradition and Transition in East Africa*. Berkeley: University of California Press, 1969.

Langlands, B.W. *Notes on the Geography of Ethnicity in Uganda*. (Department of Geography, Occasional Paper No. 62.) Kampala: Makerere University, 1975.

Mair, Lucy Philip. *African Marriage and Social Change.* London: Cass, 1969.

———. *African Societies.* London: Cambridge University Press, 1974.

Mamdani, Mahmood. *Politics and Class Formation in Uganda.* New York: Monthly Review Press, 1976.

———. "Uganda in Transition: Two Years of the NRA/NRM," *Third World Quarterly,* 10, No. 3, July 1988, 1155-81.

Martin, David. *General Amin.* London: Faber and Faber, 1974.

Middleton, John. "The Concept of Bewitching in Lugbara," *Africa* [London], 25, 1955, 252-60.

———. *The Lugbara of Uganda.* (2d ed.) (Case Studies in Cultural Anthropology.) Fort Worth: Harcourt Brace Javanovich, 1992.

———. "Political Incorporation among the Lugbara of Uganda." Pages 55-70 in Ronald Cohen and John Middleton (eds.), *From Tribe to Nation in Africa.* Scranton: Chandler, 1970.

Miers, Suzanne, and Richard Roberts (eds.). *The End of Slavery in Africa.* Madison: University of Wisconsin Press, 1988.

Mittelman, James H. *Ideology and Politics in Uganda: From Obote to Amin.* Ithaca: Cornell University Press, 1975.

Mora, Colleen Lowe. "The Revitalization of Makerere," *Africa Report,* 34, No. 2, March-April 1989, 48-51.

Moris, Jon R. *Agriculture in the Schools: The East African Experience.* Kampala: Government Printer, 1975.

Morris, H.S. *The Indians in Uganda.* Chicago: University of Chicago Press, 1968.

Morris, Henry Francis. "Buganda and Tribalism." Pages 323-38 in P.H. Gulliver (ed.), *Tradition and Transition in East Africa.* Berkeley: University of California Press, 1969.

Mudoola, Dan. "Communal Conflict in the Military and Its Political Consequences." Pages 116-40 in Kumar Rupesinghe (ed.), *Conflict Resolution in Uganda.* Athens: Ohio University Press, 1989.

Mugaju, J.B. "The Illusions of Democracy in Uganda." Pages 86-98 in Walter O. Oyugi, E.S. Atieno Adhiambo, Michael Chege, and Afrifa K. Gitonga (eds.), *Democratic Theory and Practice in Africa.* Portsmouth, New Hampshire: Heinemann, 1988.

Museveni, Yoweri Kaguta. "A New Uganda: Prospects and Opportunities. Address to the Los Angeles World Affairs Council, February 3, 1989," *World Affairs Journal,* 2, No. 4, April 1989, 1-3, 8.

———. *Selected Articles on the Uganda Resistance War.* Kampala: NRM, 1985.

National Resistance Movement. *Ten-Point Programme of NRM.* Kampala: 1985.

Obbo, Christine. "Catalysts of Urbanism in the Countryside—
Mukono, Uganda," *African Studies Review,* 31, No. 4, December 1988, 39–47.

_____. "Stratification and the Lives of Women in Uganda."
Pages 178–94 in Claire Robertson and Iris Berger (eds.), *Women
and Class in Africa.* New York: Africana, 1986.

Oyugi, Walter O., E.S. Atieno Adhiambo, Michael Chege, and
Afrifa K. Gitonga (eds.). *Democratic Theory and Practice in Africa.*
Portsmouth, New Hampshire: Heinemann, 1988.

Pain, Dennis R. "Acholi and Nubians: Economic Forces and Military Employment." Pages 41–54 in Paul D. Wiebe and Cole P.
Dodge (eds.), *Beyond Crisis: Development Issues in Uganda.* Kampala: Makerere Institute of Social Research and Makerere
University African Studies Association, 1987.

Parkin, David J. "Tribe as Fact and Fiction in an East African
City." Pages 273–96 in P.H. Gulliver (ed.), *Tradition and Transition in East Africa.* Berkeley: University of California Press, 1969.

Richards, Audrey I. *The Changing Structure of a Ganda Village.* (East
African Studies, No. 24.) Kampala: East African Institute for
Social Research, 1966.

_____. "'East African Chiefs' and Its Sequel." Pages 8–19 in
A.F. Robertson (ed.), *Uganda's First Republic: Chiefs, Adminis-
trators, and Politicians, 1967–1971.* Cambridge: African Studies
Centre, Cambridge University, 1982.

Robertson, A.F. "Conclusion: Chiefs and Administrators in Uganda's First Republic." Pages 99–128 in A.F. Robertson (ed.),
*Uganda's First Republic: Chiefs, Administrators, and Politicians,
1967–1971.* Cambridge: African Studies Centre, Cambridge
University, 1982.

Robertson, A.F. (ed.). *Uganda's First Republic: Chiefs, Administrators, and Politicians, 1967–1971.* Cambridge: African Studies
Centre, Cambridge University, 1982.

Robertson, Claire. "Women's Education and Class Formation in
Africa, 1950–1980." Pages 92–113 in Claire Robertson and Iris
Berger (eds.), *Women and Class in Africa.* New York: Africana,
1986.

Robertson, Claire, and Iris Berger (eds.). *Women and Class in Africa.*
New York: Africana, 1986.

Rupesinghe, Kumar (ed.). *Conflict Resolution in Uganda.* Athens:
Ohio University Press, 1989.

Simon, Catherine. "Un entretien avec le président Museveni,"
Le Monde [Paris], January 22–23, 1989, 4.

Southall, Aidan W. "Incorporation among the Alur." Pages 71–92
in Ronald Cohen and John Middleton (eds.), *From Tribe to Nation
in Africa.* Scranton: Chandler, 1970.

_____. "Small Urban Centers in Rural Development: What Else Is Development Other Than Helping Your Own Home Town?" *African Studies Review,* 31, No. 3, December 1988, 1–15.

_____. "Social Disorganization in Uganda: Before, During, and After Amin," *Journal of Modern African Studies* [Cambridge], 18, No. 4, October 1980, 627–56.

Southwold, Martin. "The Ganda of Uganda." Pages 81–118 in James L. Gibbs, Jr. (ed.), *Peoples of Africa.* New York: Holt, Rinehart, and Winston, 1965.

Stenning, Derrick J. "Salvation in Ankole." Pages 258–75 in M. Fortes and G. Dieterlen (eds.), *African Systems of Thought.* London: Oxford University Press for International African Institute, 1965.

Tadira, H.M.K. "Changes and Continuities in the Position of Women in Uganda." Pages 79–90 in Paul D. Wiebe and Cole P. Dodge (eds.), *Beyond Crisis: Development Issues in Uganda.* Kampala: Makerere Institute of Social Research, 1987.

Thomas, Caroline. "Challenges of Nation-Building: Uganda—A Case Study," *India Quarterly* [New Delhi], 41, July–December 1985, 320–49.

Thomas, Elizabeth Marshall. *Warrior Herdsmen.* New York: Vintage Books, 1965.

Turnbull, Colin. *The Mountain People.* New York: Simon and Schuster, 1972.

Twaddle, Michael. "The Ending of Slavery in Buganda." Pages 119–49 in Suzanne Miers and Richard Roberts (eds.), *The End of Slavery in Africa.* Madison: University of Wisconsin Press, 1988.

_____. " 'Tribalism' in Eastern Uganda." Pages 193–208 in P.H. Gulliver (ed.), *Tradition and Transition in East Africa.* Berkeley: University of California Press, 1969.

Uganda. *An Address by His Excellency the President of Uganda Yoweri Kaguta Museveni.* Entebbe: Government Printer, April 7, 1987.

_____. *An Address to the Nation by His Excellency President Yoweri K. Museveni.* Entebbe: Government Printer, May 15, 1987.

_____. *Constitution of the Republic of Uganda, Revised Edition, 1986.* Kampala: Law Development Centre, 1986.

_____. *A Note on Exchange Rate Adjustment in the Context of Stabilization and Development.* Entebbe: Government Printer, 1986.

_____. Ministry of Industry. *Strategies for Spreading Small-Scale Industries in Uganda.* Kampala: 1981.

_____. Ministry of Planning and Economic Development. *Background to the Budget, 1988–1989.* Kampala: July 1988.

Uganda Council of Women. *Law about Marriage in Uganda.* Kampala: Uganda Bookshop, 1961.

Uganda Newsletter. Washington: March–April 1989.

Uganda Protectorate. *Report of the Karamoja Security Committee.* Entebbe: Government Printer, 1961.

United States. Congress. 95th, 2d Session. Senate. Committee on Foreign Relations. Subcommittee on Foreign Economic Policy. *Uganda: The Human Rights Situation.* Washington: GPO, June 1978.

Uzoigwe, G.N. (ed.). *Uganda: The Dilemma of Nationhood.* (Studies in East African Society and History.) New York: NOK, 1982.

Vincent, Joan. *African Elite: Big Men of a Small Town.* New York: Columbia University Press, 1971.

_____. *Teso in Transformation: The Political Economy of Peasant and Class in Eastern Africa.* Berkeley: University of California Press, 1982.

Watson, Catherine. "An Approach to AIDS," *Africa Report,* 33, No. 6, November–December 1988, 32–35.

_____. "Ending the Rule of the Gun," *Africa Report,* 33, No. 1, January–February 1988, 14–17.

_____. "Trouble with the Spirits," *South,* September 1988, 42–43.

Weatherby, John M. "The Secret Spirit Cult of the Sor in Karamoja," *Africa* [London], 58, No. 2, June 1988, 229.

Welbourn, F.B. *Religion and Politics in Uganda, 1952–62.* (Historical Series No. 1.) Nairobi: East African, 1965.

Wiebe, Paul D., and Cole P. Dodge (eds.). *Beyond Crisis: Development Issues in Uganda.* Kampala: Makerere Institute of Social Research and Makerere University African Studies Association, 1987.

World Health Organization. "A Global Response to AIDS," *Africa Report,* 33, No. 6, November–December 1988, 13–17.

Wrigley, C.C. "The Changing Economic Structure of Buganda." Pages 16–63 in Lloyd A. Fallers (ed.), *The King's Men: Leadership and Status in Buganda on the Eve of Independence.* London: Oxford University Press, 1964.

(Various issues of the following periodicals were also used in the preparation of this chapter: *Africa Confidential* [London]; *Africa Contemporary Record; Africa Economic Digest* [London]; *African Defence Journal* [Paris]; *Africa Report; Africa South of the Sahara* [London]; *Defense and Foreign Affairs; Economist* [London]; Economist Intelligence Unit, *Country Report: Uganda, Ethiopia, Somalia, Djibouti* [London]; Foreign Broadcast Information Service, *Daily Report: Sub-Saharan Africa; Marchés tropicaux et méditerranéens* [Paris]; *The New Vision* [Kampala]; *New York Times;* and *Weekly Review* [Nairobi].)

Chapter 3

Adlworth, William R. *Report on the Marketing Program of the Uganda Cooperative Central Union Ltd.* Washington: Agricultural Cooperative Development International, 1984.

Banugire, Firimooni R. "Uneven and Unbalanced Development: Development Strategies and Conflict." Pages 207–22 in Kumar Rupesinghe (ed.), *Conflict Resolution in Uganda.* Athens: Ohio University Press, 1989.

Belshaw, Deryke. "Agriculture-led Recovery in Post-Amin Uganda: The Causes of Failure and the Bases for Success." Pages 111–25 in Holger Bernt Hansen and Michael Twaddle (eds.), *Uganda Now: Between Decay and Development.* Athens: Ohio University Press, 1988.

Bunker, Stephen G. *Peasants Against the State: The Politics of Market Control in Bugisu, Uganda, 1900–1983.* Urbana: University of Illinois Press, 1987.

"Country's Economic Problems Analyzed," *The Daily Nation* [Nairobi], June 30, 1989, 9.

de Vries, Fred. "Between a Rock and a Hard Place," *Africa Economic Digest,* December 4, 1989, 4.

"Donors Suspend Loans to Uganda," *Africa Analysis,* No. 85, November 10, 1989, 1–2.

Economist Intelligence Unit. *Country Profile: Uganda, 1989–90.* London: 1989.

––––––. *Country Report: Uganda, Ethiopia, Somalia, Djibouti,* Nos. 1–3, London, 1991.

Fieldhouse, David. "Arrested Development in Anglophone Black Africa?" Pages 135–58 in Prosser Gifford and William Roger Louis (eds.), *Decolonization and African Independence.* New Haven: Yale University Press, 1988.

Gertzel, Cherry. "Uganda's Continuing Search for Peace," *Current History,* 89, No. 547, May 1990, 205–28, 231–32.

"Government Aid Examined," *New Vision* [Kampala], September 13, 1989, 7.

Hansen, Holger Bernt, and Michael Twaddle (eds.). *Uganda Now: Between Decay and Development.* Athens: Ohio University Press, 1988.

Harlow, Vincent, and E.M. Chilver (eds.). *History of East Africa,* 2. London: Oxford University Press, 1965.

Holdcroft, Lane E. *Agriculture and Development in Africa: The Case of Uganda.* (Universities Field Staff International, UFSI Reports, Africa, No. 12.) Indianapolis: 1989.

"Inflation Grips Uganda," *Kenya Times* [Nairobi], August 28, 1989, 11.

Jamal, Vali. "Coping under Crisis in Uganda," *International Labour Review* [Geneva], 127, No. 6, November–December 1988.

Jamal, Vali, and John Weeks. "The Vanishing Rural-Urban Gap in Sub-Saharan Africa," *International Labour Review* [Geneva], 127, No. 3, May–June 1988, 271–92.

Kasfir, Nelson. "Land and Peasants in Western Uganda: Bushenyi and Mbarara Districts." Pages 158–74 in Holger Bernt Hansen and Michael Twaddle (eds.), *Uganda Now: Between Decay and Development*. Athens: Ohio University Press, 1988.

Low, D.A., and Alison Smith (eds.). *History of East Africa*, 3. London: Oxford University Press, 1976.

Minority Rights Group. *Uganda and Sudan—North and South*. (Report No. 66.) London: 1984.

"Museveni Interviewed on Accomplishments, Goals," *Le Monde* (Paris), January 22–23, 1989, 4. Foreign Broadcast Information Service, *Daily Report: Sub-Saharan Africa*, January 30, 1989, 9–10.

Nabudere, Dani Wadada. *The IMF-World Bank's Stabilisation and Structural Adjustment Policies and the Uganda Economy, 1981–1989*. (Research Reports, No. 39.) Leiden, Netherlands: African Studies Centre, 1990.

_____. *Imperialism in East Africa*. London: Zed Press, 1981.

Nsibambi, Apolo. "Solving Uganda's Food Problem." Pages 135–57 in Holger Bernt Hansen and Michael Twaddle (eds.), *Uganda Now: Between Decay and Development*. Athens: Ohio University Press, 1988.

Nyanzi, Semei. *The Role of State Enterprises in African Development*. (Occasional Paper No. 94.) The Hague: Institute of Social Studies, 1982.

Obbo, Christine. "Catalysts of Urbanism in the Countryside—Mukono, Uganda," *African Studies Review*, 31, No. 3, December 1988, 39–47.

O'Connor, Anthony. "Uganda: The Spatial Dimension." Pages 83–94 in Holger Bernt Hansen and Michael Twaddle (eds.), *Uganda Now: Between Decay and Development*. Athens: Ohio University Press, 1988.

Oliver, Roland, and Gervase Mathew (eds.). *History of East Africa*, 1. London: Oxford University Press, 1963.

Omoding, Ikebesi. "Uganda: Government Plan to Double Food Production," *Modern Africa*, July–August 1988, 14–15.

Opio, Chris. "Oil Exploration to Begin in Western Region," *The New Vision* [Kampala], November 9, 1988, 1.

Organisation for Economic Co-operation and Development. *Geographical Distribution of Financial Flows in Developing Countries.* Paris: 1990.

"President Outlines Nation's Economic Strategy," *The New Vision* [Kampala], May 15, 1989, 6-7.

"Rehabilitation Projects Surveyed," *New Vision* [Kampala], April 29, 1989, 4.

Rupesinghe, Kumar (ed.). *Conflict Resolution in Uganda.* Athens: Ohio University Press, 1989.

Schissel, Howard. "Africa's Underground Economy," *Africa Report,* 34, No. 1, January-February 1989, 43-46.

Shields, Todd. "Starving the South," *Africa Report,* 34, No. 1, January-February 1989, 63-65.

Southall, Aidan W. "Small Urban Centers in Rural Development: What Else Is Development Other Than Helping Your Own Home Town?," *African Studies Review,* 31, No. 3, December 1988, 1-15.

Tibazarawa, C.M. "The East African Community—A Tragedy in Regional Cooperation," *The Courier,* No. 112, November-December 1988, 48-50.

Uganda. Ministry of Planning and Economic Development. *Background to the Budget, 1989-1990.* Kampala: 1989.

_____. Ministry of Planning and Economic Development. *Background to the Budget, 1990-1991.* Kampala: July 1990.

_____. Ministry of Planning and Economic Development. *Rehabilitation and Development Plan, 1987/88-1990/91.* Kampala: May 1987.

Uganda. Office of the President. *Recovery Program, 1982-84.* Kampala: April 1982.

Uganda Commercial Bank. *UCB Rural Farmers' Scheme.* Kampala: 1987.

"Uganda: The Battle of the Banana-Bunch," *Economist* [London], July 16, 1988, 42.

"Uganda: Contractors Study Four Hydropower Sites," *Modern Africa,* July-August 1988, 8.

"Uganda: New Lease of Life for Sugar Industry," *Modern Africa,* May-June 1988, 25.

Uzoigwe, G.N. (ed.). *Uganda: The Dilemma of Nationhood.* (Studies in East African Society and History.) New York: NOK, 1982.

Watson, Catherine. "An Open Approach to AIDS," *Africa Report,* 33, No. 6, November-December 1988, 32-35.

_____. "Uganda's Women: A Ray of Hope," *Africa Report,* 33, No. 4, July-August 1988, 29-32.

(Various issues of the following periodicals were also used in the preparation of this chapter: *Africa Analysis* [London]; *Africa Confidential* [London]; *Africa Economic Digest* [London]; *Africa Report;* *Africa Research Bulletin* [Oxford]; Economist Intelligence Unit, *Country Report: Uganda, Ethiopia, Somalia, Djibouti* [London]; and *Financial Times* [Kampala].)

Chapter 4

Amnesty International. *Uganda: The Human Rights Record, 1986–1989.* London: 1989.

Apter, David E. *The Political Kingdom in Uganda.* (2d ed.) Princeton: Princeton University Press, 1967.

Avirgan, Tony, and Martha Honey. *War in Uganda: The Legacy of Idi Amin.* Westport, Connecticut: Hill, 1982.

Burke, Fred. *Local Government and Politics in Uganda.* Syracuse: Syracuse University Press, 1964.

Carter, Gwendolyn. *National Unity and Regionalism in Eight African States.* Ithaca: Cornell University Press, 1966.

Clay, Jason. *The Expulsion of the Banyaruanda.* Boston: Cultural Survival, 1984.

Doornbos, Martin. "The Uganda Crisis and the National Question." Pages 254–66 in Holger Bernt Hansen and Michael Twaddle (eds.), *Uganda Now: Between Decay and Development.* Athens: Ohio University Press, 1988.

Dunbar, A.R. *A History of Bunyoro-Kitara.* (Rev. ed.) Nairobi: Oxford University Press on behalf of Makerere Institute of Social Research, 1969.

Furley, Oliver W. "Britain and Uganda from Amin to Museveni: Blind Eye Diplomacy." Pages 275–94 in Kumar Rupesinghe (ed.), *Conflict Resolution in Uganda.* Athens: Ohio University Press, 1989.

Gertzel, Cherry. "Kingdoms, Districts, and the Unitary State, Uganda 1945–1962." Pages 65–106 in D.A. Low and Alison Smith (eds.), *History of East Africa,* 3. London: Oxford University Press, 1976.

Hansen, Holger Bernt, and Michael Twaddle (eds.). *Uganda Now: Between Decay and Development.* Athens: Ohio University Press, 1988.

Ibingira, G.S.K. *The Forging of an African Nation: The Political and Constitutional Evolution of Uganda from Colonial Rule to Independence, 1894–1962.* New York: Viking Press, 1973.

Ingham, Kenneth. *The Making of Modern Uganda.* Westport, Connecticut: Greenwood Press, 1983.

International Commission of Jurists. *Uganda and Human Rights.* (Report to the United Nations Commission on Human Rights.) Geneva: 1977.

Jørgensen, Jan Jelmert. *Uganda: A Modern History.* New York: St. Martin's Press, 1981.

Karugire, Samwiri Rubaraza. *A Political History of Uganda.* Exeter, New Hampshire: Heinemann Educational Books, 1980.

------. *The Roots of Instability in Uganda.* Kampala: New Vision, 1988.

Kasfir, Nelson. *The 1967 Constituent Assembly Debate.* Kampala: Transition, 1988.

------. *The Shrinking Political Arena: Participation and Ethnicity in African Politics.* Berkeley: University of California Press, 1976.

------. "State, *Magendo,* and Class Formation in Uganda," *Journal of Commonwealth and Comparative Politics* [Leicester, United Kingdom], 21, November 1983, 84–103.

------. "Uganda." Page 532 in *Collier's 1990 Yearbook.* New York: Collier-Macmillan, 1989.

------. "Uganda's Uncertain Quest for Recovery," *Current History,* 84, No. 501, April 1985, 169–73, 187.

Kasfir, Nelson (ed.). *State and Class in Africa.* Totowa, New Jersey: Cass, 1984.

Kiwanuka, M.S.M. Semakula (ed.). *The Kings of Buganda.* Nairobi: East African, 1971.

Kokole, Omari H., and Ali A. Mazrui. "Uganda: The Dual Polity and the Plural Society." Pages 259–98 in Larry Diamond, Juan J. Linz, and Seymour Martin Lipset (eds.), *Democracy in Developing Countries, 2: Africa.* Boulder, Colorado: Rienner, 1988.

Kyemba, Henry. *A State of Blood: The Inside Story of Idi Amin.* New York: Grosset and Dunlap, 1977.

Low, D.A. *Buganda in Modern History.* Berkeley: University of California Press, 1971.

Low, D.A., and Robert Cranford Pratt (eds.). *Buganda and British Overrule, 1900–1955.* Nairobi: Oxford University Press, 1960.

Mamdani, Mahmood. *Imperialism and Fascism in Uganda.* Nairobi: Heinemann, 1983.

------. "Uganda in Transition: Two Years of the NRA/NRM," *Third World Quarterly* [London], 10, No. 3, July 1988, 1155–81.

Martin, David. *General Amin.* London: Faber and Faber, 1974.

Minority Rights Group. *Uganda and Sudan—North and South.* (Report No. 66.) London: 1984.

Mudoola, Dan. "Communal Conflict in the Military and Its Political Consequences." Pages 116–40 in Kumar Rupesinghe (ed.), *Conflict Resolution in Uganda.* Athens: Ohio University Press, 1989.

_____. "Political Transitions since Idi Amin: A Study in Political Pathology." Pages 280-98 in Holger Bernt Hansen and Michael Twaddle (eds.), *Uganda Now: Between Decay and Development*. Athens: Ohio University Press, 1988.

Museveni, Yoweri Kaguta. *Selected Articles on the Uganda Resistance War*. Kampala: NRM, 1985.

Mutesa II, Edward. *Desecration of My Kingdom*. London: Constable, 1967.

National Resistance Movement. Secretariat. Directorate of Information and Mass Mobilisation. *NRM Achievements, 1986-1990*. Kampala: 1990.

Ogot, Bethwell A., and J.A. Kieran (eds.). *Zamani: A Survey of East African History*. New York: Humanities Press, 1968.

Omara-Otunnu, Amii. *Politics and the Military in Uganda, 1890-1985*. New York: St. Martin's Press, 1987.

Pratt, C. "The Politics of Indirect Rule: Uganda 1900-1955." Pages 161-366 in D.A. Low and Robert Cranford Pratt (eds.), *Buganda and British Overrule, 1900-1955*. Nairobi: Oxford University Press, 1960.

Roberts, A. "The Sub-Imperialism of the Baganda," *Journal of African History* [London], 8, No. 3, 1962, 435-50.

Rothchild, Donald, and John W. Harbeson. "Rehabilitation in Uganda," *Current History*, 80, No. 463, March 1981, 115-19, 134-38.

Rothchild, Donald, and Michael Rogin. "Uganda." Pages 337-40 in Gwendolyn M. Carter (ed.), *National Unity and Regionalism in Eight African States*. Ithaca: Cornell University Press, 1966.

Rowe, John A. "Islam under Idi Amin: A Case of Déja Vu?" Pages 267-79 in Holger Bernt Hansen and Michael Twaddle (eds.), *Uganda Now: Between Decay and Development*. Athens: Ohio University Press, 1988.

Rupesinghe, Kumar (ed.). *Conflict Resolution in Uganda*. Athens: Ohio University Press, 1989.

Rusk, John D. "Uganda: Breaking Out of the Mold." Africa Rights Monitor Report, *Africa Today*, 33, No. 2-3, September 1986, 91-102.

Sathyamurthy, T.V. *The Political Development of Uganda, 1900-1986*. Brookfield, Vermont: Gower, 1986.

Smith, George Ivan. *The Ghosts of Kampala*. London: Weidenfeld and Nicolson, 1980.

Tindigarukayo, Jimmy K. "Uganda, 1979-1985: Leadership in Transition," *Journal of Modern African Studies* [London], 26, No. 4, December 1988, 607-22.

Twaddle, Michael. "Museveni's Uganda: Notes Towards an Analysis." Pages 313–35 in Holger Bernt Hansen and Michael Twaddle (eds.), *Uganda Now: Between Decay and Development.* Athens: Ohio University Press, 1988.

Uganda. *Constitution of the Republic of Uganda, Revised Edition, 1986.* Kampala: Law Development Centre, 1986.

———. *Twelve Months of the NRM Government.* Kampala: Government Printer, 1987.

———. Commission of Inquiry into the Local Government System. *Report of the Commission of Inquiry into the Local Government System.* Kampala: Government Printer, 1987.

———. Commission of Inquiry into the Local Government System. *The Resistance Committees (Judicial Powers) Statute, 1987.* Kampala: Government Printer, 1987.

Uganda Elections, December 1980: The Report of the Commonwealth Observer Group. London: Commonwealth Secretariat, 1981.

United States. Congress. 96th, 1st Session. House of Representatives. Committee on Foreign Affairs. Subcommittee on Africa. *U.S. Policy Toward Uganda.* Washington: GPO, 1979.

Welbourn, F.B. *Religion and Politics in Uganda, 1952–1962.* (Historical Series No. 1.) Nairobi: East African, 1965.

(Various issues of the following periodicals also were used in the preparation of this chapter: Economist Intelligence Unit, *Country Report: Uganda, Ethiopia, Somalia, Djibouti* [London]; *Keesing's Record of World Events* [London]; *The New Vision* [Kampala]; and *Weekly Topic* [Kampala].)

Chapter 5

Adimola, D. "The Lamogi Rebellion, 1911–12," *Uganda Journal* [Kampala], 18, No. 2, 1954, 166–77.

Allen, Tim. "Understanding Alice: Uganda's Holy Spirit Movement in Context," *Africa* [Manchester], 61, No. 3, 1991, 37–39.

Amin, Mohamed. "Uganda: Children of Terror," *African Defence Journal* [Paris], August 1988, 72–74.

———. "Uganda's Children at War," *Africa Now* [London], April 1986, 8–9.

Amnesty International. *Human Rights in Uganda.* London: 1978.

———. *Uganda: The Human Rights Record, 1986–1989.* London: 1989.

———. *Uganda: Six Years after Amin.* London: 1985.

Andrade, John. *World Police and Paramilitary Forces.* New York: Stockton Press, 1985.

Austin, Herbert Henry. *With Macdonald in Uganda.* London: Arnold, 1903.

Avirgan, Tony, and Martha Honey. *War in Uganda: The Legacy of Idi Amin.* Westport, Connecticut: Hill, 1982.

Barnett, Donald L., and Karari Njama. *Mau Mau from Within.* London: MacGibbon and Kee, 1966.

Bienen, Henry. *Armies and Parties in Africa.* New York: Africana, 1978.

Boyes, John. *My Abyssinian Journey.* Nairobi: n.p., n.d.

Burrow, Noreen. "Tanzania's Intervention in Uganda: Some Legal Aspects," *The World Today* [London], July 1979, 306–10.

Bwengye, A.W.F. *The Agony of Uganda: From Idi Amin to Obote.* London: Regency Press, 1985.

By One of Them (C.J. Phillips). *Uganda Volunteers and the War.* Kampala: A.D. Cameron, 1917.

Clayton, Anthony. *Counter-Insurgency in Kenya: A Study of Military Operations Against Mau Mau.* Nairobi: Transafrica, 1976.

Clayton, Anthony, and David Killingray. *Khaki and Blue: Military and Police in British Colonial Africa.* Athens: Ohio University Center for International Studies, 1989.

Collins, Robert O. "The Turkana Patrol, 1918," *Uganda Journal* [Kampala], 25, No. 1, March 1961, 16–33.

Cooper, Carol. "Nyerere and Territorial Integrity: A Janus-Faced Approach to a Cardinal Tenet," *Horn of Africa*, 2, 1979, 55–60.

Decalo, Samuel. *Coups and Army Rule in Africa: Studies in Military Style.* New Haven: Yale University Press, 1976.

_____. *Psychoses of Power: African Personal Dictatorships.* Boulder, Colorado: Westview Press, 1989.

_____. "The Ugandan Army and Makerere under Obote, 1962–71," *African Affairs* [London], 82, No. 326, 1983, 43–59.

Dodge, Cole P., and Magne Raundalen (eds.). *War, Violence, and Children in Uganda.* Oslo: Norwegian University Press, 1987.

Doornbos, Martin R. "Protest Movements in Western Uganda: Some Parallels and Contrasts." (Conference Paper No. 416.) Kampala: East African Institute of Social Research, 1967.

Fox Bourne, H.R. *The Story of Somaliland: British Lives Squandered and Treasures Wasted.* London: The New Age Press, 1904.

Furley, Oliver W. "The Sudanese Troops in Uganda," *African Affairs* [London], 58, No. 233, October 1959, 311–28.

Galbraith, John S. *Mackinnon and East Africa, 1878–1895: A Study in the "New Imperialism".* Cambridge: Cambridge University Press, 1972.

Gertzel, Cherry. "Uganda's Continuing Search for Peace," *Current History,* 89, No. 547, May 1990, 205–08, 231–32.

Grahame, Iain. *Amin and Uganda: A Personal Memoir.* London: Granada, 1980.

Hansen, Holger Bernt. *Ethnicity and Military Rule in Uganda.* Uppsala: Scandanivian Institute of African Studies, 1977.

Hansen, Holger Bernt, and Michael Twaddle (eds.). *Changing Uganda: The Dilemmas of Structural Adjustment and Revolutionary Change.* Athens: Ohio University Press, 1991.

————. *Uganda Now: Between Decay and Development.* Athens: Ohio University Press, 1988.

Harwich, Christopher. *Red Dust: Memories of the Uganda Police, 1935–1955.* London: Stuart, 1961.

Haydon, Edwin S. *Law and Justice in Buganda.* London: Butterworths, 1960.

Hess, Robert L. "The 'Mad Mullah' and Northern Somalia," *Journal of African History* [London], 5, No. 3, 1964, 415–33.

Hodges, Geoffrey. *The Carrier Corps: Military Labor in the East African Campaign, 1914–1918.* New York: Greenwood Press, 1986.

Hordern, Charles. *History of the Great War: Military Operations, East Africa.* London: HMSO, 1941.

Hore, H.R. "The History of the Uganda Volunteer Reserve," *Uganda Journal* [Kampala], 8, No. 2, September 1940, 65–75.

International Commission of Jurists. *Violations of Human Rights and the Rule of Law in Uganda.* Geneva: 1974.

Jenkins, E.V. *A History of the King's African Rifles, Formerly Known as the Uganda Rifles.* Entebbe: Government Press, 1912.

Johns, David H. "Defence and Police Organization in East Africa." (Conference Paper No. 210.) Kampala: East African Institute of Social Research, 1964.

Jørgensen, Jan Jelmert. *Uganda: A Modern History.* New York: St. Martin's Press, 1981.

"The 'Kadogo' Generation," *Africa Events* [London], March 1989, 46–47.

Kakembo, Robert H. *An African Soldier Speaks.* London: Edinburgh House Press, 1946.

Kakwenzire, Joan. "Problems of Implementing Human Rights in Uganda." (Paper presented at Uganda Workshop on "The NRM Government: Prospects for Fundamental Reform," Dartmouth College, 1990.) Hanover, New Hampshire: Dartmouth College, 1990.

Kamau, Joseph, and Andrew Cameron. *Lust to Kill: The Rise and Fall of Idi Amin.* London: Corgi, 1979.

Keegan, John (ed.) *World Armies.* (2d ed.) Detroit: Gale Research, 1983.

Kiwanuka, M.S.M. Semakula. *Amin and the Tragedy of Uganda.* Munich: Weltforum Verlag, 1979.

Kyemba, Henry. *A State of Blood: The Inside Story of Idi Amin.* New York: Grosset and Dunlap, 1977.

Lardner, E.G. Dion. *Soldiering and Sport in Uganda, 1909–1910.* London: Scott, 1912.

Legum, Colin. "Museveni Turns to Libya and Cuba to Meet the Military Challenge by His Opponents," *Third World Reports* [Richmond, Surrey, United Kingdom], December 13, 1988.

_____. "Uganda: The Military and Politics—Why Museveni Can't Survive," *Third World Reports* [Richmond, Surrey, United Kingdom], March 3, 1988.

_____. "Uganda: Museveni's Armed Opposition," *Third World Reports* [Richmond, Surrey, United Kingdom], February 24, 1988.

_____. "Uganda Poised Between Civil War and Military Dictatorship," *Third World Reports* [Richmond, Surrey, United Kingdom], December 11, 1985.

_____. "Uganda's Army of Children," *Third World Reports* [Richmond, Surrey, United Kingdom], February 13, 1987.

Listowel, Judith. *Amin.* London: Irish University Press, 1974.

Lloyd-Jones, W. *King's African Rifles.* London: Arrowsmith, 1926.

Lofchie, Michael F. "The Uganda Coup—Class Action by the Military," *Journal of Modern African Studies* [London], 10, No. 1, 1972, 19–35.

Low, D.A., and Robert Cranford Pratt. *Buganda and British Overrule, 1900–1955.* Nairobi: Oxford University Press, 1960.

Lugard, Frederick D. *The Rise of Our East African Empire.* (2 vols.) London: Blackwood and Sons, 1893.

Lwanga-Lunyiigo, S. "Uganda and World War One," *Makerere Historical Journal* [Kampala], 3, No. 1, 1977, 27–42.

McDermott, P.L. *British East Africa or IBEA.* London: Chapman and Hall, 1895.

Martin, David. *General Amin.* London: Faber and Faber, 1974.

Martin, Michel L. "The Uganda Military Coup of 1971: A Study of Protest," *Ufahamu*, 3, No. 3, Winter 1972, 81–121.

Matson, A.T. *The Nandi Campaign Against the British, 1905–1906.* Nairobi: Transafrica, 1974.

_____. *Nandi Resistance to British Rule, 1890–1906.* Nairobi: East African, 1972.

Matthews, Lloyd. "Uganda." Pages 598–600 in John Keegan (ed.), *World Armies.* (2d ed.) Detroit: Gale Research, 1983.

Maxse, Frederick Ivoa. *Seymour Vandeleur, Lieutenant Colonel, Scots Guards and Irish Guards.* London: Heinemann, 1906.

Mazrui, Ali. *Soldiers and Kinsmen in Uganda.* Beverly Hills: Sage, 1975.

Mazrui, Ali, and Donald Rothchild. "The Soldier and State in East Africa: Some Theoretical Conclusions on the Army Mutinies of 1964," *Western Political Quarterly,* 20, 1967, 82–96.

Melady, Thomas, and Margaret Melady. *Idi Amin Dada: Hitler in Africa.* Kansas City: Andrews and McMeel, 1978.

Miller, Charles. *Battle for the Bundu: The First World War in East Africa.* New York: Macmillan, 1974.

Minority Rights Group. *Uganda.* London: 1989.

————. *Uganda and Sudan—North and South.* (Report No. 66.) London: 1984.

Mittleman, James H. *Ideology and Politics in Uganda: From Obote to Amin.* Ithaca: Cornell University Press, 1975.

Morris, Henry Francis, and James S. Read. *Uganda: The Development of Its Laws and Constitution.* London: Stevens and Sons, 1966.

Moyse-Bartlett, H. *The King's African Rifles: A Short History.* Nairobi: Regal Press, n.d.

————. *The King's African Rifles: A Study in the Military History of East and Central Africa, 1890–1945.* Aldershot: Gale and Polden, 1956.

Msabaha, I.S.R. "War on Idi Amin: Toward a Synthetic Theory of Intervention," *African Review* [Dar es Salaam, Tanzania], 12, No. 1, 1985, 24–43.

Mudoola, Dan. "Civil-Military Relations: The Case of Uganda." (Makerere Institute of Social Research, Occasional Paper No. 005.) Kampala: Makerere Institute of Social Research, 1988.

Museveni, Yoweri Kaguta. *Selected Articles on the Uganda Resistance War.* Kampala: NRM, 1985.

————. *Three Essays on Military Strategy in Uganda.* Kampala: National Resistance Army, n.d.

Mutesa II, Edward. *Desecration of My Kingdom.* London: Constable, 1967.

Mwenegoha, H.A.K., and J.P. Mbonde. *Kuanguka Kwa Fashisti Idi Amin.* Dar es Salaam: Swala, 1979.

Nayenga, Peter F.B. "Myths and Realities of Idi Amin Dada's Uganda," *African Studies Review,* 22, No. 2, September 1979, 127–40.

O'Brien, Justin. "General Amin and the Uganda Asians: Doing the Unthinkable," *Round Table* [London], 249, January 1973, 91–104.

Ofcansky, Thomas P. "Uganda: Museveni's Challenge," *African Defence Journal* [Paris], November 1989, 34–35.

Ogot, B.A. (ed.). *War and Society in Africa.* London: Cass, 1972.

O'Kane, Gerry. "With the Rebels in Uganda," *New African* [London], December 1987, 9–11.

Okoth, P. Godfrey. "The OAU and the Uganda-Tanzania War, 1978–79," *Journal of African Studies* [London], 14, No. 3, Fall 1987, 152–62.

Omara-Otunnu, Amii. *Politics and the Military in Uganda, 1890–1985.* New York: St. Martin's Press, 1987.

Patel, H.H. "General Amin and the Indian Exodus from Uganda," *Issue,* 2, No. 4, Winter 1972, 12–22.

Portal, Gerald. *The British Mission to Uganda in 1893.* London: Arnold, 1894.

Prunier, Gerard A. "Kuanguka Kwa Fashisti Idi Amin: Tanzania's Ambiguous Ugandan Victory," *Cultures et Développement* [Paris], 16, Nos. 3–4, 1984, 735–56.

Ravenhill, F.J. "Military Rule in Uganda: The Politics of Survival," *African Studies Review,* 17, No. 1, April 1974, 229–60.

Rosberg, Carl G., and John Nottingham. *The Myth of Mau Mau: Nationalism in Kenya.* New York: Praeger, 1966.

Rupesinghe, Kumar (ed.). *Conflict Resolution in Uganda.* Athens: Ohio University Press, 1989.

Smith, George Ivan. *Ghosts of Kampala.* London: Weidenfeld and Nicolson, 1980.

Soghayroun, Ibrahim Elzein. *The Sudanese Muslim Factor in Uganda.* Khartoum: Khartoum University Press, 1981.

Southall, Aidan W. "General Amin and the Coup: Great Man or Historical Inevitability," *Journal of Modern African Studies* [London], 13, No. 1, 1975, 85–105.

Steinhart, Edward I. *Conflict and Collaboration: The Kingdoms of Western Uganda, 1890–1907.* Princeton: Princeton University Press, 1977.

Strate, Jeffrey T. *Post-Military Coup Strategy in Uganda.* Athens: Ohio University Center for International Studies, 1973.

Tanner, R.E.S. "Some Problems of East Africa Crime Statistics." (Conference Paper No. 431.) Kampala: East African Institute of Social Research, 1967.

Tanzania. *Tanzania and the War Against Amin's Uganda.* Dar es Salaam: Government Printer, 1979.

Ternan, Trevor. *Some Experiences of an Old Bromsgrovian.* Birmingham: Cornish Brothers, 1930.

Thomas, H.B. "Kigezi Operations, 1914–1917," *Uganda Journal* [Kampala], 30, No. 2, 1966, 165–73.

Thomas, H.B., and Robert Scott. *Uganda.* London: Oxford University Press, 1935.

Toko, Gad W. *Intervention in Uganda: The Power Struggle and Soviet Involvement.* Pittsburgh: University of Pittsburgh Press, 1979.

Twaddle, Michael. "The Amin Coup," *Journal of Commonwealth Political Studies* [London], 10, No. 2, July 1972, 99–121.

―――. "The Ousting of Idi Amin," *Round Table* [London], 275, July 1979, 216–21.

Twaddle, Michael (ed.). *Expulsion of a Minority: Essays on the Ugandan Asians.* London: Athlone Press, 1975.

Twining, E.F. "Uganda Medals and Decorations," *Uganda Journal* [Kampala], 2, No. 3, January 1935, 209–25.

Uganda. Civil Reabsorption and Rehabilitation Committee. *Report.* Entebbe: Government Printer, 1945.

―――. Civil Reabsorption Organisation. *Civil Reabsorption: Progress Report.* Entebbe: Government Printer, 1946.

―――. Civil Reabsorption Organisation. *Civil Reabsorption: Progress Report.* Entebbe: Government Printer, 1948.

―――. Commission of Inquiry into Disturbances in the Eastern Province, 1960. *Report.* Entebbe: Government Printer, 1960.

―――. Forest Department. *Uganda Forests and the 1939–45 War.* Entebbe: Government Printer, 1947.

"The Uganda Army: Nexus of Power," *Africa Report,* 11, December 1966, 37–39.

Ullman, Richard H. "Human Rights and Economic Power: The United States Versus Idi Amin," *Foreign Affairs,* 56, No. 3, April 1978, 529–43.

Umozurike, U.D. "Tanzania's Intervention in Uganda," *Archiv des Volkerrechts* [Tübingen, Germany], 20, No. 3, 1982, 301–13.

United Kingdom. *Preliminary Report by Her Majesty's Special Commissioner on the Protectorate of Uganda.* London: HMSO, 1900.

―――. *Report by Her Majesty's Commissioner in Uganda on the Recent Mutiny of the Sudanese Troops in the Protectorate.* London: HMSO, 1898.

―――. Ministry of Information. *The Official Story of the Conquest of Italian East Africa.* London: HMSO, 1942.

―――. War Office. *Official History of the Operations in Somaliland, 1901–04.* (2 vols.) London: HMSO, 1907.

United States. Committee for Refugees. *Three Papers Presented Before the Commission of Inquiry into Violations of Human Rights, February 15–16, 1990, Kampala, Uganda.* Washington: 1990.

Uzoigwe, G.N. "The Kyanyangire, 1907: Passive Revolt Against British Overrule." Pages 179–214 in B.A. Ogot (ed.), *War and Society in Africa.* London: Cass, 1972.

_____. *Revolution and Revolt in Bunyoro-Kitara.* London: Longmans, 1970.

Vandeleur, Seymour. *Campaigning on the Upper Nile.* London: Methuen, 1898.

Wallis, H.R. *The Handbook of Uganda.* London: Crown Agents for the Colonies, 1913.

_____. "The War in Uganda," *National Review* [London], 74, 1919, 556–61.

Wani, Ibrahim J. "Humanitarian Intervention and the Tanzania-Uganda War," *Horn of Africa,* 3, No. 2, 1980, 18–27.

Watson, Catherine. "How the War in the North Began." (Paper presented at Uganda Workshop on "The NRM Government: Prospects for Fundamental Reform," Dartmouth College, 1990.) Hanover: New Hampshire: Dartmouth College, 1990.

_____. "The Lakwena Movements of Northern Uganda: 1986–1990." (Paper presented at Uganda Workshop on "The NRM Government: Prospects for Fundamental Reform," Dartmouth College, 1990.) Hanover, New Hampshire: Dartmouth College, 1990.

Wells, Rick. "Uganda's Security Nightmare," *Africa Report,* 29, No. 2, March–April 1984, 24–26.

Whitehead, E.F. "A Short History of Uganda Military Units Formed During World War II," *Uganda Journal* [Kampala], 14, No. 1, March 1950, 1–14.

Wild, J.V. *The Story of the Uganda Agreement.* Nairobi: Eagle Press, 1950.

_____. *The Sudanese Mutiny.* Nairobi: Eagle Press, 1950.

_____. *The Uganda Mutiny.* London: Macmillan, 1954.

Winter, Roger P. "The Armies of Uganda and Human Rights—A Personal Observation," *Cultural Survival,* 11, No. 4, 1987, 46–48.

Worker, J.C. "With the 4th (Uganda) K.A.R. in Abyssinia and Burma," *Uganda Journal* [Kampala], 12, No. 1, March 1948, 52–56.

Young, M. Crawford. "The Obote Revolution," *Africa Report,* 11, No. 6, June 1966, 8–14.

(Various issues of the following periodicals also were used in the preparation of this chapter: *Africa Analysis* [London]; *Africa Confidential* [London]; *Africa Contemporary Record; African Defence Journal* [Paris]; *Africa Economic Digest* [London]; *Africa Events* [London]; *Africa News; Africa Now* [London]; *Africa Report; Africa Research Bulletin* (Political, Social, and Cultural Series) [London]; Foreign Broadcast Information Service, *Daily Report: Sub-Saharan Africa; The Guide*

[Kampala]; *Indian Ocean Newsletter* [Paris]; International Institute for Strategic Studies, *The Military Balance* [London]; *Keesing's Contemporary Archives* [London]; National Resistance Army, *The 6th of February* [Kampala]; *The New Vision* [Kampala]; *New York Times; Star* [Kampala]; *Third World Reports* [Richmond, Surrey, United Kingdom]; *Times* [London]; *Uganda Journal* [Kampala]; Uganda Police Force and Uganda Prison Service, *Annual Reports* [Kampala]; *Washington Post;* and *Weekly Review* [Nairobi].)

Glossary

age-set—A group of persons of the same sex and approximately the same age who have been initiated together or who have passed through other social experiences together.

clan—A group whose members are descended in the male line from a putative common male ancestor (patriclan) or in the female line from a putative common female ancestor (matriclan—not reported in Uganda). Clans may be divided into subclans organized on the same principle or into lineages (q.v.) believed to be linked by descent from a remote common ancestor.

fiscal year (FY)—Uganda's fiscal year runs from July 1 to June 30. Fiscal year dates of reference correspond to the year in which the period ends. For example, fiscal year 1990 began July 1, 1989, and ended June 30, 1990.

gross domestic product (GDP)—A measure of the total value of goods and services produced by a domestic national economy during a given period, usually one year. Obtained by adding the value contributed by each sector of the economy in the form of profits, compensation to employees, and depreciation (consumption of capital). Only domestic production is included, not income arising from investments and possessions owned abroad, hence the use of the word "domestic" to distinguish GDP from gross national product (q.v.). Real GDP is the value of GDP when inflation has been taken into account. In this book, subsistence production is included and consists of the imputed value of production by the farm family for its own use and the imputed rental value of owner-occupied dwellings. In countries lacking sophisticated data-gathering techniques, such as Uganda, the total value of GDP is often estimated.

gross national product (GNP)—The total market value of all final goods and services produced by an economy during a year. Obtained by adding the gross domestic product (q.v.) and the income received from abroad by residents and then subtracting payments remitted abroad to nonresidents. Real GNP is the value of GNP when inflation has been taken into account.

International Monetary Fund (IMF)—Established along with the World Bank (q.v.) in 1945, the IMF is a specialized agency affiliated with the United Nations; it is responsible for stabilizing international exchange rates and payments. The main business of the IMF is the provision of loans to its members (including industrialized and developing countries) when they experience balance-of-payments difficulties. These loans frequently carry conditions that require substantial internal economic adjustments by the recipients, most of which are developing countries.

lineage—A group whose members are descended through males from a common male ancestor (patrilineage) or through females from a common female ancestor (matrilineage—not reported in Uganda). Such descent can in principle be traced. Lineages vary in genealogical depth from the ancestor to living generations; the more extensive ones often are internally segmented.

Paris Club—The informal name for a consortium of Western creditor countries that have made loans or have guaranteed export credits to developing nations and that meet in Paris to discuss borrowers' ability to repay debts. The organization has no formal or institutional existence and no fixed membership. Its secretariat is run by the French treasury, and it has a close relationship with the World Bank (*q.v.*), the International Monetary Fund (*q.v.*), and the United Nations Conference on Trade and Development (UNCTAD).

patrilineage—A group of male and female descendants of a male ancestor, each of whom is related to the common ancestor through male forebears.

special drawing right(s) (SDRs)—Monetary unit(s) of the International Monetary Fund (IMF—*q.v.*) based on a basket of international currencies consisting of the United States dollar, the German deutsche mark, the Japanese yen, the British pound sterling, and the French franc.

Uganda shilling—USh; basic unit of currency divided into 100 cents. The Uganda shilling was introduced in 1966 and was tied to the United States dollar until 1975, when its value was tied to the special drawing right (SDR; *q.v.*) of the IMF (*q.v.*). In 1986 the Uganda shilling was officially valued at US$1 = USh1450. A new Uganda shilling was introduced in May 1987. It involved an effective devaluation of 76 percent, was given an official value equal to 100 old shillings, and had an international exchange rate of US$1 = USh60. Successive devaluations in 1988, 1989, and 1990 reduced the official dollar value to US$1 = USh510 by late 1990.

World Bank—International name used to designate a group of three affiliated international institutions: the International Bank for Reconstruction and Development (IBRD), the International Development Association (IDA), and the International Finance Corporation (IFC). The IBRD, established in 1945, has as its primary purpose the provision of loans to developing countries for productive projects. The IDA, a legally separate loan fund administered by the staff of the IBRD, was set up in 1960 to furnish credits to the poorest developing countries on much easier terms than those of conventional IBRD loans. The IFC, founded in 1956, supplements the activities of the IBRD through loans and assistance designed specifically to encourage the growth of productive private enterprises in the less-developed countries. The president and certain senior officers of the IBRD hold the same positions in the IFC. The three institutions are owned by the governments of the countries that subscribe their capital. To participate in the World Bank group, member states must first belong to the IMF (*q.v.*).

Index

Acak, Opon, 206
Acholi people, 9, 66; agriculture of, 67; cattle of, 67; discrimination against, 35; ivory trade by, 10; killed under Amin, 26–27, 232; languages of, 50, 66; lineages of, 67; marriage among, 67; origins of, 67; as percentage of population, 67; social structure of, 77–78; soldiers, 26, 36, 213
Acholi region, 65; conquered by British, 12; religion in, 77
Achwa River, 46
acquired immune deficiency syndrome (AIDS), xxvii, 41, 89–90, 93; deaths from, 47, 89; distribution of, 89; effect of, on population growth, 90; effect of, on society, 90; infection rate of, 89; prevention programs for, 89; and religion, 41, 76; treatments for, 90; and women, 83
Action for Development, 83
Activist, The, 234
Adoko, Akena, 24
Adrisi, Mustafa, 30
African Development Bank, 136
African Socialism, 24
Agency for International Development. *See* United States Agency for International Development
agricultural cooperatives, 55, 78–80; credit by, 111, 135; marketing by, xxvi, 104, 110
agricultural development, 144
Agricultural Enterprises Limited, 114
agriculturalists, 4, 7, 59; ancient, 6; migration of, 6; political system of, 6; trade of, with pastoralists, 6
agricultural production (*see also under individual crops*), 97; ancient, 98; under British, 14; decline in, 110; during the Great Depression, xxii; growth in, xxvi; methods of, 110; by smallholders, 16, 110; during World War I, xxii
agricultural products, 110–16; bananas, 6, 52, 54, 56, 136; beans, 65; cassava, 54, 56, 66, 67, 68, 110; corn, 54, 51, 65, 66, 67, 68, 110, 136, 211; eleusine, 65, 67; exports of, 137; fruit, 110;

government supports for, xxvi; legumes, 56, 68, 110; marketing of, xxvi, xxvii, 103; millet, 54, 56, 61, 65, 66, 67, 68, 110; peanuts, 54, 61, 65, 67, 110, 127; potatoes, 66; prices for, 99; rice, 58; sesame seeds, 67, 110, 127; sorghum, 65, 68, 110; sunflowers, 127; sweet potatoes, 54, 56, 65, 67, 110; trade in, xxii
agricultural sector, 97; growth in, 100, 101; problems in, 125; regional cooperation in, 143, 144
agriculture, 108–23, 181; in Buganda, 52; in Bunyoro, 55–56; diversification of, 97; in Karamojong culture, 61; loans for, 142; in the north, 110; promotion of, 131; regional cooperation in, xxv, 144; in the south, 42, 110; wage earners in, 110
agriculture, commercial: diversification in, 111; as percentage of gross domestic product, 100; wage earners in, 110
agriculture, subsistence (*see also under individual crops*), xxii, 54, 80, 97; growth of, 100; for survival, 101, 107
AID. *See* United States Agency for International Development
AIDS. *See* acquired immune deficiency syndrome
air cargo service: government control of, xxvii
air force: equipment, 216; established, 216; training, 216
Air France: hijacking, 29, 187, 190, 218
airlines: energy consumption by, 125; government control of, xxvii, 104
Air Tanzania, 133
Akaramojong language, 60
al Bashir, Umar Hasan Ahmad, 185, 223
Albert Nile, 46
Algeria: trade with, 139
Ali, Moses, 157
Alur people, 66, 67–68; influences on, 68; languages of, 50; marriage among, 68; political system of, 67–68
Amin Dada, Idi, 3, 24, 25, 224; aid to Anyanya rebels by, 25; ancestry of, 66, 185; arms smuggling by, 23, 186,

275

189-90; attempt of, to return from exile, 186, 221; coup d'état by, 25-26,
167, 190, 202; exile of, 30-31, 99, 195,
204; fear of counterattack from Obote,
28; hatred of, 81; illiteracy of, 29; as
protégé of Obote, 22, 201
Amin administration: Air France hijacking under, 29, 187, 190, 218; army under, 210, 213; army mutiny under, 30;
Asians expelled under, 28, 70, 73, 80,
98, 187, 203; courts under, 166;
defense spending under, 27-28; disappearances under, 3; dissipation under,
xxii, 3, 28, 187; districts under, 161;
economic damage by, xxii, 98,
100-101, 141, 147; foreign policy under, 27-28, 195; human rights abuses
under, 233-34; illiteracy in, 29; international recognition of, 26, 187; international opposition to, 26, 180-81;
invasion of Tanzania by, 30, 203; massacres under, 3, 195; military under,
203; military recruitment under, 80,
203; Muslim heritage of, 73; organization of, 26; overthrown, 99; rivalries in,
26; terror under, xxii, 97, 203, 231
Amnesty International, 35, 232, 233,
235-36
ancestors: religious significance of, 74, 75
Anglican Cathedral, 72
Anglican Church. *See* Church of England
Ankole kingdom, 12, 21, 34, 59-60, 69,
152; British treaty with, 13; landowning classes in, 78; military service in,
59; police in, 227; prison in, 232
Anyanya rebels, 25, 27, 202
Apac, xxiv, 209, 230
Arab Bank for Economic Development in
Africa, 120
Arabic, 51, 69
archaeology, 7
Armed Constabulary, 226
armed forces (*see also* army; air force; military): Africanization of officer corps in,
200, 212-13; cost of maintaining, xxiii,
197, 201; crimes by, 213; human rights
violations by, 195; mutinies by, 213;
number of troops in, 31-32; racial separation in, 197; role of, in political development, 195, 210; role of, in social
development, 195, 210; women in, 212
Armed Services Act (1964), 214
army, 25; under Amin, 202, 210; Brit-

ish officers in, 200, 212-13; Bugandan,
8; cattle rustling fought by, 202; child
soldiers in, 214-16; as coalition of rebel armies, 210; conditions in, 205; coup
d'état by, 24; crimes by, 205, 209,
231; demobilized, 199; ethnic favoritism in, 25, 35; expansion of, under
Amin, 27; under first Obote administration, xxii; foreign training of, 25,
213; human rights abuses by, xxiii,
xxiv, 205; internal security by, 230; involvement in politics, 199-200; looting
by, 30, 36; luxury items for, under
Amin, 28, 187; under Museveni, 154;
mutiny in, 22, 30, 197; northerners in,
171; political education for, 148; purges
of, 27; rebels in, xxiii; recruitment,
xxiii, 27, 199, 201, 202; reduction of,
xxiii; reorganization of, 201-2; rivalries in, 203; Rwandans in, xxv; terrorism by, 30
Arua, 92, 125, 133, 205, 222
Asians, 5, 70, 78, 80; in army, 197; coffee
processing by, 70; cotton ginning by,
16, 70; deprived of citizenship, 154; expelled by Amin, 28, 70, 73, 80, 98, 114,
187, 203; sugar plantations of, 16, 70;
tea production by, 114; as traders, 70
Astles, Bob, 28
Aswa River, 46
Ateso language, 60
austerity measures, 34
Australia, 116, 228
Austria, 93
Azidothymidine (AZT), 90
AZT. *See* Azidothymidine

Baamba people, 58
Baganda people, 14; British admiration
of, 11; dominance by, 41, 52; languages
of, 50, 51-54; literacy rate of, 51; *mai-
lo* estates of, 14, 78; as percentage of
population, 51; prosperity of, under
British, 14-15; riots by, 16; as tax col-
lectors, 8, 13, 14, 51
Bagisu people, 54-55; as percentage of
population, 54
Bagwere people, 55
Bahai, 72
Bahima. *See* Hima people
Bairu. *See* Iru people

Museveni, xxiv; with Rwanda, xxv 185–86; with the Soviet Union, 190–91; spending on, 106; with Sudan, 185; with Tanzania, 182, 184; with the United States, 188–89; with Zaire, xxv, 186–87

foreign trade, 137–40; precolonial, 9–10

forest, 122–23; area, 122; poaching, 123; production, 122; products, 122, 124; rehabilitation, 122–23; resources, 122

Former Uganda National Army (FUNA), 205, 206, 209

Fort Portal, 28, 130

France: debt to, rescheduled, 142; exports to, 128, 137; police training by, 230

Frelimo. *See* Front for the Liberation of Mozambique

French, 133

Frente de Libertação de Moçambique. *See* Front for the Liberation of Mozambique

Freshwater Fisheries Research Organization, 121

Front for the Liberation of Mozambique (Frelimo): Museveni's training under, 34, 150

FUNA. *See* Former Uganda National Army

Ganda culture (*see also* Baganda people; Buganda): agricultural economy of, 52; authoritarian control among, 51; cultural chauvinism of, 13; divorce in, 54; history, 8; home territory, 52; individual achievement among, 51; influence of, 52–53; lineages in, 52; marriage in, 52, 54; religion in, 75; social diversity in, 53–54; social organization in, 52, 53; villages, 52

gasoline subsidies, 106

Gayaza, 15

Gazette, 165

GDP. *See* gross domestic product

General Service Department (GSD), 228

General Service Unit (GSU), 24, 201; disbanded, 26

generational conflict, 15

geography, 42–45

German East Africa, 227

Germany, 12

Ghana Airways, 132

"ghost" employees, xxvii, 133

GNP. *See* gross national product

gourds, 65

government (*see also under individual administrations*), 155–65; borrowing, 135; coalitions in, 4, 21, 22; under constitution of 1962, 152; under constitution of 1966, 153; control over Buganda, 172; as employer, 108; hostility of, toward labor unions, 21; interim (1979–80), 31–33, 187; involvement of, in economy, 101–7; northerners in, 171; revenues, xxvi, 78; single-party, 35; subsidies, 106

government, local, 161–65; under British, 161; chiefs in, 161; divisions in, 161

government spending, 99; attempts to cut, 105; under Museveni, 158, 211; in 1990, 106

grain, 58; milling, government control of, xxvii

Great Depression: agriculture during, xxii, 16; police in, 227

Great Lakes, 45, 50

Great Rift Valley, 5, 45

Grindlays Bank, 134

gross domestic product (GDP), 100, 101; agriculture as percentage of, 100; export earnings as percentage of, 110

gross national product (GNP), 211

GSD. *See* General Service Department

GSU. *See* General Service Unit

guerrilla movements: fears of Ugandan support for, 185, 196; Popular Resistance Army, 150

Guide, The, 210

Guweddeko, Smuts, 27

Gulu, xxiv, 169, 170, 208, 209, 219, 230, 236

guns, 10, 196; tax on, 13

Habyarimana, Juvénal, xxv, 186, 196, 226

Hall, Sir John, 16

Hassan, Shaykh Muhammad Abdullah, 198

Harare, 143

health, public (*see also* acquired immune deficiency syndrome; population): birth rate, 47; cancer, 88; causes of death, 88; death rate, 47, 88; fertility rate, 47;

Mpigi district, 210; hospitals in, 90
Mpologoma River, 46
Mpoma: telecommunications system in, 133
MPPU. *See* Mobile Police Patrol Unit
Mubende, 7
Mubuku Power Scheme, 124
Muhammad, 73
Mukono district: hospitals in, 90
Mukwano Industries, 128
Mulago Hospital, 91, 190
Munno (Your Friend), 15, 19
Murchison Bay Prison, 233
Murchison (Kabalega) Falls, 46; hydroelectric power station, 124
Murchison (Kabalega) National Game Park, 68, 124, 130
Musazi, I.K., 17
Museveni, Yoweri Kaguta, xxii, 32, 35, 175, 195; background of, 150; coup attempts against, 210; coup d'état by, 36, 81, 210; foreign policy of, 179; international reaction to, 180; mediation of, in Sudanese civil war, 185; meetings of, with Moi, 183, 184; Muslims under, 74; private army of, 32, 204; revolutionary training of, 150; roles of, 155; Uganda People's Movement formed by, 149; visit of, to Britain, 188; vow of, to overthrow Obote, 33–34
Museveni administration (*see also* National Resistance Movement government; Ten-Point Program), 147; accused of corruption, 103; army under, 231; cabinet under, 158; debt under, 134; foreign aid to, 97, 142; foreign relations under, xxiv, 190, 219; goals of, xxii; improvements in military by, 213, 214; police under, 229–30; policy making under, 158; privatization under, 103; women under, 83
Muslims (*see also* Islam): under Amin, 29–30; under British colonial government, 197; under Museveni, 74; number of, 73; as percentage of population, 70, 73; rivalry of, with Christians, 5, 11, 30, 72, 147; as victims of anti-Amin revenge, 74
Mutebi, Ronald, 174, 175
Mutesa I (Kabaka), 11, 51, 196; conversion of, to Islam, 73
Mutesa II, Frederick Walugembe (Kabaka Freddie), 16; exiled, 18, 24, 172; as

head of state, 20; power of, 18–19; reinstated, 18
Mutesa, Edward, 200, 202
Mutukula military prison, 232
Muwanga, Paulo, 32, 234
Mwanza, 131
Mwinyi, Ali Hassan, xxiv

Naguru, 228
Nairobi: flights to, 132; telecommunications system in, 133
Nakasongola, 125
Nakawa, 127
Nalukolongo Diesel Workshop, 131
Namilyango, 15
Namirembe Hill, 72
Namuwongo, 92
National Assembly, 153
National College of Business Studies, 85, 87
National Consultative Council (NCC), 31, 204, 205; quarrels in, 31
National Executive Committee (NEC), 160–61
national income, 4
national integration: obstacles to, 4–5
nationalism: absence of, 4, 5; local, 5
National Military Leadership Academy (Tanzania), 219
National Mining Commission, 128
National Resistance Army (NRA), xxii, 33–34, 36, 205; background of, 148, 149–50; capture of Kampala by, 147, 183; counterinsurgency campaign, 209; foreign training for, 219; formation of, 150; government overthrown by, 195, 206; human rights violations by, 235–36; internal security by, 229; organization of, 212; peace accord signed with Military Council, 206; rebel activities of, 206; Rwandans in, 224–26; self-sufficiency of, 211; size of, 212; women in, 83
National Resistance Army Council (NRAC), 154; interim period extended by, 154–55, 177–78
National Resistance Council (NRC), 83, 158–61, 178; authority of, 154, 159, 160; candidates for, 168–69; elections, 160, 168; expanded, 160; hierarchy of, 156, 211; members of, 154; women in, 83, 160, 163, 168, 169

112, 134, 136, 158; exchange rate of, 136; floated, 99, 104, 135, 136; linked to special drawing right, 136
Siedle, Robert, 27
Simba Battalion, 27, 203
Singapore, 25, 202
Sino-Uganda Fisheries Joint Venture Company, 121
slaves, 59; slave trade, xxii, 10, 77
sleeping sickness epidemics, 16, 76
smuggling, 111, 186; under Amin, 28, 80, 182; arms, 23, 186, 189–90; coffee, 28, 111, 112, 182; to Kenya, 28; percentage of population engaged in, 81; steps to eliminate, 28, 111, 229
social change, 77–81; role of armed forces in, 195, 210
social services: under Ten-Point Program, 99
social welfare, 92–93
Société Générale de Surveillance, 140
Society of Missionaries of Africa (White Fathers), 11, 12, 72
Somalia, 144, 181
Sor, 75
Soroti District, 170, 209, 230, 236
south (*see also* north-south conflict): agriculture in, 110; autonomy of, xxii; dominance of, xxii, 171; fertility rate in, 47; land use in, 42; language groups in, 49; under Museveni, 195–96; occupations in, 80; political control by, 148; rainfall in, 46, 110; temperatures in, 46, 110
South Africa: moratorium on trade with, 140, 188
Soviet Union: Amin's coup denounced by, 190; matériel from, 190, 217, 218, 219; military assistance from, 190, 217–18; military relations with, 216; military training by, 190, 217; relations with, 180, 190–91, 219
special drawing right, 136, 143
Special Force Units, 24, 25, 35, 227
Speke, J.H., 10–11
SPLA. *See* Sudanese People's Liberation Army
SRB. *See* State Research Bureau
Ssekandi, Edward, 234
Ssemogerere, Paul Kawanga, 32, 157
Staffordshire Regiment, 201
Standard Bank, 134
standard of living; of Baganda, 51

Stanley, Henry M., 8, 11
State Research Bureau (SRB), 26, 228–29; disappearances by, 29, 228–29; killing by, 203, 228–29; mercenaries in, 229; prisoners of, 232; terror by, 203, 228–29; torture by, 35, 228–29
steel industry: attempts to rehabilitate, 126; government control of, xxvii, 104
Stroh, Nicholas, 27
structural adjustment program, xxiii, 142, 158, 180
Sudan (*see also* Nubians), 5, 42, 60, 204; cattle rustlers in, 205; civil war in, xxv, 5, 25, 185, 189–90, 196; drought in, xxv; in IGADD, 144, 181; immigrants from, 49; influence of, on Alur people, 68; nonaggression pact with, 185, 223; refugee camps in, 36; refugees in, 49, 185, 189, 205, 222; relations with, 185, 189, 220, 222–23; religion in, 76; support for Amin in, 185
Sudanese People's Liberation Army (SPLA), 222, 223
sugar, 116; as cash crop, 97; imports of, 116, 127; plantations, 16, 70, 98; production, 58, 116, 125, 127; subsidies, 106
sugar industry: government control of, xxvii; neglect of, under Amin, 28; rehabilitation of, 127
Suicide Battalion, 203
Sumba Island, 224
Supreme Court of Uganda, 165–66
Swahili, 51, 69, 133
Sweden, 206

Tabasiat Peak, 45
Tamteco. *See* Toro and Mityana Tea Company
Tanganyika (*see also* Tanzania), 10, 16, 18, 22, 199; army mutiny in, 201
Tanzania (*see also* Tanganyika; Zanzibar), 3, 7, 10, 23, 28, 30, 32, 42, 70, 180; Amin administration opposed by, 26, 180–81; cattle purchased from, 117; in East African Community, 98, 143; in East African Development Bank, 134; fighting along border with, xxv; invaded by Amin, 30, 182, 203; in Kagera Basin Organization, 144, 181; military assistance from, 219; military training

by, 184, 219; Obote exiled to, 26, 182; relations with, 181–84, 184, 196, 219, 220; shipping through, 130, 131, 183

Tanzanian People's Defence Force (TPDF), 31, 32, 203; Amin overthrown by, 99, 182, 195, 203–4, 218; training by, 218

taxes, 68; government control of, 162; under *kabakas,* 52; reform of, 105

tea, 113–16; barter for, 139; as cash crop, 97; expansion of, 114–16; exports, 137; payment for, 104; prices, 104, 114, 140; producers, 114; production, xxvi, 98, 110, 113–14; under Rehabilitation and Development Plan, 110

teachers, 84, 85; shortage of, 87

telecommunications, 133; contribution of, to economy, 100; government control of, xxvii; regional cooperation in, 143

telephones, 133

television: broadcasts, 133; programs, languages of, 51, 133; stations, 133

temperature, 46, 110

Ten-Point Program, xxiii, 147–48, 149–52, 161, 174, 180; broad-based government under, 158; courts under, 166; democracy under, 150, 163; economic development under, 99; economic goals of, 99, 151, 155; elimination of corruption under, 151; national unity under, 150–51; political parties under, 175; regional cooperation under, 151, 180–81; rehabilitation under, 151; resistance councils under, 162; ten points of, 150–51; written, 150

Tepeth people, 60, 64–65; religion of, 75

terrorism: under Amin, 81, 229, 231; by army, 30; under Obote, 34; state, 29, 211, 229

Teso District, 21, 60; area of, 65; cotton production in, 14

Teuso people, 60, 64

textile production, 125; government control of, xxvii; rehabilitation of, 126; Soviet aid for, 190

tobacco, 116; barter for, 139; as cash crop, 56, 68; exports, 137; industry, rehabilitation of, 127; prices, 140; production, xxvi, 61, 110, 116, 125; under Rehabilitation and Development Plan, 110

topography, 42–45; altitude, 42

Toro and Mityana Tea Company

(Tamteco), 114, 116

Toro kingdom, 58, 69, 152, 227; agriculture in, 58; British treaty with, 13; land-owning classes in, 78; police in, 227; political organization of, 58; prison in, 232

Tororo, 28, 235, 236; cement production in, 126; oil mill in, 127

torture, 147, 200; under Amin, 26; by army, 206; under Obote, 35; by police, 229; punishment for, 234; by State Research Bureau, 35, 228–29

Total, 125

tourist agencies: government control of, xxvii

tourist industry, 97, 124, 128–30; contribution of, to economy, 100; destroyed, 130; foreign exchange from, 130; loans for, 142; number of tourists in, 128, 130; rehabilitation of, 130; revenue from, 128, 130

trade (*see also* balance of trade): in agricultural products, xxii; barter for, 130, 138–39, 179; between agriculturalists and pastoralists, 6, 65; contribution of, to economy, 100; ivory, xxii; regional cooperation in, xxv; routes, 178; slave, xxii, 10

tradition, 41

transportation, 130–33, 137; air, 130, 131–33; contribution of, to economy, 100; energy consumption by, 124–25; freight, 131, 183; infrastructure, disrepair of, 130; network, 4; regional cooperation in, xxv, 143, 144

tribalism. *See* nationalism, local

Tutsi people (*see also* Hima), 69, 185–86; as refugees, 186

UDCM. *See* United Democratic Christian Movement

UEB. *See* Uganda Electricity Board

UFM. *See* Uganda Freedom Movement

Uganda: etymology of, 51

Uganda African Farmers Union, 17

Uganda Airlines, 131–33

Uganda Armed Constabulary Ordinance (1903), 197

Uganda Association of Women Lawyers, 235

Uganda Bata Shoe Company, 128

Published Country Studies

(Area Handbook Series)

550-65	Afghanistan	550-87	Greece	
550-98	Albania	550-78	Guatemala	
550-44	Algeria	550-174	Guinea	
550-59	Angola	550-82	Guyana and Belize	
550-73	Argentina	550-151	Honduras	
550-169	Australia	550-165	Hungary	
550-176	Austria	550-21	India	
550-175	Bangladesh	550-154	Indian Ocean	
550-170	Belgium	550-39	Indonesia	
550-66	Bolivia	550-68	Iran	
550-20	Brazil	550-31	Iraq	
550-168	Bulgaria	550-25	Israel	
550-61	Burma	550-182	Italy	
550-50	Cambodia	550-30	Japan	
550-166	Cameroon	550-34	Jordan	
550-159	Chad	550-56	Kenya	
550-77	Chile	550-81	Korea, North	
550-60	China	550-41	Korea, South	
550-26	Colombia	550-58	Laos	
550-33	Commonwealth Caribbean, Islands of the	550-24	Lebanon	
550-91	Congo	550-38	Liberia	
550-90	Costa Rica	550-85	Libya	
550-69	Côte d'Ivoire (Ivory Coast)	550-172	Malawi	
550-152	Cuba	550-45	Malaysia	
550-22	Cyprus	550-161	Mauritania	
550-158	Czechoslovakia	550-79	Mexico	
550-36	Dominican Republic and Haiti	550-76	Mongolia	
550-52	Ecuador	550-49	Morocco	
550-43	Egypt	550-64	Mozambique	
550-150	El Salvador	550-35	Nepal and Bhutan	
550-28	Ethiopia	550-88	Nicaragua	
550-167	Finland	550-157	Nigeria	
550-155	Germany, East	550-94	Oceania	
550-173	Germany, Fed. Rep. of	550-48	Pakistan	
550-153	Ghana	550-46	Panama	

550-156	Paraguay	550-53	Thailand
550-185	Persian Gulf States	550-89	Tunisia
550-42	Peru	550-80	Turkey
550-72	Philippines	550-74	Uganda
550-162	Poland	550-97	Uruguay
550-181	Portugal	550-71	Venezuela
550-160	Romania	550-32	Vietnam
550-37	Rwanda and Burundi	550-183	Yemens, The
550-51	Saudi Arabia	550-99	Yugoslavia
550-70	Senegal	550-67	Zaire
550-180	Sierra Leone	550-75	Zambia
550-184	Singapore	550-171	Zimbabwe
550-86	Somalia		
550-93	South Africa		
550-95	Soviet Union		
550-179	Spain		
550-96	Sri Lanka		
550-27	Sudan		
550-47	Syria		
550-62	Tanzania		

☆U.S. GOVERNMENT PRINTING OFFICE: 1992 311-824/60010